The Beach Boys On CD: vol 3 - 1985-2015

Andrew Hickey

BY THE SAME AUTHOR:

- Sci-Ence! Justice Leak!

- The Beatles In Mono

- The Beach Boys On CD: vol 1 - 1961-1969

- The Beach Boys On CD: vol. 2 - 1970-2011

- An Incomprehensible Condition:An Unauthorised Guide To Grant Morrison's Seven Soldiers

- Monkee Music

- Preservation: The Kinks' Music 1964-1974

- Ideas and Entities

- California Dreaming: The LA Pop Music Scene and the 1960s

- Faction Paradox: Head of State

- The Black Archive: The Mind Robber

- Welcome to the Multiverse: An Unauthorised Guide to Grant Morrison's Multiversity (ebook only)

- Fifty Stories for Fifty Years: An Unauthorised Look at Doctor Who

For Holly

Contents

Introduction

In this book and its two companion volumes, I am attempting to analyse, track by track, every available Beach Boys CD, including the solo albums, to try to provide a buyer's guide to the band's music.

This is an attempt to provide an analytical look at this music, but one that gives equal weight to all the band members, rather than just focusing on one or two. If Dennis Wilson's solo work is spoken of less harshly than Mike Love's, that's not because of a personal bias for Wilson or against Love, it's based purely on my assessment of them as artistic works.

But as anyone who read the first two volumes will be aware, this will be a very personal assessment. I make no claim to objectivity here. While I have tried to note where I go against established consensus, this is a critical analysis from a single point of view.

Since volume one of this series was published, there has been a huge amount of change in the Beach Boys world – the band have reunited, recorded a new album, toured and split up again. This has meant a change from the original plan for these three books. When volume one was published, the Beach Boyswere in the past tense, with a definite end point on the band's career. That is no longer the case – even after the latest split, Brian Wilson, Al Jardine, Blondie Chaplin, and David Marks collaborated on Wilson's most recent "solo" album.

This volume attempts to trace the story of the band's music, both together and solo, from 1985 through to 2015; it follows their brief wave of success in the late 80s, the band's acrimonious and painful collapse into irrelevance, and the revitalisation of Brian Wilson as a solo artist. It also looks at the many archival releases which were as much a part of the band's story during that period as the new music, and which contributed to the band's critical reassessment as one of the most creative bands of the rock era. (Many of these archival releases, of course, contain different versions of songs already covered in this series. My policy in this book is only to look in detail at songs that haven't already been covered, although exceptions may be made for startlingly different versions).

Some recordings are outside the scope of this book – while I've tried to include all Beach Boys and solo works, band-members' collaborations with others outside the band are not included here. So for example Mike Love and Dean Torrence's duets, Carl Wilson's album with Gerry Beckley and Robert Lamm, and Brian Wilson's collaboration with his daughters on *The Wilsons* are not included.

Most of these are minor works, but one that definitely isn't is *Orange Crate Art*, an album by Brian Wilson and Van Dyke Parks. That album is at times stunningly beautiful, but it's also an album on which Wilson is merely a guest vocalist – the songs, production, and arrangements are all Parks – and should rightfully be considered a Van Dyke Parks album first and foremost. Its omission here should not be taken to mean it's a bad album – it's better than the majority of what is covered here – just that it's outside the boundaries of this work.

Much of the new music discussed here was not up to the standards of the best of the Beach Boys' pre-1980s work. But even at their lowest point in the mid 1990s, the Beach Boys were still intermittently capable of greatness. If this book is sometimes harsh about the less great material, it's only because it stands in such sharp contrast to the best music discussed here.

The Beach Boys

1985 saw the Beach Boys making their first album in five years, but the band making it was very different from the one that had recorded *Keepin' the Summer Alive*. In the intervening years, both Brian and Dennis Wilson had hit lower points in their mental and physical health than either had experienced before. Brian's life had been saved by the band getting psychiatrist Dr Eugene Landy back in to get him off street drugs and start him on a programme of exercise and healthy eating that saw him become physically healthier than he had been in decades.

Sadly, however, by 1985 Landy had already started his well-documented abuses of Wilson, which would within a few years lead to Landy having his license to practice removed, and he was insisting on getting songwriting credit for Wilson's new songs. Landy's credits, along with credits for his girlfriend Alexandra Morgan, have apparently since been removed from the songs (though they were still credited for some on the most recent CD issue) and in these essays songs for which Landy was originally credited will be marked with an asterisk, while songs for which both Landy and Morgan were credited will be marked with a †, but the assumption throughout will be that neither made any substantial contribution.

Dennis Wilson was not even as lucky as Brian. Reeling from a succession of personal problems, including the break-up of his sixth marriage (to Shawn Love, a teenager who claimed to be Mike's illegitimate daughter – a claim which he denies), Dennis turned increasingly to alcohol, and on December 28, 1983, he went diving after drinking a large amount of vodka, and never came back up. He was thirty-nine.

The tragic loss of Dennis seems to have spurred the rest of the band into one of their increasingly rare acknowledgements that the world had moved on since 1965 (though they had already been making plans for a new album before his death), and by June 1984 they were in the studio again, this time to record an album with the first outside producer to take sole charge of a Beach Boys album in more than twenty years.

Steve Levine had been a protégé of Bruce Johnston in the late 70s, and

9

considered that he largely owed his career to Johnston's encouragement, but by 1984 he was briefly one of the hottest producers in the world, thanks to his production of Culture Club's massively successful albums *Kissing to Be Clever* and *Colour by Numbers*. He, along with arranger Julian Lindsay, helped the Beach Boys create a truly up-to-the-moment sounding album, with the bulk of the instruments (and, according to some, a fair chunk of the backing vocals) created using Fairlight sequencers.

The results sound incredibly dated now, as precisely of their moment as the back-cover photo (in which the band look like five Republican Senators heading for a casual team-building exercise at the golf course), and much of the material seemed sub-par even at the time – Brian Wilson was writing again, but nothing he came up with here would threaten the claims of "God Only Knows" or "Good Vibrations" to be his most important work – but the album gave the band their biggest hit with new original material since "Do It Again", with Love and Terry Melcher's "Getcha Back", and proved that even without Dennis, the Beach Boys *could* continue making music in the 1980s.

line-up

Brian Wilson, Carl Wilson, Al Jardine, Mike Love, Bruce Johnston

Getcha Back

Songwriters: Mike Love and Terry Melcher

Lead vocals: Mike Love with Brian Wilson

The album starts with this Frankenstein's monster of a track, which sounds like it has been bolted together in the most cynical manner possible to produce a perfect facsimile of what people in the 1980s thought a "Beach Boys record" should sound like.

Thus we start with an 80s "sonic power" update of the drum sound from "Do It Again", and then get a backing track reminiscent of "Don't Worry Baby", before Love's vocal comes in. The basic shape of the melody line is taken from Bruce Springsteen's "Hungry Heart", his own hit attempt to replicate the Beach Boys' formula, while the chorus hook is taken from Billy Joel's contemporary Four Seasons pastiche "Uptown Girl", but over the rising progression that made up the chorus to "Sail On Sailor". Then add in lyrics about trying to recapture the lost glories of a bygone adolescence, and you've got the perfect focus-group-approved Beach Boys track.

Everything is processed to hell – they've managed to get one half-decent take of Brian Wilson singing a few bars of wordless falsetto and used that same recording over and over – but somehow it works.

Partly this is because of Love's vocal, which is nasal to the point of self-parody, but precisely because of that works in a way that most of his recent vocals at that point hadn't. (Love himself dislikes his vocal on this, and on recent tours has often had either David Marks or Love's son Christian take the lead.) There's also the joy of hearing the last gasp of Brian's husky late-70s voice on the tag.

But mostly it's because of Levine's production. This is an odd thing to say, as the production on the album hasn't dated well. But it's only dated precisely as badly as anything else from the time period, and no worse, and there's an aesthetic sense here that's missing from a lot of their contemporaries' recordings of the time. Levine has noticed things about Brian Wilson's production sound that get missed by a lot of the less competent pasticheurs – the way he uses almost no cymbal on his recordings, for example, and the way that a lot of his basslines are played on instruments other than guitar – and adapted them for an 80s audience, so this has a wonderfully simple drum machine part and a great honking sax bassline.

The song itself may be a cynical one, but there's a lot of joy in the recording, and taken as a single it's probably the best they'd put out since "It's OK", if not earlier. It reached number 26 in the US, and number two on the Adult Contemporary chart.

It's Gettin' Late

Songwriters: Carl Wilson, Myrna Smith-Schilling and Robert White Johnson

Lead vocals: Carl Wilson

The second song is a dull affair, based around a three-chord minor-key chorus and a two chord major-key verse. It plods so much it actually sounds at times like the drum machine is slipping out of time. The horns on here sound like synths though they're live, and the vocals sound sequenced, especially the opening stack of Brians where you can almost hear the keys being pressed and released on the synth triggering them.

It's not a terrible song – it would have fit onto either of Carl Wilson's solo albums and been better than much of the material on them – but it's tired and dull. Released as a single, it didn't chart.

Crack At Your Love

Songwriters: Brian Wilson and Al Jardine *

Lead vocals: Al Jardine and Brian Wilson

A minor piece, but a fun one, this track more than most sounds like Levine's work with Culture Club, having a generic upbeat synth-pop backing.

But while the lyrics to this track are simplistic ("I'm goin' crazy/Would you be my baby?"), the vocals, by Jardine, are the best on the album to this point – until Brian Wilson comes in for the middle eight, again singing plaintively in the husky voice that would soon be gone for good, "Lonely nights, lonely days..."

It's one of those little moments that lift an adequate song for a moment or two into greatness, and while this is never going to be anyone's favourite Beach Boys song, it's far, far better than anything on *Keepin' the Summer Alive* or much of *MIU Album*.

It may also be the first recording to feature the band's touring falsetto vocalist Jeffrey Foskett, who had joined the band when Carl had temporarily quit a few years earlier, and who would be a major part of the band's story throughout the 80s, and again from 1998 on. While no full vocal credits for this album have ever been made available, Foskett has often claimed to have provided backing vocals on several tracks, and the falsetto on the intro sounds more like him than any of the actual Beach Boys, though everything's so processed it's hard to be sure.

Maybe I Don't Know

Songwriters: Carl Wilson, Myrna Smith-Schilling, Steve Levine and Julian Stewart Lindsay

Lead vocals: Carl Wilson

Possibly the blandest thing on the album, this has the dull, loping, swing of much 80s jazz/soul influenced AOR, an unimaginative descending chord sequence, and meaningless lyrics. While Gary Moore was capable of greatness as a guitarist, his cursory squealing here adds little, and the whole thing isn't even saved from banality by Carl Wilson's lead vocal.

She Believes In Love Again

Songwriter: Bruce Johnston

Lead vocals: Bruce Johnston and Carl Wilson

Johnston's only song on the album is also the second-best thing he's ever contributed to the Beach Boys. A simple ballad, based around a keyboard part that sounds like Johnston's own playing (he's one of three keyboard players credited on the track, along with Lindsay and Levine), this is the most craftsmanlike song on the album. There's nothing here that's massively innovative, but it's put together beautifully, with the only crack in the facade coming with the "God I'm sorry" in the middle eight – an interjection that throws the melody out, and provides just enough of a sense of real emotion that it gives the whole carefully-constructed song a sense of conviction it would otherwise be missing.

Johnston's voice helps in this, too. Between *Keepin' the Summer Alive* and the recording of this album, his voice had grown notably huskier, and here he sounds almost like Rod Stewart at times – but this is a good thing, as especially given the death of Dennis and Brian's usual absence on tour, Johnston's voice now provided a little of the grit that the harmonies needed.

Both he and Carl Wilson are in fine form here, subtly multitracked in ways that only become apparent when listening with headphones but which give the vocals a real richness, and while sonically this has the same 80s sheen as the rest of the album, the arrangement (with a slow build from single keyboard through to guitars, strings, and trombone) is much better thought-out, and more organic, than much of the album.

California Calling

Songwriters: Brian Wilson and Al Jardine

Lead vocals: Al Jardine and Mike Love

Another strong track, featuring Ringo Starr on drums, this is yet another rewrite of "California Girls" and "California Saga" (and also lyrically references "Surfin' USA"), with nothing particularly interesting about it musically, but it's done with such enthusiasm that it's hard not to be swept along. Al Jardine's voice is stunningly good, and while Love's tenor lead sections are weak, his "callin' me, ring ring ring" bass vocal in the chorus is wonderfully goofy

Passing Friend

Songwriters: George O'Dowd and Roy Hay

Lead vocals: Carl Wilson

This, on the other hand, is utterly worthless. Written by Boy George and Roy Hay of Culture Club, who were at that time very briefly one of the biggest bands in the world, this is a fairly typical example of Boy George's songwriting, one of the many interminable songs he wrote at the time about how everyone else was a phoney, with what sound like several digs against Boy George's boyfriend, Culture Club drummer Jon Moss.

The track is, at five minutes, at least double the length that the musical material demands, and Carl Wilson sounds embarrassed singing lines like "through the child's eyes there were feelings touching my violet skin".

In fact here, as we'll see again later, we have Carl Wilson on autopilot. The track was originally recorded by George and Hay (who provides almost all the instrumentation), and George's guide vocal was replaced by Carl Wilson. It sounds like Wilson didn't bother thinking about the song at all, and just imitated the guide vocal as closely as possible – the phrasing, and even many of the vowel sounds, are far closer to George's than to any other vocal Wilson ever did. It's a lazy performance, but no worse than this profoundly tedious song deserves.

I'm So Lonely

Songwriter: Brian Wilson *

Lead vocals: Brian Wilson and Carl Wilson

Starting with a sax solo that sounds suspiciously like the one from Sade's then-recent hit "Your Love Is King", this song is about the most perfunctory thing imaginable, with a verse shuffling between I, IV, and V, a chorus that just goes through standard doo-wop changes, and lyrics along the lines of "I'm so lonely, really, really so lonely" and "I wish/since you went away/that you'd soon be back to stay". And while Brian's vocal on the verses is quite good for his shouty, husky, early/mid-80s voice, his attempts at falsetto in the chorus are painful.

This sounds like an exercise to get Brian writing again, and while there's nothing horrible about the song itself, it's clearly not the work of someone who's actually trying.

Where I Belong

Songwriters: Carl Wilson and Robert White Johnson

Lead vocals: Carl Wilson and Al Jardine

Carl Wilson's final songwriting contribution to the Beach Boys is also arguably his best. Certainly the other band members seem to have warmed to it – this is the only track on the album to feature an instrumental contribution by a Beach Boy who didn't write the track, with Brian adding keyboards, and it's also one of the few on which every band member's voice can be heard.

In fact every band member shines vocally here – it's Carl's best lead on the album, but Al's counter-vocals on the later choruses lift the track immensely, and the two-chord section after the second chorus, where Brian and Bruce sing wordlessly over Mike's doo-wop bass might be the last appearance of Brian's young voice, in all its nasal whining glory.

But they're all rising to the occasion because of the song. The song is allegedly about John-Roger, the cult leader who was Carl's "spiritual adviser" for much of the later period of his life, but the lyric shows little sign of that, being instead a generic love lyric, albeit one about having drifted through life until finding the right person.

Musically, though, this sounds like an expansion on, and progression from, the musical ideas on Carl's first solo album. There's a strong similarity to both "Heaven" and "Hurry Love", but this is more musically sophisticated, with a bassline rising almost independently of the chords in the first part of the verse, where the singer is confused. The bass note then stays on the tonic while the chords change, on the line "you just could be my anchor", before it descends under simple IV, V, and I chords to get to the simpler, more broad-strokes emotions of the chorus.

The sparse instrumentation, allowing the gorgeous vocals to do the work, makes this the least dated-sounding track on the album, and this is the one thing on the album that can legitimately stand up with the band's very best work.

I Do Love You

Songwriter: Stevie Wonder

Lead vocals: Carl Wilson and Al Jardine

And then the album slumps into this. Stevie Wonder, who wrote this and played almost every instrument (and it also sounds like he provided uncredited backing vocals on the tag), is one of the great geniuses of popular music of the last fifty years, and even though this sounds like something he tossed off in about as long as it takes to listen to it, it's still one of the catchiest things on the album. Mediocre Stevie Wonder is still Stevie Wonder, after all.

The problem is that Stevie Wonder isn't the Beach Boys, and the style just doesn't fit. Both Carl Wilson (who takes the bulk of the lead vocals) and Al Jardine (who sings the "I do love you" sections) seem to be imitating a guide vocal by Wonder – much as with "Passing Friend", the vocals sound far more like the songwriter than like the singers normally sound.

The result is not a combination of Stevie Wonder and the Beach Boys – rather, it's two of the greatest voices in popular music turning themselves into a Stevie Wonder tribute act. There's nothing of the Beach Boys in here, and why would I want to listen to a Stevie Wonder impersonator, when I have *Innervisions, Songs in the Key of Life*, or *Talking Book* that I could be listening to instead?

It's Just a Matter of Time

Songwriter: Brian Wilson *

Lead vocals: Mike Love and Brian Wilson

A generic doo-wop track, this passes two minutes and twenty-two seconds perfectly acceptably, and that's about all that can be said about it.

Male Ego

Songwriter: Brian Wilson and Mike Love *

Lead vocals: Brian Wilson and Mike Love

This song was only included on the CD version of the album, not on the vinyl or cassette releases, and was originally the B-side to "Getcha Back".

Musically, this is utterly fantastic, with more energy than almost anything on the album, some great analogue-sounding squelchy synth bass, a baritone sax honking away in the lower register, tuned percussion, and the most enthused vocal from Brian we've heard on anything since *Love You* – which this sounds very like. It's almost impossible to believe that this is from the same producer – or indeed the same band – as the album proper. If the rest of the album sounded like this, it would have been one of their all-time classics.

Sadly, the lyrics are about how great it is to sexually harass women in the street. Oh well.

Brian Wilson

As soon as "Doctor" Eugene Landy was taken on for a second time, in 1983, to "treat" Brian Wilson's increasingly severe mental illness, he started taking control of both Wilson's personal life and his professional life. Landy fancied himself a songwriter – or at least, wanted to get a writing credit and the concomitant royalties – and so started inserting himself into Wilson's writing process, as "therapy".

The end game of this was to create a solo career for Wilson, ideally in parallel with continued membership of the Beach Boys, so that albums could be released with as much Landy involvement as possible, and without the other Beach Boys getting involved in the songwriting process (or, worse – from Landy's point of view at least – starting to object to the level of control Landy had over Wilson). But Brian was not considered in a fit mental state at that point to take complete control over a project, and so collaborators had to be brought in.

At first, Brian's old friend Gary Usher, who had recently returned to the music industry, was contacted, and he worked with Brian to shape his ideas into music that would have commercial appeal in the changed industry landscape of the mid-80s. Only three tracks saw any kind of release, though: a Beach Boys/Fat Boys collaboration on "Wipe Out"; a track called "The Spirit of Rock & Roll", co-written by Tom Kelly (who had earlier co-written Madonna's hit "Like A Virgin"), which was used on a Beach Boys TV special; and a single called "Let's Go To Heaven In My Car", used in the soundtrack for *Police Academy 4*. Usher was abruptly sacked by Landy after he started asking for actual payment for his services – Usher suspected that this was because he was too independent for Landy's tastes.

The Usher demos did, though, get Brian a contract for a solo album on Sire Records, a division of Warner Brothers, and Lenny Waronker, the label's president, took a personal interest in the project. Waronker co-produced one track himself, and paired Wilson up with two major collaborators. Russ Titelman, who co-produced most of the album, was an industry veteran with whom Wilson had collaborated in the 60s (Titelman had written lyrics for "Guess I'm Dumb" and the then-unreleased "Sandy She Needs Me") and who had worked with Waronker on several projects, most notably Randy Newman's 70s albums.

The other collaborator, who would be a major force in Wilson's musical life for the next fifteen years, was the powerpop songwriter Andy Paley. Paley was a very talented songwriter and multi-instrumentalist in his own right, and as well as co-writing several songs, he also played most of the guitars, bass, and drums on the album — while there were many additional session musicians on odd tracks, the core backing tracks were mostly performed by Paley and synthesiser programmer Michael Bernard, with Wilson adding keyboards.

And this is where we have to discuss what is a potentially inflammatory topic — the question of exactly how much involvement Brian Wilson's collaborators have in his music. Up to this point, Wilson's collaborators had mostly been lyricists, with Wilson writing all the music. From this point on, however, his major songwriting collaborations have all been with people who were capable of writing both words and music themselves, and in several cases (including Paley) those people have also been capable of writing convincing pastiches of Wilson's own style.

This has led, understandably, to some people questioning whether Wilson himself has much involvement in the songs for which he is credited. I believe that for the most part he does, and will be taking that view in this book, except where the evidence points another way on a specific song. The nature of the collaborations has varied over the years, with some collaborators having more influence over the music than others, but I think it is possible to see a clear through-line through all Wilson's late-period work (and we are here at the precise half-way mark in his career as a songwriter as of the time of writing).

So in all discussions of Wilson's songwriting, I shall be treating him as the *auteur*, and his collaborators as (very talented) assistants. I shall sometimes try to make a best assessment of who contributed what, and may say for example that a particular melody line sounds more Paley than Wilson, but Brian Wilson will be treated as the overall primary creative force, and I shall be looking at the music in the context of his body of work.

And in that context, *Brian Wilson*, the album that came out in 1988, is remarkably good. It's certainly the best thing he had been involved with since *The Beach Boys Love You* eleven years earlier, and the most consistent. It's not, however, a particularly easy listen. It has a *very* 80s sound, with many of the tracks being built almost entirely out of digital synths, and many of the tracks were mixed by Hugh Padgham (the engineer who was responsible for the drum sound on Phil Collins' "In the Air Tonight").

Along with that, Wilson's voice has changed again. This is neither the gruff, shouty, but enthusiastic and tuneful Brian of the late 70s and early 80s, nor the sweet falsettist of the 60s. Rather, this sounds more like Randy Newman than anyone else, but with both slurring and clipping – these are the vocal equivalent of pressured speech, and he sounds like what he was: a man on incorrectly-prescribed psychiatric medication. The attempts to go into falsetto are often painfully off, but even the normal range sounds uncomfortable.

But listen past that, and this is the best collection of relatively straight-forward pop songs that Wilson had recorded since *Pet Sounds*, and the circumstances of its creation make that achievement all the greater.

Love and Mercy

Songwriter: Brian Wilson †

The album's opening track is apparently inspired by a quote from the Bible – Isaiah 63:9. "In all their distress he too was distressed, and the angel of his presence saved them. In his love and mercy he redeemed them; he lifted them up and carried them all the days of old."

And it appropriately has a hymnal feel, at least when one takes into account the 80s production sound. Musically, the proximate influence was Burt Bacharach's "What the World Needs Now", but the song actually bears a far stronger resemblance to Brian's brother Dennis' "Forever", being based around the same descending scalar bassline, and with the first few chords identical once one takes the difference of key into account.

The song, both verse and chorus, is based around a repeating I/iii7/vi7/iii7/IV/vi7/ii7/V7 pattern, with lyrics alternating between verses about everyday life ("I was lying in my room and the news came on TV") and observations of the suffering in the world ("a lot of people out there hurting and it really scares me"), and choruses wishing "love and mercy to you and your friends tonight".

The only escape from this repetition is in the largely *a capella* section before the last two repetitions of the chorus, where from out of nowhere what sounds like a choir of angels (or as close as Wilson's 80s voice could come) descends and wordlessly seems to heal the narrator's pain.

Of all Wilson's solo songs, this is the one that has come closest to having the same reputation as his Beach Boys work, and the song has been the closing song at almost every one of his solo performances. The 2015 film based around Wilson's life was titled after the song, and it remains his best-known solo work, despite being unsuccessful when released as a single.

Some early live performances of this song had an extra verse ("I was praying to a God who just never seems to hear/The things we need the most are what we most fear"). This was supposedly the work of Landy, and thankfully never made it to the finished version.

Walkin' the Line

Songwriters: Brian Wilson and Nick Laird-Clowes *

An uninspired song dating from the Usher sessions, this is catchy enough, but is based around simple, repetitive, I-IV and I-V shuffles (though with quite a pleasant bassline). The one real musical piece of interest, the bridge, is actually taken from a then-unreleased Al Jardine song from a decade or so earlier, "Looking Down The Coast" – the lines "If I don't get my way this time I'll die/And that's no lie" and "Sittin' at a place called Nepenthe we can see it there/Mountain lion's lair" are almost identical, musically. Then-hot pop star Terence Trent D'Arby adds some backing vocals.

Melt Away

Songwriter: Brian Wilson *

Easily the best song on the album, this is also the track where a lyrical collaborator would have been most beneficial. Musically this is spectacular (though again marred by the shoutiness of the vocals), and most of the lyrics (originally credited to Landy, but these are *clearly* Wilson's lyrics) rise to the challenge, but there are a few infelicities (like the overuse of melisma – the word "why" is stretched out over six notes in the first line) that could easily have been improved.

That's nitpicking, though. This is a beautiful song, and the lyrical tone matches the music perfectly, with the confusion and pain of the earlier lines of the verses turning into the relief of "and my blues just melt away" mirroring the chord sequence, which makes the song appear to be in B♭ at first, but with several "wrong" chords, before the resolution at the end of the verse makes it clear it's really in F.

Lyrically this is yet another return to the muse who is too good for the singer, and very much part of a continuum with Wilson's earlier work, but knowing of his personal situation at the time makes the middle eight, where he sings "I won't let you see me suffer/No not me/I won't let you hear me crying/No not me", utterly heartbreaking.

When the CD was reissued with bonus tracks in 2000, this song and several others were included in the wrong mixes, at least on early pressings. Most differed so little that I've never noticed an audible difference between them, but "Melt Away" on the 2000 reissue is missing some prominent vocal parts on the round-like tag.

Baby Let Your Hair Grow Long

Songwriter: Brian Wilson *

This song had been around for a few years when it was recorded, and had been recorded during the Usher sessions, though Usher called the song, whose lyrics he attributed to Landy, "nonsensical, immature, and childish".

That's probably an accurate description of the lyrics (though the version on the album makes a lot more sense than the demo lyrics did), but musically the track is quite interesting, especially the bridges, where Wilson changes key up a fourth, runs through a slight variation of the standard doo-wop chord sequence, and then has a passage similar to the verses of "Love and Mercy" where he allows the descending scalar bassline to take him back to the original key.

It's not the most coherent of Wilson's songs lyrically, but for those of us who enjoy his more eccentric work, there's plenty of pleasure to be found here in the cleverly-constructed music.

Little Children

Songwriter: Brian Wilson

This song dated back at least to 1976, when it was recorded during the demo sessions for *The Beach Boys Love You*. Apparently written for his daughters Carnie and Wendy, by the time the song was actually released "poor little Carnie" and "little Wendy" were nineteen and eighteen, respectively, and estranged from their father thanks to "Doctor" Landy.

The song is slight, consisting of a three-chord verse and a chorus that is stolen from the middle eight of "Mountain of Love", but at one minute and fifty seconds it doesn't outstay its welcome.

One for the Boys

Songwriter: Brian Wilson

Another 1:50 song, this one has far more musical interest. A totally *a capella*, wordless, track, this showcases Wilson's vocal arrangement ability, which was as good as ever, on a piece which sounds like it was inspired by "Rhapsody in Blue". One of the highlights of the album.

There's So Many

Songwriter: Brian Wilson †

Another highlight of the album, this song is probably the one that sounds most "Brian Wilson" to the average listener. While it's a mistake to go into falsetto at the end of each verse, and the lyrics are utter gibberish, if one ignores the differences in production style the music manages to split the difference between his mid-60s *Pet Sounds* and *Today!* style romantic ballads and the more idiosyncratic material on *Love You*. The moment at the end of the middle eight where he sings "planets are spinning around", the music drops into waltz time for a moment, and the chord sequence goes from G♭maj7 to Gm7/C to C, is simply transcendent.

Night Time

Songwriters: Brian Wilson and Andy Paley †

Apparently one of the songs Wilson was most enthused about, this is one of the weaker tracks on the album, with a faintly "tropical" feel in the percussion that seems almost like a response to the Beach Boys' recent success with "Kokomo", though the release date, before that song became the massive hit it did, seems to make that unlikely.

Not a particularly strong track, and not one that has dated well.

Let it Shine

Songwriters: Brian Wilson, Jeff Lynne

Apparently Sire didn't think that Wilson had enough strong material to make a full album, and insisted that some work from outside songwriters be brought in. In the case of "Let It Shine", they turned to Jeff Lynne, who was at that time having some success as a producer and writer for veteran artists – around the same time period he also worked on albums by George Harrison, Randy Newman, Tom Petty, and Roy Orbison, all of which had a great deal of success.

Lynne has recently talked about writing this together with Brian at the piano, but all other information seems to suggest that the song was written by Lynne on his own, with Brian merely contributing the "Let it shine, oh let it shine" section later. Certainly, it sounds far more like Lynne's work than Wilson's. It does, however, have some of Wilson's strongest vocals on the album, presumably because of Lynne's co-production, although it's easy to tell that the vocals were edited together from multiple takes.

Oddly, other than "Love and Mercy" and "Melt Away" this is the only song from the album to have been performed live by Wilson since he started touring solo in 1999.

Meet Me in My Dreams Tonight

Songwriters: Brian Wilson, Andy Paley, Andy Dean

Another song brought in by an outside writer, this is apparently largely (or totally) the work of Paley, and again sounds more like him than it does Wilson. If Wilson contributed anything, I'd suggest it was either the "lullaby baby/goodnight baby" section (which obviously references "Wouldn't It Be Nice", and doesn't sound like Paley melodically) or the last, staccato, "meet me in my dreams tonight" of the chorus, which like many of Wilson's songs on the album features a scalar, descending, bassline.

Rio Grande

Songwriters: Brian Wilson and Andy Paley

And the album itself ends with an eight-minute-long suite. One of Lenny Waronker's conditions for putting the album out was apparently that it have something reminiscent of *Smile* on it. As Wilson was simply not capable yet of structuring something like that, the job fell to Andy Paley. Paley took several fragments of unfinished songs Wilson had lying around, some dating back years or even decades, and combined them with new material he wrote himself. Paley and Waronker then added sound effects to help smooth over some of the transitions, and the result was a fairly plausible piece of pseudo-*Smile* – a suite with several different melodic themes, and with lyrics about the old West.

The more one examines the song, the less there really is there – the "night blooming jasmine" section, for example, has no musical or lyrical relationship to anything else in the piece (understandably, as it was taken from a totally unrelated song) – but Paley does a great job of making the disparate pieces *seem* to hold together, and each of the sections by itself is a musically interesting one. The result is a fine, though not great, closing track for a fine, though not great, album.

Bonus Tracks

Brian Wilson on "Love and Mercy"

A section of interview from 1988, with Wilson talking about the song.

He Couldn't Get His Poor Old Body to Move

Songwriters: Lindsey Buckingham, Brian Wilson

A song that Wilson had written early in the Usher sessions, this was res-
urrected as the B-side of "Love and Mercy". The original version had
lyrics about exercise and eating healthily; Lindsey Buckingham, who was
brought in to rework it and co-produce, rewrote nearly all the lyrics. The
new lyrics, while not great, are a vast improvement, but the song itself
will never be a great one – it has a nice triplet feel to it, but it's not got
anything particularly interesting about it.

Being With the One You Love

Songwriter: Brian Wilson

The B-side to "Melt Away", this was originally written as "Doing Time on
Planet Earth", intended for the flop film of the same name (though rather
oddly Gary Usher claimed that he had given Brian Wilson that title). When
it wasn't accepted for the film, it was given a light rewrite. The melody
has some promise, but between the dud vocals, the 80s production and
the dreadful lyrics, a B-side was probably the fate it deserved.

Let's Go to Heaven in My Car

Songwriters: Gary Usher, Brian Wilson

Gary Usher used this song as an example of why Brian Wilson needed a
collaborator to shape his ideas. In actual fact, though, it seems to prove
the opposite.

In an early session with Usher, Wilson brought in a song called "Water
Builds Up", allegedly written with Landy. The song was later recorded for
Wilson's unreleased second solo album, *Sweet Insanity*, and the bootlegs of
that reveal a rather charming little song. No "God Only Knows", perhaps,
but definitely worth a place on an album. Usher, on the other hand,
thought it "had a nice verse, but the rest of the song was very mediocre".

A while later, however, Usher was speaking with Bruce Johnston, who told him that Wilson had a song title that was so great Johnston was tempted to buy it off him. The title was "Let's Go to Heaven in My Car".

Usher asked Wilson about the title, and Wilson played him a few bars of chorus, which was all he had of the song. Usher's solution was to take the verse of "Water Builds Up" and the chorus of "Let's Go to Heaven in My Car", and put them together and create. . .a horrible mess.

The song simply doesn't work. The chorus itself is terrible, with the scansion of the lyrics all wrong, and with no real interesting musical features. Worse, though, the verse and chorus simply don't go together in any sensible way. When one listens to "Water Builds Up", the verse, chorus, and middle eight all progress naturally one into the other. Here, though, the chorus comes out of nowhere and sounds like what it is, a jarring interruption from a less interesting song. For the final touch, Usher's production adds the kind of dull 80s rawk guitar that adorned much of the Beach Boys' near-contemporary *Still Cruisin'* album, as it did the work of so many 60s pop stars who were lost and musically confused in the 1980s.

The song was released as a single, and found its natural home on the soundtrack to *Police Academy 4*, the fourth-least-dreadful of the "comedy" franchise.

Too Much Sugar

Songwriter: Brian Wilson

The B-side of "Let's Go To Heaven in My Car", this sounds like a mildly-overdubbed demo, with a simple keyboard and beatbox backing track lightly adorned with some keyboard and backing vocal overdubs.

Had it been any more produced, this silly little song about health, exhorting you to "move it all around just like Jane Fonda" and warning you that if you eat "too much sugar and too much cake/you'll end up with a belly-ache", would seem ridiculous. As it is, it's rather charming, and while Wilson's vocals on the middle eight are more than a little strained, his vocals on the verses are some of the most natural-sounding of anything he recorded between about 1985 and 1998. Charmingly eccentric, if slight.

There's So Many (demo)

Songwriter: Brian Wilson

A rather lovely demo, with just keyboard, vocals, and some overdubbed harmonies. Compared to the released version, the lyrics are even worse, and Wilson can't hit the notes on "planets are spinning around". The end of each verse is simpler, too, without the lovely little chord changes under the last word of the line, making the song harmonically much simpler. But on the plus side, that also means that Wilson can actually *sing* the last lines of the verses, without the soaring into a falsetto that's out of his range. The released version probably wins on points, but it's nice to have both.

"Walkin' the Line" (demo)

Songwriter: Brian Wilson

A vocal/keyboard/beatbox demo recorded with Gary Usher, this is mostly fully-formed – even in this primitive version it's very easy to hear what the record will become. There are some slight lyrical improvements on the finished version (presumably the work of Nick Laird-Clowes, who is credited as a co-writer there but not on the demo), but they amount to about three lines being altered. The only musical element missing is the "wah wah wah" that on the finished version leads from the chorus back into the verse.

Melt Away (early version – alternate vocal)

Songwriter: Brian Wilson

A demo featuring very slightly different lyrics, with Brian, a keyboard, and a stack of backing vocals adding "dit"s and "ooh"s. Not especially revelatory – it sounds exactly as one would imagine a demo for the song would sound.

Night Time (instrumental track)

Songwriters: Andy Paley and Brian Wilson

The instrumental track and backing vocals for "Night Time". Nothing especially interesting if one has heard the finished version.

Little Children (demo)

Songwriter: Brian Wilson

Another demo with little to reveal about the finished song.

Night Bloomin' Jasmine (demo)

Songwriter: Brian Wilson

This, on the other hand, is a very different matter. This is a recording from 1979, with Brian's older, gruff, voice, and is a fascinating song in its own right. It consists of three sections – the "night bloomin' jasmine, it comes a creeping through my window" chorus, which was reused in "Rio Grande", a much more uptempo verse section ("I smell, I smell, I smell it for the very first time"), and then an even faster instrumental section, with a bass riff similar to "Help Me Rhonda", and fast clusters of boogie-style piano chords augmented by Moog.

Vocally and production-wise, this is head and shoulders above anything else on the CD, even though it's clearly an unfinished demo. Unlike some of the patchwork songs I've discussed earlier, the three disparate sections here feel of a piece. Quite a fascinating track, and evidence that even at his lowest, Brian Wilson had been musically very inventive.

Rio Grande (early version – compiled rough mixes)

Songwriters: Andy Paley and Brian Wilson

This isn't really an early version of the song, nor is it a compilation of rough mixes as such. Rather, it's a selection of bits of instrumental takes and vocal parts, arranged into something resembling the final form of the song (though two minutes shorter), along with some discarded elements that didn't make the final song, and allowing one to hear different parts of the instrumentation more clearly. It manages to reveal both the fragmentary nature of the pieces that made up the track and the inventiveness of those pieces – what we hear here is several thirty- or sixty-second fragments, most unmistakably Brian Wilson, with very little connection to each other. But those fragments are often gorgeous, and large parts of this are very reminiscent of the *Holland* album, with its combinations of banjo, Moog, and piano.

Brian on "Rio Grande"

Excerpts of an interview with Brian Wilson, clearly pressured in speech and uncomfortable, explaining the meaning behind "Rio Grande".

Brian on "The Source"

Another excerpt from an interview, with Brian saying "art is intangible...art is not a finite thing". This is followed by two hidden tracks

– a Christmas message from 1987, and a very short excerpt from "Doing Time on Planet Earth" (a stack of Brians singing "join the human race", to the same melody that in "Being With the One You Love" would be "in our private space").

Still Cruisin'

While Brian Wilson's comeback was receiving critical acclaim but little commercial success, something rather strange was happening to the rest of the band...

The Beach Boys had spent much of the 1980s releasing odd one-off singles, often for film soundtracks or as collaborations with other artists. These were pretty much uniformly awful, and didn't trouble the charts, and the band generally dropped them out of their live sets after a perfunctory few weeks or months at most.

But then came "Kokomo", a song the band recorded for the Tom Cruise film *Cocktail*, which was itself a massive hit. But while the film was big, the song – written and recorded without the presence of Brian – became a massive phenomenon, selling over a million copies, and becoming the band's first US number one in twenty-two years, making them the record holders for the longest gap between number one records.

As a result, the band got a one-off album deal with Capitol, to put out an album of songs that had featured in recent films. The resulting album was the result of much horse-trading between various interested parties, and ended up featuring a mix of recent minor hit singles, new songs, and three old hits ("Wouldn't It Be Nice", "I Get Around", and "California Girls") that had recently appeared in successful films. It's a strange mix of styles and sounds, which went gold mostly because it featured "Kokomo", but which has been out of print for a long time, with very little demand for a reissue.

This review will only deal with the 1980s tracks on the album, as I dealt with the 60s ones on their respective albums (though note that the version of "Wouldn't It Be Nice" here is an alternative mix, included by mistake, which can now be found on the *Pet Sounds Sessions* box set).

Unless otherwise mentioned, all tracks were produced by Terry Melcher.

line-up

Brian Wilson, Carl Wilson, Al Jardine, Mike Love, Bruce Johnston (and Dennis Wilson on the three 1960s tracks)

Still Cruisin'

Songwriters: Terry Melcher and Mike Love

Lead vocals: Mike Love and Carl Wilson

The album opens surprisingly strongly, with Love's "come on let's cruise, you got nothin' to lose" hook, on a song that John Phillips referred to as "Still Kokomoin'". In truth, this is a better song than the one it's patterned after – while both have a repetitive Love bass vocal hook and Carl Wilson singing a high chorus line, this one is far catchier, and has a better groove to it than the earlier single.

We do, though, here see the final end of Mike Love's ability to write a lyric without referencing both the environment ("you got a greenhouse effect on me") and the titles of earlier, better, Beach Boys songs ("hop in my hot rod and *do it again*", "party *all summer long*"). This will get much, much worse on the next album.

But while the song itself is pleasant (and makes occasional returns to the Beach Boys' live set to this day), and the vocal arrangement is strong (each of the four Beach Boys on the track – Brian Wilson is not present – is clearly audible and in strong voice), the problem is the production. Whether the blame lies with Terry Melcher, or with Keith Wechsler, who engineered and also provided the keyboards and drum programming, the result is a treble-heavy, thin, jangly mess. There are things that purport to be solos here, but they're just lost in a trebly mush of reverb.

While the track made the top thirty in a few countries, it barely scraped into the Hot 100 in the US.

Somewhere Near Japan

Songwriters: Terry Melcher, John Philips, Bruce Johnston and Mike Love

Lead vocals: Mike Love, Al Jardine and Carl Wilson

Another attempt to recapture lightning in a bottle, this time by rewriting another song by John Phillips, who had provided the basic idea for the song that became "Kokomo". Love, Johnston, and Melcher took a song, "Fairy Tale Girl", which Phillips had originally written as a baroque pop song[1], and ditched everything but the second verse, which became the first three lines of the new song, and the general subject matter.

The subject of Phillips' song was the first honeymoon of his daughter, Mackenzie, who had married her drug dealer, and had called Phillips from Guam asking for help when the drugs and money ran out. Phillips' original version saw the "fairy tale girl's" drug addiction as not entirely negative – "sometimes you have to leave a place, and head on out into inner space".

The Beach Boys make the girl's plight far more obvious, while also increasing the drug references – "and now she's tripping on some Chinese junk/Her world is spinning and all hope is sunk... strung out in no man's land". They also replace Phillips' plinky baroque-pop-by-numbers with a generic eighties rock sound, overlaid with a little Hollywood orientalism.

The song is widely regarded by fans as the last truly great Beach Boys track, at least until 2012. I disagree myself, but that may well be because of my own distaste for thin layers of "exotic" faux-Japanese music overlaid on rock songs. It's one of the few songs on this album or its successor that actually has any musical or lyrical coherence, or aims any higher than providing a not-too-unpleasant soundtrack for a beach party, and for that it should be applauded, but I still don't think it's actually all that good.

Island Girl

Songwriter: Al Jardine

Lead vocals: Al Jardine, Mike Love and Carl Wilson

...and here's where the album gets really bad. Al Jardine, possibly the world's whitest man, trying to write tropical music – since "Kokomo", the Beach Boys had clearly decided to go after some of the Jimmy Buffett money. The melody is derivative of both "The Tide Is High" (the Paragons song that Blondie covered and had a hit with) and "Every Day" by Buddy Holly, but the song is actually not too bad, and Jardine's production has more depth to it than the two Melcher tracks that preceded. We also have our first bit of Brian Wilson on the album, as he appears with Carl and Al on the intro (though not on the rest of the song).

The problem is, surprisingly enough, Carl Wilson. Carl was always a great vocalist, but as the eighties drew to an end he didn't seem any longer to have the ability to rise above mediocre material. Here he distorts his vowels in a way that suggests he is trying for a Caribbean accent.

This is the Beach Boys' equivalent to "Ob-La-Di, Ob-La-Da", but for the 1980s, synthesised steel drums and all. Between this and the last

---

[1] Phillips' version can be heard on the album *Many Mamas, Many Papas*. It's not very good.

track, one starts to wonder if this album should not have been called *The Beach Boys Appropriate Other Cultures.*

In My Car

Songwriter: Brian Wilson †

Lead vocals: Brian Wilson, Al Jardine and Carl Wilson

This track, produced by Brian Wilson and, allegedly, Eugene Landy, was apparently a late addition to the album, and is sonically completely different from everything else on the album. This makes sense, as it's a Brian solo track, onto which Al and Carl have dubbed chorus lead vocals (Carl takes the first chorus, Al the second, and both the ending choruses). It shouldn't be confused with "Let's Go To Heaven In My Car", which is a completely different song – and which actually *would* have fit the theme of the album, as it appeared in *Police Academy IV.* That said, Brian does make an attempt to fit in with the rest of the record, echoing the "still cruisin' after all these years" line from the title track.

This could have been a fun track, had the band been more involved. Sadly, we have a wall of Brians – and while Brian sounds great on the second and third verses (or at least "great for Brian in 1989"), on the opening verse he's practically incomprehensible, and the attempts to go into falsetto for the bridges are just painful.

The last Brian Wilson track released by the Beach Boys in their original incarnation should have been better than this.

Kokomo

Songwriters: John Phillips, Scott McKenzie, Terry Melcher and Mike Love

Lead vocals: Mike Love, Carl Wilson and Bruce Johnston

And this is the last time the Beach Boys made any significant cultural impact on the world with something new...

"Kokomo" started as a song written by John Phillips of the Mamas and the Papas, with his friend Scott McKenzie (for whom Phillips had earlier written the song "San Francisco"). Phillips' song was a gentle lounge song about nostalgia and memories. In his song, he looks back on trips to Kokomo, "where we used to go to get away from it all", with a lost love, and compares it to his present life. "At least we gave it a try" is the refrain, which ends the middle eight and which is repeated at the end of the song.

Love and Melcher took Phillips' verse melody and about a third of his lyrics (the first two lines of the first verse, much of the last verse, and odd phrases from elsewhere), and changed it to a straightforward fantasy – whereas Phillips sang about "where we *used* to go", Love sings about "where we *wanna* go", and he wants to take you there with him.

While the verse lyric changes were sometimes minor (and oddly one of the lines Love always claims for himself, "by and by we'll defy a little bit of gravity", which he claims to be a reference to yogic flying, is clearly based on the line "Everybody's tryin' to break loose from gravity" from the original), they change the focus dramatically, from being about specific times with a specific, remembered, lost lover to being about a fantasy of the future with a generic "pretty mama" to whom Love and Carl Wilson are singing.

But the verses aren't what made the song – what made the song a hit is Love and Melcher's major contribution, the two-part chorus. Love apparently came up with the "Aruba, Jamaica," section – a list of places in the style of "Surfin' USA" or "California Girls", which opens the song as a bass vocal hook, sung by Love alone, and then becomes a mass chorus on subsequent repeats – while Melcher came up with Carl Wilson's "Ooh I wanna take you down to Kokomo" section. This chorus, far more than McKenzie and Phillips' verses, is what made the song into the hit it became.

And it became a *massive* hit. When released as a single, backed not even with a Beach Boys track but with Little Richard's "Tutti Frutti", it reached number one in the US, and went on to sell more copies than anything the band had done since "Good Vibrations". While it didn't have the long-term cultural or critical impact of the earlier song, and is now mostly remembered as a piece of 80s kitsch, it could easily be argued that it was as big a hit.

And it did deserve to be a hit; there's no question of that. Personally, I find the song at best uninteresting, at worst actively unpleasant, depending on my own mood, but as a crafted piece of work it's extraordinarily well done. As it was being made for a big-budget film, even the demo was far more crafted than most of the finished tracks on this album, with Melcher cutting an instrumental track with such big names (and long-term colleagues) as Ry Cooder, Van Dyke Parks, and Jim Keltner – although it says everything about 80s attitudes that Keltner was hired, not to play the drums, but to come up with the drum machine part. Over this Love, Johnston, Jeffrey Foskett (who also played acoustic guitar), and Melcher layered vocals, and the demo was used to get the song on the *Cocktail* soundtrack. Only once that had been agreed did Jardine and Carl Wilson drop in their own vocals.

And the vocals are quite remarkable – Love, in particular, is in far better voice than normal, singing in his more comfortable baritone rather than his increasingly-strained tenor voice, while Johnston doubles him on the "everybody knows..." section, and Carl's vocal on his short section is possibly the most memorable part of the track.

Brian Wilson, on the other hand, was not involved. Sources differ as to why that was – either the band deliberately excluded him because they considered him unreliable or, more likely, Landy kept him away from the session and didn't inform him of it. Either way, this meant that when the track got to number one, Love had irrefutable proof that he could make a hit record without Brian Wilson...

Wipe Out (with the Fat Boys)

Songwriters: Bob Berryhil, Pat Connolly, Jim Fuller and Ron Wilson

Lead vocals: Prince Markie Dee, Kool Rock-Ski, Buff Love a.k.a. The Human Beatbox, and Brian Wilson

Oh dear...

The story goes that this track, from 1987, was originally going to be a collaboration with Run DMC, who approached the Beach Boys after the hip-hop act's earlier success working with Aerosmith on "Walk This Way". One can only imagine what such a collaboration would have been like – certainly, there was every chance it could have been dreadful, but it also could have revitalised the Beach Boys' career in the same way that "Walk This Way" had for Aerosmith.

Instead, allegedly because Mike Love thought it would be more commercial, though reliable information about this track is hard to find, it was decided that the Beach Boys should guest on a track by novelty rappers The Fat Boys, whose main claim to fame was that they were, indeed, fat.

The chosen track for the collaboration was a remake of the Surfaris' classic instrumental "Wipe Out", whose most distinctive aspect was its frenzied, bacchanalian, drumming – so naturally it was decided to take the track at a slower speed and use a dull drum machine part instead. While the Fat Boys rapped about going for a ride to the beach and meeting "the real Beach Boys", a stack of overly-processed Brians sing the words "wipe out" and "wah wah wah" over and over, all feeling drained from the vocal by the production in a desperate attempt to make him sound something like in tune.

While Love, Jardine, and Johnston all appear in the video (there were apparently some lows to which Carl Wilson wouldn't stoop), Jardine and Johnston are not audible on the track. While Gary Usher, who assisted in the production (credits: "Produced by Albert Cabrera and Tony Moran (Little Rascals) in association with the Beach Boys, co-produced by Darren Robinson and Damon Wimbley"), claimed that all the Beach Boys were present for at least one session, all that can be heard is multi-tracked Brian and what may be Love on the bass part.

Rather surprisingly, the track reached number twelve on the Billboard chart (and number ten on their R&B chart), and actually made number two in the UK, becoming their biggest hit here other than "Do It Again" and "Good Vibrations". This meant that the song stayed in the band's live repertoire for far longer than was decent, with Billy Hinsche rapping.

Diabolical.

Make it Big

Songwriters: Terry Melcher, Bob House and Mike Love

Lead vocals: Carl Wilson and Mike Love

And the final new song on the album is a track that was recorded for the film *Troop Beverly Hills*. The song is built around a synth riff that sounds like... well, like every other bad rock song built around a synth riff for a poor eighties film. It could be Huey Lewis, or Kenny Loggins, or Survivor, or any of a thousand other identical awful excuses for music.

Over this riff is... not a song, exactly, because "song" implies something more structured than this. There are several things that seem to be trying to be hooks, joined together into a twelve-and-a-half-bar pseudo-chorus sung with more gusto than it deserves by Carl Wilson, there's a sixteen-bar verseish sung by Mike (with a bit of Al), and there are some repetitions of the main "make it big" line. But at no point does this cohere into anything like a workable song, rather than a few half-arsed ideas glued together by synth riffs and sax solos. The lyrics, meanwhile, are motivational-poster pabulum.

I really don't like talking about what, despite appearances, are my favourite band like this. But the fact is, *Still Cruisin'* as a whole, and this song in particular, are lazy, half-thought-out and bland, the epitome of "will this do?" MTV-era mediocrity. And sadly, this was not the worst they would do. There was still a further depth to which they would sink...

Summer in Paradise

The early 90s were a terrible time for the Beach Boys. Critically, they were at their lowest point, before their late-60s and 70s work had been reevaluated and seen for the clever, beautiful, music it was. Artistically, they were even lower – trudging through oldies shows with a backing band that was steadily getting worse, and making Hawaiian-shirted guest appearances on family sitcoms. And their interpersonal relations were at their worst.

Brian Wilson was completely uninvolved with the band at this point. He'd recorded a second solo album (the rather decent *Sweet Insanity*), which remained unreleased, and his family were finally extricating him from the clutches of "Doctor" Landy. But a whole series of lawsuits surrounding Landy (and publishing credits for songs dating back to the 60s) strained his relationships with all the other band members. Meanwhile, for a while, Al Jardine was "suspended" from the band because of an "attitude problem" (Mike Love's assessment of the situation).

Jardine was thus absent during the initial sessions for what became *Summer in Paradise*, the worst album, by a long way, to ever be released under the Beach Boys' name. Essentially a Mike Love/Terry Melcher album, to which Jardine, Johnston, and Carl Wilson added some vocals, it's the only Beach Boys album with no Brian Wilson involvement whatsoever (apart from his writing credit on the re-recorded "Surfin'"), and it's truly terrible.

The really sad thing is that it's clearly not *intended* to be terrible. The people involved clearly thought they were doing something good – and one can even follow the thinking. "Kokomo" had been a massive hit, and *Still Cruisin'* had been a commercial, if not critical, success. So an album of stuff that sounded just like "Kokomo", written by Love and Melcher, with a few remakes of oldies thrown in, should have made commercial success. And then to combine the fun in the sun theme with advocacy for environmental causes – something about which Love was and is commendably and genuinely passionate – and a little of Love's spiritual beliefs, should at least have created something with some artistic integrity. Commercial *and* artistic – how could it miss?

Instead, what we end up with is just awful; an album that the band themselves have quietly disowned (in the video screens and programmes for their 2012 reunion tour, every album except this one had its cover displayed, and in the two career-spanning box sets they've released there are no recordings from this), and which is generally, and rightly, regarded as the worst thing the band ever did.

While quite a few people ended up owning copies of this thanks to a QVC sale bundling it in as a freebie with the 1993 *Good Vibrations* box set, according to Terry Melcher, who produced, it sold fewer than a thousand copies total through normal channels. And it's easy to see why. It's terrible without being *interestingly* terrible – frequently crass, horribly recorded (it was recorded on a beta copy of Pro-Tools, one of the very first albums to be made entirely using that software), and unimaginative. It was released on the band's own Brother Records, and the US distributor soon went out of business, which didn't help.

It was re-released in a substantially different form in Europe, through EMI, with five of the tracks partially re-recorded, and that version is better, but still not good. The main difference is that Al Jardine features on more tracks in the European release, as he probably would have on the original release had he been in the band for the whole recording.

Either version, however, is unpleasant, and nearly unlistenable. An album that can safely be ignored by even the biggest fan. For twenty years it sat as the ignominious end of the band's studio career – thankfully, the 2012 reunion means that this no longer even has that significance.

line-up

Carl Wilson, Al Jardine, Mike Love, Bruce Johnston

Hot Fun in the Summertime

Songwriter: Sylvester Stewart

Lead vocals: Mike Love, Carl Wilson, and Adrian Baker

Sly and the Family Stone's original of this is a glorious, slow-grooving, funky soul track, which one can listen to over and again, just glorying in the interplay of the voices and the swing feel of the instrumental track.

This, on the other hand, is a mess of synth drums, lounge sax, and over-processed vocals, with Carl Wilson sounding bored out of his head (as he does throughout most of the album), and Adrian Baker (the band's touring falsettist for brief periods in the early 80s, very early 90s, and very late 90s/early 2000s) getting as close as he ever does to being on key. There's horrible tinkly percussion all over the stereo spectrum, and all the vocals sound like they've been sung through a tin can thanks to all the processing.

Amazingly, this is one of the better tracks on the album.

Surfin'

Songwriters: Brian Wilson and Mike Love

Lead vocals: Mike Love and Carl Wilson

A remake of the band's first single, slowed down enormously, with terrible synth drums and a crunchy 80s rawk guitar riff. One could possibly find a use for this song as part of a conceptual art piece of some sort – showing the difference between a gang of teenagers with a single acoustic guitar, double bass, and bin lid, and a bunch of men in their late forties and fifties, who even with the most up-to-date technology in the world couldn't replicate the simple joy of their teens. One could perhaps call it "The Pro-Tools of Dorian Gray", or simply "Death".

What this track *isn't* useful for, though, is gaining any pleasure by listening.

Bruce Johnston said online, around 2001, that the vocal tracks from this were being used in a "Britney Spears-style" remix by the producers of "Macarena", for a potential fortieth anniversary single release. That this never happened is evidence that no matter how bad things are, they indeed *could* always be worse.

Summer of Love

Songwriters: Terry Melcher and Mike Love

Lead vocals: Mike Love

This is the absolute nadir of recorded sound. I can't really emphasise that enough. One can analyse the song – pointing out that the "sum sum summer" hook (if that's the right word for anything involved in this track) is a reuse of a hook that had already been used in "Some of Your Love" on *Keepin' the Summer Alive*, and before that on "Almost Summer" by Love's side project Celebration. One can talk about the fact that the song was intended as a duet with Bart Simpson, but turned down, or about the dreadful appearance on *Baywatch* lip-syncing the track. There are a lot of things one can say about this.

But nothing can prepare you for the experience of Mike Love's "Well it's a LOVE THANG" bass vocal, or robo-Bruce singing "Girls are always ready" (because girls, apparently, are always ready for a summer of love). But those aren't the worst things.

This song features Mike Love rapping.

And not just that, but the lyrics he's rapping are things like "Well, I'll take you to a movie, but I'm no fool/First I'll get you on the beach or in a swimming pool/Doing unto others is the golden rule/But doing it with you would be so very cool".

I cannot possibly convey how incredibly terrible this track is. Please do *not*, however, take this as some sign that this is "so bad it's good", or that you need to listen to this to see how awful it really is. There is nothing good here. It's just terribly, terribly sad.

Island Fever

Songwriters: Terry Melcher and Mike Love

Lead vocals: Mike Love and Carl Wilson (Love and Al Jardine on European version)

Compared with the last track, this is astonishingly beautiful. However, compared with any other music ever made, it's a dull retread of "Kokomo". Structurally, the two songs are almost identical, but this has none of "Kokomo"'s admittedly limited charms.

The USA version sounds, frankly, like a demo, and the European version, with its much fuller production, rewritten lyrics, and new bridge (with a solo line for Al, his first lead vocal line on the album and the best thing on it so far), is much more listenable. But both are, essentially, just "Kokomo" with lyrics that attempt a metaphor about wanting a prescription to treat "island fever". Dull, but not unlistenable.

Still Surfin'

Songwriters: Terry Melcher and Mike Love

Lead vocals: Mike Love

Another diabolical song, this time about someone with a law degree who's quit to become an oceanographer and save the whales while also surfing. Or something. The song doesn't make much sense, and it's not helped that it's a patchwork of other, better songs. The "duh duh" backing vocal comes from "Heroes & Villains", "that's where the girls are" from "Palisades

Park", and the chorus is the chorus of "Cherry Cherry Coupe", just with a ii substituting for the IV chord.

The track as a whole, though, is a dreary, sludgy, mess of midtempo nothing.

Slow Summer Dancin' (One Summer Night)

Songwriters: Bruce Johnston and Danny Webb

Lead vocals: Bruce Johnston and Al Jardine

Easily the best thing on the album to this point, this is Johnston's last songwriting contribution to the band as of 2015. Johnston writes new verses, in his usual style, and uses the verse/chorus of the doo-wop classic "One Summer Night" (originally a hit for the Danleers) as a chorus. It actually works pretty well, if one ignores the horrible drum sound and lounge sax solo.

There's always an element of *schmaltz* to Johnston, even at his best, and that shows up in the verses he sings, but Jardine, who takes lead on the "one summer night" sections, sounds extraordinary – unlike everyone else involved in the album, he seems to be really *trying* with his vocal.

The result isn't a great track, but it's one that could, with a remix and with the drums replaced, be a good one.

Strange Things Happen

Songwriters: Terry Melcher and Mike Love

Lead vocals: Mike Love and Al Jardine

This is, at least in the European version, one of the less offensively bad songs on the album. The lyrics, about a New Age woman who "believes in God, and karma too/paranormal powers..." and who travels to the Rio climate summit, are not too awful, and Jardine again sounds fantastic on the chorus. The US version, though, is spoiled by a hugely extended fade containing no musical ideas at all.

The track, in the European version, is merely bland, with annoying amounts of reverb on the vocals, and the usual annoying guitar licks from Craig Fall (who played as large a part in this album as in *Still Cruisin'*). The US version, with its extra 84 seconds, tries the patience considerably.

Remember (Walking In The Sand)

Songwriter: George "Shadow" Morton

Lead vocals: Carl Wilson

The original version of this song, by the Shangri-Las, is one of the greatest singles ever, with its sudden changes in mood and tempo, its sense of drama, its portentous opening chords, and its stop-start "oh no no no" section.

So of course, the best thing to do was to get rid of half the chorus lyrics, keep everything at a constant tempo, have the same godawful sax part Joel Peskin has played on every other track on this album (and most of *Still Cruisin'*), have a horrible drum machine, synth percussion, and a voice sounding like a robot from a children's cartoon saying "remember".

Vile.

Lahaina Aloha

Songwriters: Terry Melcher and Mike Love

Lead vocals: Mike Love and Carl Wilson

Whenever someone makes a half-hearted attempt to defend *Summer in Paradise* among Beach Boys fans, one thing is always said: "well, 'Lahaina Aloha' is quite good..."

It isn't. It's merely not terrible. Carl Wilson takes much of the lead vocal on the chorus, and sounds considerably less bored than on much of the rest of the album, and the accordion part (played by Van Dyke Parks, of all people) makes the arrangement slightly less generic than some of the other tracks. But this is still the same mid-tempo AOR, with the same lyrical themes (mysterious dancing women, ships sailing away, temporary affairs) as everything else on the album, and the same bad generic rawk guitar.

Unlike much of the rest of the album, this at least sounds vaguely competent, like more than ten seconds' thought has gone into it, but on almost any other Beach Boys album this would be the worst thing by a long way.

Under the Boardwalk

Songwriters: Artie Resnick and Kenny Young (new lyrics Mike Love)

Lead vocals: Mike Love and Carl Wilson (with Al Jardine on the European version)

Yet another absolute classic song turned into a mess of skittering electronic percussion, with a bored Carl Wilson and an unimaginative sax solo from Joel Peskin. For some reason Love decided to get rid of the second verse of the Drifters' original (possibly the line about tasting the hot dogs conflicted with his vegetarianism) and replace it with two new verses about walking on the beach.

The US version of this has no redeeming features at all. The European version restores the bridge (which was replaced by even more Peskin solo in the US version), and has Jardine take the lead on that section, immediately lifting it up. It's also considerably shorter, which is a mercy.

Summer in Paradise

Songwriters: Terry Melcher, Craig Fall, and Mike Love

Lead vocals: Mike Love (Love and Roger McGuinn on European version)

This is the closest thing to a decent new song on the entire album. What starts out as more nostalgia ("our masterplan was having fun fun fun as America's band/We came out rockin' with Rhonda and Barbara Ann") soon turns into a rather more interesting song about wanting to fix the world's environmental problems "so we can bring back summer in paradise".

Other than Van Dyke Parks' accordion, the US version of the track sounds like a poorly-thought-out demo, but the European version, which is largely re-recorded and features Roger McGuinn on vocals and twelve-string guitar, is much more listenable, and has slightly less ridiculous lyrics (only slightly – "surfers recycle now, don't you know/like everyone from California to Kokomo" becomes "everybody knows that you reap what you sow/all the way from California to Kokomo" – this is still not subtle).

The tempo of the song is still too plodding in either studio version, but a rather nice live version from 1993, with Johnston singing the parts that McGuinn sings here, available on the *Made in California* box set shows that there is the germ of a good track here, and on the rare occasions the band have performed it live it's been enjoyable enough.

Forever

Songwriters: Dennis Wilson and Gregg Jakobson

Lead vocals: John Stamos

And the album ends with a remake of Dennis Wilson's most popular song. John Stamos, a teen heartthrob in mediocre family sitcom *Full House*, was a fan of the Beach Boys, and had guested with them on drums occasionally for several years. The band had also featured in the TV series on several occasions, and he had performed "Forever" on the show more than once, including in a scene at his character's wedding the year before this album came out (a version of the song that's rather nicer than this one).

It therefore made sense to have Stamos sing the song here, and he does a competent enough job. It's a hard song to mess up, and while there are once again too many squealing rock guitars, if you hadn't heard the original you could be forgiven for thinking "this is quite good".

In a world where the original exists, of course, this is utterly pointless, but it still stands head and shoulders above the rest of the album because it's a great song and they don't do anything to deliberately sabotage it. On an album like *Summer in Paradise*, that's as close as you can get to a success.

Good Vibrations: Thirty Years of the Beach Boys

The 1990s saw a huge change in the image of the Beach Boys – or, rather, in the image of Brian Wilson. While the Beach Boys were performing, largely without Brian, on shows like *Full House* and having hits like "Kokomo", the CD reissue programme of the early 90s which saw the twofer CD releases and *Pet Sounds* released on CD for the first time led a new generation of music fans to reevaluate the band's mid-sixties music.

Hipster and indie music fans were now name-checking *Pet Sounds* and *Smile,* and the band's more artistic music was now considered vital listening even if the band themselves were the epitome of uncoolness. This period really saw the first significant split in the Beach Boys' fanbase – now there were "Beach Boys fans" who liked the early hits, and "Brian Wilson fans" who liked only the music from 1966 and 67 (revaluation of the later music would have to wait another few years). This divide would only become greater as the years went on, but *Good Vibrations: Thirty Years of the Beach Boys* added a lot of fuel to the debate.

On its release in 1993, this five-CD box set was the definitive collection of the Beach Boys' music, and it's still a fascinating, worthwhile collection. It contained every top thirty hit the band had had in the US, most of the notable album tracks, and a lot of previously-unreleased material, including a CD of outtakes and demo versions. Most interesting for most fans was its presentation of thirty minutes of *Smile* music – the first time almost any of it had seen legitimate release. (That material will be dealt with in the *Smile* ,essays later in this book.)

The box set was put together by David Leaf (writer of an early Brian Wilson biography), Andy Paley (Wilson's songwriting partner at the time), and Mark Linett (the sound engineer who worked on the reissue programme and on Wilson's solo recordings at the time). Unsurprisingly, given those who worked on it, it presents, both in song selection and packaging, a very Brian-centric view of the band, in which Brian is a romantic tortured genius and the other band members just some hangers on (in the fifty-nine-page booklet, Al Jardine is mentioned by name eight times, for example (five of them on one page about the band forming) and Bruce Johnston five. In comparison, Paul McCartney is mentioned seven times). The story being told is clearly "big hits, Brian gets good and becomes a genius, then he crashes and burns and nothing much happens". CD one is devoted to the years 1961-64, two to 65-67, three to late 67-72, and disc four covers 1972 through 1988 (nothing from the five years between "Kokomo" and the box set's release is included). Disc five, the outtakes disc, contains alternate versions of songs on the first two discs, so a full sixty percent of the box covers the first five-and-a-bit years of the band's existence, while the seven albums released after *The Beach Boys Love You* are covered by six songs in total. (A limited edition version with a sixth CD was briefly available in Europe. That sixth CD contained songs like "Bluebirds Over the Mountain" which had been hits outside the US)

This sounds like I am being harsh on the box set, and it's really not intended that way. For the twenty years until the release of the six-CD *Made in California* set this was *the* definitive Beach Boys collection, and it still contains some great music which is unavailable elsewhere. The fact that it tells one particular story of the band's career is unavoidable – every possible collection would be governed by the viewpoint of whoever selected the songs – and Leaf, Paley, and Linett did an extraordinary job in putting this together.

The songs I discuss below are a very small portion of the box set – only those songs which had not had a CD release earlier, and which are not covered in the *Smile* essays later in the book (I also don't cover a couple of fragments of radio station jingle recorded by the band and included between proper tracks). There's much to love in the alternate takes of songs like "In My Room", or the vocals-only and instrumental-only versions of well-known songs, and of course in the hundred or so previously-released songs on the box set.

Little Surfer Girl

Songwriter: Brian Wilson

Lead vocals: Brian Wilson

A thirty-second fragment, just Brian's voice, organ, and a snare drum. Not the same song as "Surfer Girl", this just has two lines of a rather pretty melody, a song which seems to have been intended as a duet between a "surfer boy" and a "surfer girl".

Punchline

Songwriter: Brian Wilson

An utterly generic organ-led surf instrumental, with various band members pretending to laugh over the top.

The Things We Did Last Summer

Songwriters: Sammy Cahn and Jules Styne

Lead vocals: Brian Wilson and Mike Love

An old standard, recorded by Dean Martin, Jo Stafford and others, this version is arranged very much in the style of the Four Freshmen, with a light orchestral backing, and was recorded for a TV appearance. Brian and Mike dominate in the harmonies, and it's a very pleasant example of the kind of easy-listening music that influenced Brian's arrangements.

Ruby Baby

Songwriters: Jerry Leiber and Mike Stoller

Lead vocals: Brian Wilson

A cover version of the Drifters' song, recorded during the *Party!* sessions and very much in the style of that album, with interjections, jokes, and forgotten words. Billy Hinsche adds harmonica, and the whole thing is fun, if hardly the band's greatest work.

San Miguel

Songwriters: Dennis Wilson and Gregg Jakobson

Lead vocals: Carl Wilson

A castanet-driven uptempo song with a vaguely Spectorish sound to it, this was recorded in 1969, and originally released on the now-out-of-print compilation *Ten Years of Harmony* in 1981. It's an unusual song for Dennis – light and fun – though an overly-muddy mix makes it something less than it otherwise could have been. Dennis later returned to some of the musical material in this track during the *Bambu* sessions, turning it into "Time For Bed", though this is superior to the later track.

Games Two Can Play

Songwriter: Brian Wilson

Lead vocals: Brian Wilson

One of several tracks recorded during the band's spurt of creativity around the time of *20/20* and *Sunflower*, this is a very silly, Latin-flavoured, song with an utterly charming vocal from Brian, and with lyrics that make songs like "Busy Doin' Nothin'" seem almost profound – "In the morning people are so happy/and that's the time when I'm a mister businessman/later on I really get to going/I get my legs to moving".

Utterly daft, but fun.

I Just Got My Pay

Songwriter: Brian Wilson

Lead vocals: Mike Love

A rewrite of the verse melody of "All Dressed Up For School", and one which would itself later be reworked into "Marcella", this is the least convincing of the three versions of the song. The verses alternate between a unison *a capella* chant, almost like a worksong, and fairly standard instrumentation with a Love lead, but there's not much of musical interest here. It was recorded during the sessions for *Sunflower* in early 1970, but shares little of that album's lush prettiness.

Unfortunately, what really lets it down are the lyrics, which are an attempt to imagine what the life of somebody in a normal job is like, written and performed by people who have never had that experience.

HELP is on the Way

Songwriter: Brian Wilson

Lead vocals: Mike Love

A song originally recorded in summer 1970, this is a rather charming little song about Wilson's occasional obsession with health food. Over a minimal backing consisting mostly of tack piano and "ooh" backing vocals, Love sings "Stark naked in front of my mirror/a pudgy person somehow did appear/Seems lately all I've eaten's sugar and fat/It's getting obvious that's not where it's at". The song goes on to warn of the "doughy lumps, stomach pumps, enemas too" that will result from a junk food diet, and to recommend H.E.L.P (a healthfood store which is also mentioned in "Take a Load off Your Feet" from around this time) and the Radiant Radish (another healthfood shop, this one owned at the time by Wilson himself).

4th of July

Songwriters: Dennis Wilson and Jack Rieley

Lead vocals: Carl Wilson

Originally recorded during the sessions for *Surf's Up*, this is one of Dennis Wilson's most beautiful ballads. It's about the US government's attempt to censor the New York Times' publication of the Pentagon Papers, though you couldn't tell that from listening — Rieley's lyrics are, as so often, cryptic in the extreme. They do, though, convey a more general feeling of disillusion with the US failing to live up to its ideals, quoting and paraphrasing "The Star-Spangled Banner".

Carl Wilson turns in one of his best vocals, over a string backing, and this would have been a perfect fit for *Surf's Up*, but it was apparently pulled (along with Dennis' "Wouldn't It Be Nice To Live Again") due to a conflict between Carl and Dennis over the album's sequencing.

It's Over Now

Songwriter: Brian Wilson

Lead vocals: Carl Wilson, Brian Wilson, and Marilyn Wilson

This is one of two songs on the box set from an unreleased album from 1977, *Adult/Child*. *Adult/Child* was a fascinating project, something like *The Beach Boys Love You*, but with many of the songs having full orchestrations (by Dick Reynolds, who had previously arranged the band's original Christmas album and had worked with the Four Freshmen). The combination of Brian's most idiosyncratic writing with lush big band arrangements is truly astonishing, and one has to hope that at some point the full album will see an official release.

The two songs chosen for the box set, though, are probably the best on the album, and certainly the most commercially acceptable. "It's Over Now" is a gorgeous ballad of lost love, mostly sung by Carl, with Brian taking the repeated last verse line "shades of blue and purple haunt me", while Brian's wife Marilyn sings the middle eight ("Heaven, heaven is far away/Angels no longer play").

For many years some fans assumed that this track was left unreleased in part because it was evidence of Carl Wilson's substance and drinking problem of the late 70s. He had a very brief period, during the collapse of his first marriage, when he was sometimes known to slur on stage and sing badly, and his vocal here does sound slightly drunk on this release. It turned out, though, that the master tape used had been slowed down about three percent. A corrected-speed version was included on *Made in California*, and is a much better listening experience than this one.

Still I Dream of It

Songwriter: Brian Wilson

Lead vocals: Brian Wilson

The second track from *Adult/Child* on the set, this track was unfortunately left off *Made in California*, making this the only absolutely essential track on this box which isn't available elsewhere.

One of Brian's most haunting ballads, this is one of the most heart-breaking pieces of music ever written, the work of a man who is clearly in pain, clearly mentally ill, but still also one of the greatest craftsmen in popular music.

It's a beautifully crafted piece, starting out almost sounding like the kind of slice of life songs that Brian wrote for *Friends* – he's waiting for supper and feels like eating, he can hear the maid whistle in the kitchen. In the second verse, he claims to be feeling "young and beautiful, like a tree that's just been planted", but after both verses there's a chorus which says that all is not right in the singer's world.

And then we get to the middle eight: "When I was younger, my mother told me Jesus loved the world/But if that's true then why hasn't he helped me to find a girl and find my world?" It's a punch in the gut, the sound of someone broken by the world. It's one of those moments which makes music writing frustrating, because it's impossible to describe the emotional effect of this, other than to say "just listen".

In the final verse, Brian's convinced himself that everything will all be OK, somehow, and that, as he sings as the song ends, "some day I'll find my world" – there's a clear, strong, narrative, emotional arc to this song that the apparently random lyrics at first seem to be hiding, but it's there. The song as a whole continues the theme of lost, broken, longing optimism that we see in "I Just Wasn't Made For These Times" or "Til I Die", where the reaction to the world being against you is to sing "hey hey hey".

Heartbreakingly beautiful.

Our Team

Songwriters: Brian Wilson, Dennis Wilson, Carl Wilson, Mike Love, Al Jardine

Lead vocals: Al Jardine, Brian Wilson, and Group

A fun little nothing that was an outtake from the *MIU Album*, and was used over the end credits of a making-of documentary about the album. While the writing is credited to all five band members, it's likely to be mostly the work of Brian, Mike, and Al, as Carl and Dennis were basically absent for the *MIU* sessions.

This is one of several sports-themed songs Brian wrote or co-wrote around this time (of which the most well-known is the widely-bootlegged "Baseball" (also known as "It's Trying To Say") from *Adult/Child*). Al takes lead on this paean to team spirit, but Brian belts out an enthusiastic "the girls in the stands/and all of our fans" at the end of every verse (he sounds surprisingly like Dennis on these lines). There's a verse of "ba ba ba"s with party noises, a la *Beach Boys Party!*, and the whole thing makes almost no impression but is impossible to dislike.

I Just Wasn't Made For These Times

An interesting thing happened in the early 1990s. The image of the Beach Boys began to split into two – and this split would determine much of the rest of the band's career.

On the one hand, there was the image in the general media, of America's band having fun, fun, fun and bringing good vibrations to Kokomo. Rightly or wrongly, this image was associated primarily with Mike Love, and was the focus of many of the band's TV appearances at the time.

But there was another image that was being created, one that was appearing in the music magazines and was increasingly becoming the received wisdom about the band. In this version of history, largely promoted by Brian Wilson's biographer and friend David Leaf, the Beach Boys were at best a decent vehicle for Brian Wilson's unique genius, and at worst active saboteurs. Brian Wilson was a unique genius (although in this version of history his genius was only really expressed to its fullest in *Pet Sounds* and *Smile* before being destroyed by the evil Mike Love) and the band's story was a variant on the Orson Welles one of a great genius never living up to his full potential after an early masterwork, because of the petty minds of petty people.

Both these stories have a certain amount of truth to them, of course, but in the 1990s more than at any other time, there wasn't a nuanced view of the band's career in the public eye. Those who bought the CD reissues of the band's sixties albums, with liner notes by Leaf, felt like they were getting the real truth about a romantic genius who was just too good for this world.

But while the legend of Brian Wilson was growing enormously, Wilson himself had been almost absent from the public eye for several years, except for stories about his problems. His proposed second solo album, *Sweet Insanity*, was rejected by the label and never released (bootlegs show that while it wasn't a great album, it was very solid, and certainly better than many things that *did* get released). Wilson was also the subject of a prolonged court battle, with his family attempting to save him from Landy, who had by this point thoroughly taken control of Wilson's life.

That court battle, and the other litigation around that time, put a permanent strain on Wilson's relationship with the Beach Boys, especially his brother Carl (who had been the biggest force trying to extricate him from Landy, and who had therefore become a source of stress in Brian Wilson's eyes). But by the mid-1990s, everything had settled down. Wilson had married Melinda Ledbetter, who had become a stabilising force in his life, and bridges were starting to be built with the other Beach Boys.

But while attempts were being made to record a new Beach Boys album, led by Brian, it was also very clear that his relationship with the band was still fragile, and so a second attempt was being made to build a solo career for him, to give him a public identity outside the Beach Boys.

The first fruits of this were two projects that came out in 1995. The first, *Orange Crate Art*, was an album by Van Dyke Parks which was jointly credited to Parks and Wilson, and on which Brian Wilson sang all the lead vocals and much of the backing, though he had no other creative input. That album is outside the scope of these essays, as it is far more of a Van Dyke Parks album, but it's a beautiful, astonishing record (as so much of Parks' work is), and should be listened to by anyone who loves music.

The second project was *I Just Wasn't Made For These Times*, a film and accompanying soundtrack CD, produced and directed by Don Was, which attempted to show the wider public why Wilson was a genius.

The film featured interviews with him, his family, and many of his peer group (although Carl Wilson was the only other Beach Boy interviewed in the film). The highlights, though, were the musical performances.

Unfortunately, the three best of these (performances of "God Only Knows" and "In My Room" by the two Wilson brothers and their mother, Audree, around a piano, and a piano/vocals performance of "Orange Crate Art" by Wilson and Parks) were left off the soundtrack CD, and what is left is a very 1990s take on Wilson's music.

I Just Wasn't Made For These Times is, essentially, an "Unplugged" album. It's a collection of remakes of many of Wilson's best songs, from 1963 ("The Warmth of the Sun") through to 1988 ("Love and Mercy" and "Melt Away"), all recorded in very polite, slick arrangements by some of the leading session players of the day, with top session vocalists replacing the Beach Boys' parts (although on "Do It Again" Wilson's daughters, Carnie and Wendy, add backing vocals as well). Everything's very tasteful, but the album is somewhat lacking in the sheer *oddness* of much of Wilson's best work. This is an album with all the rough edges carefully sanded off (except for Wilson's vocals, which were still as idiosyncratic as on his first solo album) – an album designed to be listened to in the car along with Eric Clapton's *Unplugged* album, or Crowded House's *Woodface*, or Paul Simon's *Graceland*.

The image it presents is definitely *part* of why Wilson is a great artist, but to me at least it's not the most interesting part. This is just a collection of Wilson's most obviously good songs, re-recorded without anything (other than his voice) that might be distracting or indigestible. It's Wilson being fit neatly into a mould, and with anything that doesn't fit being cut off.

With one exception.

Still I Dream of It had originally been released on the *Good Vibrations* box set in a fully-orchestrated version, recorded during the sessions for the unreleased *Adult/Child* album. It had been a quiet highlight of that box's fourth disc, but had been overshadowed by the half hour of *Smile* material on the set.

Here, the original mid-70s demo is released, and it's heartbreaking. A simple piano and vocal demo, recorded on what sounds like a fourth- or fifth-generation cassette copy (bootleg copies of the demo exist in much better, though far from perfect, quality, without the break in the tape close to the end, so it must have been an aesthetic decision to use this version), the track has Brian's voice at its 1977 croakiest, hammering out piano chords while singing those glorious but broken stream-of-consciousness lyrics about hearing the maid whistling and how "the hypnosis of our minds can take us far away". Hearing that shattered voice, coming from a shattered man, singing "young and beautiful, like a tree that's just been planted I've found life today", is indescribably moving, and when he gets to the middle eight, and sings "a little while ago, my mother told me Jesus loved the world/And if that's true then why hasn't he helped me to find a girl/And find my world?" I would defy anyone not to cry.

Where the rest of the album smooths the rough edges down to something that could almost be used in a car commercial, "Still I Dream of It" is nothing *but* rough edges, and all the better for it, and merely by being on the album it manages to validate the whole thing, artistically. This, it says, is the same man – the craftsman who wrote "Meant For You" or "Warmth of the Sun", and the mentally ill man croaking about how it's time for supper are both the same person, and both deserving of recognition as great art.

I Just Wasn't Made For These Times will never be my own favourite Brian Wilson album – even with the addition of "Still I Dream of It", many of these tracks are simply too polite for my own tastes – but as we'll see with the next few albums, as an album of remakes it could have been much, much worse.

Stars & Stripes Vol. 1

And so we come to what seemed, for sixteen years, as if it would be the last ever new Beach Boys album.

Brian Wilson had spent much of the mid-1990s working with Andy Paley on several dozen new songs, intended for a Beach Boys record, recording what were, depending on who you ask, either very fully-fleshed-out demos or stripped-down completed records that just needed the Boys' vocals added. Two of these songs saw release at the time – the Paley instrumental "In My Moondreams", which appeared on a compilation titled *Pulp Surfin'*, and a rather lovely song called "This Song Wants to Sleep With You Tonight" which, in a Don Was-produced version, became the B-side of the "Do It Again" single from *I Just Wasn't Made For These Times*.

And Brian was slowly being integrated back into the group. Tentative plans for a thirtieth-anniversary *Pet Sounds* tour, performing the whole album, were abandoned because Carl Wilson didn't believe his brother was in a fit state to tour at the time, but Brian performed with the band on a collaboration with Status Quo – a remake of "Fun, Fun, Fun" with a new verse written by Love – and, importantly, on a remake of "The Warmth of the Sun" with Willie Nelson on lead vocals.

But the plan was still to do an album based on the Paley material, probably with a then-hot producer collaborating on it. Johnston brought in Sean O'Hagan of the High Llamas (a lounge-revival band whose albums *Gideon Gaye* and *Hawaii* had both been critically acclaimed, and who were very influenced by *Pet Sounds*, *Smile* and *Friends*), but personality clashes meant that that collaboration went no further, and it was eventually decided to have Don Was produce the backing tracks, and Brian to produce the vocals. Love and Wilson collaborated on reworking at least some of the Paley material, and everything was looking good for what would be the best new Beach Boys album in twenty years.

Right up until they went into the studio.

The sessions, in November 1995, were intended to produced five songs

– "Must Be A Miracle", "Turn on Your Love Light", "Soul Searchin'", "It's Not Easy Being Me", and "You're Still A Mystery". The Beach Boys, plus Matt Jardine (Al Jardine's son, who was the band's touring falsettist at the time, and had a voice that was spookily similar to a young Brian), managed to get vocals for two tracks done – the two best tracks they had recorded since 1977 – before Carl Wilson walked out of the studio, saying the new material was no good and he refused to work on it any further.

Carl had been unwell for some time, and would, within months, be diagnosed with the cancer that would eventually kill him, and one can only suppose that this was part of his decision. Either way, that decision meant the end of the Beach Boys as a creative force in the studio, apart from the brief 2012 reunion.

But the band still wanted to record with Brian, and so there was a quick change of plans. The Willie Nelson collaboration, originally intended as a one-off single, now became the start of a new album, the optimistically-named *Stars & Stripes vol. 1*, titled in the expectation of future volumes, on which the Beach Boys would collaborate with country singers on remakes of their earlier classics.

This *could* have been a good idea, if the band had been paired with a sympathetic producer and the true greats of country music. One can imagine Johnny Cash singing "Til I Die", perhaps, or Steve Earle and Emmylou Harris duetting on "God Only Knows".

Sadly, the producer they worked with was Joe Thomas (a figure who will return several times in our narrative), a mulletted ex-wrestler who gave almost all the songs a terrible, unimaginative, 80s-rock backing suitable for a Kenny Loggins B-side, all crunchy guitar and "sonic-power" drums. And the choices of vocalist were similarly uninspired – Toby Keith, Collin Raye, Ricky van Shelton, and a bunch of other interchangeable "hat acts".

To make matters worse, two of the best collaborations – Rodney Crowell singing "Sail On Sailor" and Tammy Wynette singing "In My Room" – were left off the album for volume two. Both those can be seen on the documentary *Nashville Sounds*, which is the best way to experience this album, if for some reason you have to, if only so you can see Mike Love trying to teach Willie Nelson how to sing, or Al Jardine bravely attempting to defend the album as being in some way creative by talking about how they used to sing "Ooh rah rah rah" on "Be True To Your School" but were now only singing "Ooh rah rah".

But apart from unintentional comedy on the video, is there anything at all about this album that is actually worth hearing?

Surprisingly, there is. While James House singing "Little Deuce Coupe" or Doug Supernaw on "Long Tall Texan" are as wince-inducingly awful as one would imagine, there are three tracks on the album with the involvement of actual talented people other than the Beach Boys, and those three are really quite good.

The first, obviously, is "The Warmth of the Sun" with Willie Nelson on vocals. Not only is Nelson head and shoulders above everyone else involved, but the arrangement is far more subtle than anything else on the record, with a rather lovely harmonica part, and Nelson's aged vocals give the song a very different feel from the youthful innocence of the original, which makes it an actually worthwhile performance.

Junior Brown's "409" is the polar opposite of Nelson's poignant subtlety, but in a good way. Brown rips out rockabilly solos on his guit-steel (an instrument of his own invention, combining electric and pedal steel guitars in one), and sings in a deep voice full of vibrato. It's hilarious, ridiculous, fun, and an absolute joy to listen to.

And the band must have realised those two were the best things on the album, because in the documentary those are the two tracks Jimmy Webb mentions listening to before his contribution. Webb didn't sing on the album, but did provide the glorious orchestral arrangement for "Caroline, No", sung by Timothy Schmit of the Eagles, which closes the record, and which for the first time features the other Beach Boys' vocals on what had originally been a solo Brian track.

While there are many, many, faults with this album, its closing isn't one of them, as for the last time ever we hear those family vocals, with Brian, Carl, and Mike singing "Caroline, no" in a round like the end of "God Only Knows", with Schmit over the top, and the album fades out not to a train or dogs, but just to the voices of two brothers and their cousin.

They did tell us it wouldn't last forever. But still... it's kinda sad.

The Pet Sounds Sessions

Of the spate of archival releases by the band in the 1990s, possibly the most fascinating for fans was *The Pet Sounds Sessions*, a four-CD box set dedicated to the *Pet Sounds* album, put together by Mark Linett and David Leaf.

Originally intended to come out in 1996 for the album's thirtieth anniversary, the box set was delayed eighteen months due to various band members' dissatisfaction with Leaf's original liner notes (apparently even Brian Wilson super-fan Bob Hanes felt moved, on reading them, to ask Leaf "you do know there were five other guys singing on the album too?"). When it finally came out in November 1997, though, it was definitely worth the wait.

Whatever the original liner notes were like, the two booklets eventually included with the box, both by Leaf, were a superlative resource, including interviews with almost all the surviving session players, comments from the band members, discussions of each track by Carol Kaye (the session bassist who played on many of them), and a reprint of a run of *Doonesbury* comic strips in which a character dies happy after finally hearing *Pet Sounds*, his favourite album, on CD.

But it was the music that was important, and where the box really deserved the "Best Historical Recording" Grammy it won for Leaf , Linett, and Brian Wilson. One disc of the album was simply *Pet Sounds*, presented in its original mono mix (though not my favourite mastering of the album – while some dislike the noise-reduction processing used on some other CD reissues, to my ears that's preferable to this overly-hissy version), but the other three discs were the draw for fans.

The first disc contains what was the first ever true stereo mix of *Pet Sounds* – a mix put together by Mark Linett in what was a remarkable feat for the mid-nineties. By syncing together the four-track tapes on which the instrumental tracks were recorded and the eight-tracks containing the vocals, he was able to recreate the original balances but in stereo, while also improving the sound quality – the original mono mix was the result of much bouncing down of multitrack recordings to single tracks, and by going back to the originals Linett was able to remove several generations of tape hiss.,

There are some flaws in these mixes − some parts, notably Love's vocals on the middle eight of "Wouldn't It Be Nice" and one of the two tracks for Brian Wilson's lead vocal for "You Still Believe in Me", don't exist on the multitracks, and these are missing from these stereo mixes (Love's missing vocal part on "Wouldn't It Be Nice" is replaced by a take of Brian Wilson singing the same part). Later releases of the album have restored some of these parts by digitally extracting them from the mono mix, with mixed results, but getting as close as this in 1996 was a feat in itself.

Following from this there is a disc and a half devoted to the instrumental recording sessions for the album. Each track from *Pet Sounds*, plus "Trombone Dixie" and an early run-through of "Good Vibrations", is represented by several minutes of session chatter and false starts, before stereo versions of the instrumental tracks, *sans* vocals, are presented. (The two actual instrumentals, "Pet Sounds" and "Let's Go Away For A While", are presented in versions without an important instrumental overdub, giving the same effect). This disc-and-a-half long section is perhaps the most impressive part of the set, though also the least relistenable − it's invaluable for those who want to study Wilson's work habits in the studio, or for those who want to make out every detail of the instrumental track − hearing the buried honky-tonk piano line in "I Just Wasn't Made For These Times", for example.,

There's then half a disc of stereo vocal-only mixes of all the songs (with the obvious exception of the two instrumental tracks), showing the extraordinary vocal gymnastics the band went through on this album, and allowing for the same kind of detailed analysis that the instrumental tracks provide.

(It also allowed for a certain amount of mythbusting − at the time this set came out, there were still many articles which claimed that Brian Wilson performed most or all of the backing vocals on the album by himself. Hearing the isolated vocals, in stereo separation, makes it very easy to pick out individual voices − Bruce Johnston, for example, stands out in the vocal stack on "Wouldn't It Be Nice" in a way he doesn't in the final mix.),

And finally the box finishes with a set of alternative mixes and takes − if you've ever wanted to hear "Sloop John B" with Carl Wilson singing lead on the first verse, "I'm Waiting For The Day" with Mike Love on lead, or "God Only Knows" with a really terrible saxophone solo, you can hear them here. These examples of choices not taken are interesting, but mostly show that Wilson made the correct decisions with the final album.,

There have been several reissues of *Pet Sounds* since this release – most recently a fiftieth anniversary box set that rejigs this one, adding a Blu-Ray disc and some mediocre live tracks – but this is the box set that set the standard for how to do archival projects about a single album.

Mike Love, Bruce Johnston and David Marks of the BEACH BOYS Salute NASCAR and Union 76 Gasoline

And so we come to February 1998, the worst month in the Beach Boys' history.

Mike Love and Al Jardine had, over the previous few years, grown increasingly distant, to the point where it was almost impossible for the two men to work together, with Carl Wilson being the peacemaker who could allow them to be on the same stage. For some time, Love had been planning to replace Jardine with David Marks, who had shown up for occasional shows (notably a performance for *Baywatch* in 1995).[2] Love and Marks had remained friendly, and Marks had become a remarkably proficient guitarist in the decades since he had left the band.

But all these plans became up in the air when in early 1997 it was announced that Carl Wilson (who had been seeming increasingly unwell for some time) had cancer. Carl continued to perform until the end of August, often having to sit through the performance and use an oxygen mask between songs (though he always stood for "God Only Knows", no matter how much effort it took him, according to those who were at the shows). But after August, he was no longer capable of performing, and David Marks replaced him, rather than Jardine, for the last few shows of 1997.

---

[2] Love claims that Jardine was likewise planning to replace Love, with Peter Cetera from Chicago

After that, Love performed a few shows as The California Beach Band, with the Beach Boys' backing band members, and sometimes with either Marks, Bruce Johnston, or both, but without Jardine. And Love was making plans to have a "Beach Boys" that would no longer involve Jardine at all.

The first that Jardine realised this might be a possibility was when watching the Super Bowl on TV, on January 25th, 1998, when he saw the pre-game show, featuring "A Tribute To The Beach Boys Featuring Mike Love, Bruce Johnston, David Marks, Glen Campbell, Dean Torrence, and John Stamos". He'd not been told about the show.

And also watching the Super Bowl together were Brian and Carl Wilson. They discussed Brian's forthcoming solo album, *Imagination*, on which Carl had been planning to guest on a track. Carl told Brian that he wouldn't be able to do it, and that he was dying. He said "You know, Brian, I'm not gonna be able to make it", and Brian's response, the last thing he ever said to his brother, was "I think I'm gonna stay for a while".

Carl Wilson died on February 6, 1998. Other than a single previously-contracted private show[3], Al Jardine wouldn't appear with the Beach Boys again until 2011. Mike Love would soon get the license to use the Beach Boys' name for his own touring band (featuring Johnston and, at first, Marks), but the Beach Boys as an actual band died with Carl Wilson.

And the evidence of this came almost straight away.

Love had, over the years, recorded many tracks with Adrian Baker (who had been the touring falsettist with the band in 1981-82 and 1990-92, and would rejoin in 1998, staying with Love's band until 2004). Various of these tracks have turned up over the years on promo recordings and limited-edition releases. The most well-known of these, because of its February 1998 release date, is *Mike Love, Bruce Johnston and David Marks of the BEACH BOYS Salute NASCAR and Union 76 Gasoline*, a CD that was available for a limited time through participating petrol stations only, released by Love's MELECO label.

This CD is, in this series of essays, standing in for all the various releases of material from the Mike and Adrian sessions, such as *Summertime Cruisin'* (a CD that was given away free in 2001 by participating Canadian Chrysler dealerships to people who test-drove a car). Other than two Baker originals on *Summertime Cruisin'*, these CDs all consisted of re-recordings of Beach Boys hits, along with a few covers of similar-sounding 60s hits.

While the CD claims Love, Johnston, and Marks as artists, Marks is

---

[3]Oddly, on the same day as Brian's first solo show, a TV taping to promote the *Imagination* album, at which Johnston also appeared.

inaudible on the album – it's claimed he supplied guitars for the album, but the guitars sound identical to the guitars credited to Baker on other such CDs, and I suspect he's not present at all. Johnston's only musical contribution is apparently the keyboard on "Don't Worry Baby", the closing track (some of the backing vocals, especially on "Little Deuce Coupe", sound like him, but I'm reliably informed he wasn't present for any vocal sessions).

I specify "musical" contribution, because Johnston *is* present on the excruciating intro, in which over a synthesised instrumental backing similar to, but legally distinct from, "Good Vibrations", we hear the following spoken:

> Hi, this is Mike Love of the Beach Boys. As you've probably figured out by now, cool cars and hot fun at the beach have always been close to my heart. That's why I'm pleased to have recorded, with the help of Beach Boys Bruce Johnston and David Marks, and our buddy Dean Torrence of Jan & Dean, some of our all-time favourites.

> This is Bruce Johnston of the Beach Boys. Beach lover, NASCAR lover, and the fuel that fuels me from high school all the way to my family life? 76. A million thank yous to Adrian Baker, our music producer, and I hope you enjoy our music.

> [Mike again] This CD is brought to you by 76, the official fuel of NASCAR, and I'm hopin' these songs will bring you as many good vibrations as a chequered flag at Daytona Beach.

This will give you an idea of the level of the whole CD.

There are ten tracks proper on the album, eight of them remakes of Beach Boys car songs, plus two covers of Beach Boys-sounding car hits from the 60s: "Little Old Lady From Pasadena", with Dean Torrence guesting on vocals, and a version of Ronnie & The Daytonas' "Little GTO".

"Little GTO" is one of only two listenable tracks – it actually has quite a bit of energy, and Adrian Baker sounds surprisingly like mid-60s Brian Wilson on it. The other track worth a listen is the surprising inclusion of "Ballad of Ole Betsy". This is a song that Love has always had a strong personal affection for, and which he regularly includes in his band's shows (usually now sung by his musical director Scott Totten). Here, Love takes the lead, in his lower register, and he actually manages a remarkably affecting performance – were it not for the cheap drum sound, this version might actually be better than the original.

But past those two – neither of which is great, but which are both not unpleasant – the CD is dire. The harmonies, mostly by Baker and session singer Paul Bergerot, are horrible. Baker's tone is all wrong, sounding more like Frankie Valli than the Beach Boys; his vowel sounds are all off, as he's a British person putting on an unconvincing American accent; and his pitching is inconsistent. He can occasionally (as on "Little GTO") sound OK in a backing vocal role, but when he takes lead parts, as on the chorus to "I Get Around", he just sounds unpleasant. His version of "Don't Worry Baby", the final track here, is astonishingly poor.

Love doesn't sound much better. In the late 90s and early 2000s Love was having his own pitching problems, and sounding almost self-parodically nasal. And the backing tracks are rough approximations of the originals, but created largely digitally, with bad drum programming, and with Baker's guitars sounding like the only live instruments. The tracks sound like karaoke backing tracks to which Love has added lazy vocals.

These days, Love sounds as good as he ever has, and the touring Beach Boys are once again a band that more than does the music justice. But in 1998, with this coming out within weeks of Carl Wilson's death, the album seemed to be a tacky plastic tombstone on the Beach Boys' career.

But while the Beach Boys were winding down, Brian Wilson's solo career was restarting itself. . .

Imagination

As the Beach Boys were falling apart, Brian Wilson's solo career was getting a second wind. After the abortive efforts to produce a Beach Boys album, he guested on four tracks on an album, *The Wilsons*, by his eldest daughters Carnie and Wendy, who a few years earlier had had a brief career as pop stars as part of Wilson Phillips.

For those four tracks, Wilson once again worked with Joe Thomas, the producer with whom the Beach Boys had collaborated on *Stars & Stripes vol 1*, and shortly after the Wilsons' album was released, it was announced that Wilson and Thomas were collaborating on an album together, and that Wilson had moved to St Charles, Illinois, to be close to Thomas to aid in their collaboration.

The result was the first album of new material from Wilson in a decade, and it's mixed at best. Joe Thomas, who co-wrote almost every track and produced (he was officially credited as co-producer, but from the descriptions of their working methods it seems Wilson had fairly little input), has an aesthetic which is very different from that which Wilson's fans had grown to expect. The collaborators Thomas brought in were (with the exception of shock-jock Steve Dahl) almost all people who had had their greatest success in the early 80s, making "adult contemporary" or yacht-rock tracks, and that is very much the feel of the album as a whole.

The album is full of close-mic'd nylon-string guitar, tinkling percussion, keyboards, and snare drums with gated reverb – a sound which had been popular, if not critically acclaimed, in the mid 80s, but even by 1998 sounded horribly dated. And it was clear that the album – with its airbrushed-to-death cover photo – was trying to pitch Brian Wilson's music at a mainstream market, on the theory that the same baby boomers who had bought Beach Boys records in the 60s were the people who'd bought records by REO Speedwagon, Styx, or Billy Joel in the 80s, and might be tempted back to Brian Wilson if he made records that sounded something like that.

The problem is, of course, that by this time Wilson couldn't, vocally, sound commercial. The slurring, straining, forced vocalisation and pitch problems are all here, and Wilson sounds more like a slightly more eccentric Randy Newman than the over-slick production and songwriting can really cope with.

The result is an album with a few very good tracks on it, but much more that's weaker than it should be. Wilson said, even in interviews promoting the album at the time, that "it's not my kind of music. . . well, *vocally* it is", and ten years later was saying "I didn't really like that 'Imagination' album as much as I did some of mine."

In retrospect, *Imagination* is far more important for the musicians it brought into Brian Wilson's life than for the album itself. Three of the musicians who played on this album – Scott Bennett, Paul von Mertens, and Bob Lizik – remained core members of Wilson's touring band for many years, and von Mertens and Lizik remain in the band, while a fourth (Todd Sucherman) played on his early solo tours.

Because for the first time, as a result of this album, Brian Wilson had started touring solo. And the results were quite spectacular. . .

Your Imagination

Songwriters: Brian Wilson, Joe Thomas, Steve Dahl (and, uncredited on the sleeve, Jim Peterik)

The opening track – and first single – is really rather good. One wouldn't expect that from the writing team (Steve Dahl is a shock-jock, best known for starting the "Disco Sucks" campaign, and his previous musical highlight was a Rod Stewart parody called "Do Ya Think I'm Disco?", while Jim Peterik is best known for co-writing "Eye of the Tiger" for his band Survivor), but the fact is this is a very respectable pop song.

The song is built around a fairly standard trick – using a descending scalar bassline and moving the chords above it as little as possible while making musical sense with the bass note – one that Brian's brother Dennis had used on "Forever", and which is used in scores of other pop tracks. Over this, Brian sings a melody reminiscent of "Love and Mercy", but noticeably more upbeat and exuberant.

The lyrics are mostly a mixture of nostalgia ("another car running fast, another song on the beach") along with what will regrettably become a cliché of Wilson's late-period solo work, references to his past difficulties ("I miss the way that I used to call the shots around here"). Banal as they are, though, they work, and the transition between the verses and bridges, where the same word is held from the end of one line to the beginning of the next ("And when I feel all alone, sometimes I think about/you take my hand", "I took a trip through the past and got to spend it with/you take my hand") is actually moderately clever, although set against that is the fact that the lyric wavers arbitrarily between first and second person.

All Joe Thomas' production tics are here – crunchy electric guitar, too many woodwinds, tinkling percussion, and two separate truck-driver's key changes for the last chorus – spiced up with some referencing of old Beach Boys classics (the "oom bop didit" backing vocal line being taken from "This Whole World") and some baroque trumpet on the fade. There's nothing at all original here, it's built entirely from parts – but those parts work together, and the result is a fun track that would be pretty much what a casual Beach Boys fan would expect Brian Wilson circa 1998 to sound like.

She Says That She Needs Me

Songwriters: Brian Wilson, Russ Titelman, Carole Bayer Sager

The second song dates back to 1965, when Wilson and Russ Titelman wrote the song as "Sandy She Needs Me", and recorded a backing track, but no lead vocals. It was revived in the 70s as "Sherry She Needs Me", and in the 80s as "Terri She Needs Me", and Mike Love even recorded a solo variant as "Trisha", but none of these had been released as of 1998.

And it's amazing it was never released, because in any version this is one of Brian Wilson's most lovely melodies (though in the "Sherry" version its debt in the chorus to the Four Seasons' "Sherry" is perhaps a little too obvious). Going from a plaintive minor key verse to a massive major key chorus a semitone up, it has the emotional surges of a Phil Spector classic, but with a self-awareness that Spector's songs never had.

Unfortunately, the version here is not the song at its best. Carole Bayer Sager (the lyricist best known for co-writing "Arthur's Theme (Best That You Can Do)" for Christopher Cross) was brought in to rewrite the lyrics, and while she only made a few small changes, one was to introduce the line "it's too late and you know there's nothing here for you and I", in place of the original "before we both start crying I'll just walk away".

Sager's change has the advantage of rhyming with the previous line's "wanna cry", but it has the disadvantages of being both overlong and grammatically incorrect. A professional lyricist, someone whose job it is to work with words, should understand the difference between the accusative and the oblique – grammatically the sentence should be "there's nothing here for you and me". This could perhaps be let go if the line was otherwise great, but it isn't – and the fact that this was a change made to a previously reasonable lyric makes it even less excusable.

The other major problem with the track is the production, which is full of nylon-string guitars, and which has a thumping four-on-the-floor kick drum on the chorus which sounds like someone smashing a hammer on your head.

But these things aren't enough to wreck what is a truly lovely song, one of Wilson's best, and vocally he rises to the challenge, giving perhaps the sweetest vocal performance he's given since about 1970. It's the only track on the album where vocally one doesn't have to make allowances – this isn't "a good lead vocal for Brian", it's just a good lead vocal by any standards. And the clarinet part (reportedly arranged by Brian rather than Thomas) is nice.

The result is imperfect, but so far we've had the best two-song opening run on a Beach Boys (or solo) album since 1979. Can the run of quality continue?

South American

Songwriters: Brian Wilson, Joe Thomas, Jimmy Buffett

No.

We descend here into yacht rock, and three-chord yacht rock at that (a fourth chord is introduced, briefly, in the middle eight). Presumably an attempt to get some of that "Kokomo" money a decade later, this has un-convincing vaguely-mariachi horns as the only vaguely interesting element in a backing track that's otherwise a mass of AOR guitars strumming away. The lyrics, by yacht-rock star Jimmy Buffett (who is more-or-less unknown outside North America, but was at one point truly massive in the US, with hits such as "Margaritaville"), are full of supposedly-"aspirational" boasts about "doing lunch with Cameron Diaz" and going sailing in "a little piece of heaven near the Argentine".

The sound of mass-produced corporate fun-like substance.

Where Has Love Been?

Songwriters: Brian Wilson, Andy Paley, J.D. Souther

The only track to be included that dates from Wilson's mid-90s songwrit-ing with Andy Paley, this is a pleasant but unremarkable ballad. The lyrics, at least partly rewritten by J.D. Souther (who co-wrote several of the Ea-gles' biggest hits) are a bland mush of Hallmark card lines like "making love can always get you through the night, but true love's there to catch you when you fall". There's also an example here of a problem that comes up occasionally in Brian's later work, where a melody has been written for which it's very difficult to write singable lyrics – while the tune is pretty, the scansion on the line "I know that even if I tried I couldn't hide my love inside" and the others that follow the same pattern is so off that it breaks the flow of the song.

Keep an Eye on Summer

Songwriters: Brian Wilson, Bob Norman (aka Bob Norberg)

The first of two old Beach Boys tracks redone for the album is an utterly pointless remake of what was never even one of the better songs on its album. No-one listening to the *Shut Down vol. 2* album ever thought "this is a nice track, but what it really needs is a much sloppier lead vocal, a horrible drum sound, and an over-busy guitar line".

Dream Angel

Songwriters: Brian Wilson, Joe Thomas, Jim Peterik

Jim Peterik co-write? Check.
    Truck-driver's key change for the last chorus? Check.
    Horrible guitar sound? Check.
    This is a song so bland and generic that even my criticisms of it have to be bland and generic. Supposedly written for Brian's baby daughter, it's hard to detect the slightest trace of human emotion in the finished product. Some interesting horn parts are buried in a mix that's otherwise guitar crunch, while Brian sings lyrics that rhyme "girl" and "world", "alright" and "tonight".

Cry

Songwriter: Brian Wilson

One of the two tracks on the album that are solo Brian Wilson compositions, this is a pretty little tune with an incoherent lyric, inspired by a row Wilson had with his wife Melinda.
    Interestingly, like "Your Imagination", it's both based on a descending bassline – though chromatic rather than scalar here – and has a lyric which confuses persons (in this case the second and third person).
    Unfortunately it's around two minutes of actual decent song, followed by a further three minutes of vaguely bluesy guitar noodling.

Lay Down Burden

Songwriters: Brian Wilson, Joe Thomas

This is a song whose origins for a long time caused some confusion among fans. It was known that in the early stages of the album's recording, there had been plans for Carl Wilson to guest on a track called "Lay Down Burden". When the album came out, however, Wilson and Thomas referred to the song as being about Carl Wilson's death.

The explanation for the contradiction only became public in 2012, during interviews for the *That's Why God Made the Radio* album, in which Thomas explained that "Lay Down Burden" was originally the title given to a gospel-flavoured song (which was later reworked as "Spring Vacation") which they'd planned to give to Carl to sing, but that they'd applied the title to a new song after Carl had died.

The song as recorded seems more about generic loss than a specific loss (and, indeed, Wilson had also lost his mother only months before his brother's death), and seems to be about the end of a love affair rather than a death, but the sense of loss is palpable, and while the track shares most of the faults of the rest of the album, the song itself is a pretty one, and other than the title track is the only song from the album that remained in Wilson's live set any length of time (in a piano-only arrangement much more suited to the song).

Let Him Run Wild

Songwriters: Brian Wilson, Mike Love

The second Beach Boys remake here is less pointless than the first. Wilson's vocal is strong, and the arrangement is relatively faithful to the original, give or take a few skittering hi-hats. Since Wilson never liked his vocal on the original (although personally I think it's one of his best) there was at least some reason for re-recording it, and while it'll never replace the original, it's at least a listenable version of a great song.

A snippet of an early working track for this version, with Brian apparently playing all the instruments, circulates, and it would be interesting to hear the full track in that rawer style, but this is OK.

Sunshine

Songwriters: Brian Wilson, Joe Thomas

This is a song about which there is a split in Beach Boys fandom. On the one side, there is me, and on the other side (as far as I can tell) is everyone else.

I think this is lovely. Not to be confused with the Beach Boys song of the same name on *Keepin' the Summer Alive*, this starts out as an utterly charming, fun track. This first two minutes is almost always dismissed by fans, but in fact it's one of the most Brian-feeling bits of the record, at least for me – a song clearly written as a Fats Domino style shuffle, though given a vaguely reggae-ish production, with Brian singing nonsense like "Here's my number, number one/Dial it honey let's have some fun". It's lightweight froth, but *fun* lightweight froth, and Brian sounds like he's enjoying himself.

The extended tag of the song, on the other hand, got a lot of praise from fans until it was revealed that it was composed by Joe Thomas. Whoever composed it, the idea (taking the basic piano riff from the intro to Dennis Wilson's "River Song" and adding a massive stack of Brians singing a round over it, with strings) works beautifully, though it has nothing to do with the rest of the song.

Happy Days

Songwriter: Brian Wilson

And at the end we get to the one true masterpiece on the album. "Happy Days" is made up of sections from all over Wilson's career, but somehow manages to have a unity to it that allows us to be guided from great despair to deep joy.

The song starts with a simple, happy instrumental melody, recycled from the then-unreleased *Smile* track "Holidays", but after this instrumental intro everything changes.

We move into a verse/chorus taken from a song dating from the 70s, "My Solution". But where that song had been a joke – a comedy song about a mad scientist, this is the darkest, densest, thing Brian Wilson has ever been involved with.

Over a verse consisting of a single minor chord, an electronic noise beeps out the Morse code for SOS over and over, a saxophone skronks atonally, while a massive stack of Brians, mostly hideously distorted, chant in dissonant unison "dark days were plenty, never-ending sorrow", sounding like a choir of demons, while buried in the mix Joe Thomas recites chunks of Dante's *Inferno*[4].

---

[4]Specifically, since many people have been unable to figure out what he's saying, it's these two passages from Dr Robert Pinsky's translation:

In the first verse, from Canto XIII

Mixed with sad words?" It answered, "O souls–you two who arrive to see this shameful havoc crush my leaves and tear them from me–gather them now, and bring them to the

After eight bars of this, there's what seems like some respite – there's a change to the relative major for the chorus, and an actual melody and chord changes. The fact that someone singing "Oh god the pain" actually feels like a relief from the gloom tells you how oppressive the verses are.

We have a repeat of this verse and chorus, and then some new musical material comes in – a mid-tempo rock groove, shuffling between closely related chords – actually for a while a minor-key transposition of the same basic two-chord shuffle that underpins the chorus to "Good Vibrations", though it later goes in a different direction – over which we get a lounge sax solo and plinky electric piano, before a mass of Brians come in "Ooh"ing.

We then get a short section, with the same basic feel as the lounge sax section, but with Brian singing about how "happy days are here again" and "everybody I talk to says 'man you're looking cool'", before suddenly going into yet another section, similar in instrumentation and tempo, but with Brian lamenting "nature, oh nature, please let me feel..."

And then into the final section, we have an uptempo, sing-along, almost nursery rhyme section with Brian singing "Oh my gosh, happy days are here again", and Brian Wilson may be the only rock star in history ever to unironically sing "oh my gosh", and for that alone one has to love both him and this song. While Joe Thomas co-produced this track, the song is Brian Wilson communicating without any filters, as he does on all his best material, and the utter joy and despair, and the wild swings between them one experiences in less than five minutes, do a wonderful job of communicating the mental experiences of someone with Wilson's particular set of mental health problems.

Imagination is not, by any reasonable standards, a very good album at all. But in the first two and last two tracks at least, it still manages, almost despite itself, to show why Brian Wilson is an artist that matters.

---

foot of this wretched bush. In life I was of the city that chose to leave Mars, her first patron, and take the Baptist: for which the art of Mars will always make her grieve."

In the second verse, from Canto XII

Guarded by the feral rage that I defied and quelled just now. Know then: that other time I journeyed here, this rock had not yet slid. It must have been a little before He came to Dis, if I have reckoned rightly, to take the great spoil of the upper circle with Him– when the deep, fetid valley began to shake

Symphonic Sounds: Music of the Beach Boys

With the split between Mike Love and Al Jardine in 1998, the Beach Boys effectively ended their existence as a creative band producing new music. "The Beach Boys" became a trademark, licensed by Mike Love's company MELECO, and applied to a band that initially consisted of Love, David Marks, Bruce Johnston, Adrian Baker, and a handful of backing musicians.[5]

Brian Wilson and Al Jardine both started touring with their own bands, both of whom released live albums we will deal with shortly, so combining those with Love's NASCAR CD we have an idea of what three of the four living principal band members felt were the Beach Boys' strengths in the very late 90s.

But what of Bruce Johnston? Well, he was touring with Love, of course, as he does to this day, but he also put out his own album reinterpreting the Beach Boys' music. *Symphonic Sounds: Music of the Beach Boys* by the Royal Philharmonic Orchestra would normally not be covered in this book, as it's neither a Beach Boys album nor a solo album by a Beach Boy, but an outside project, but given that it features both Johnston and Love, along with Matt Jardine, Adrian Baker, and various longtime touring band members, and that it forms a useful parallel with the recordings by the other three members, it's worth looking at.

It's not, however, worth listening to. This is Muzak pure and simple, as one might guess from the press release put out at the time, which compared it to the same label's other "classical crossover" album, *Orinoco Flow: The Music of Enya*, as though such a comparison was something to be proud of, rather than something to hide like an embarrassing disease.

---

[5]The band as it tours today, featuring Love, Johnston, and very occasionally Marks, but with only keyboardist Tim Bonhomme remaining from this backing band, is extremely good, and any negative comments I make about the late-90s touring band should not be taken to refer to the current line-up.

The album consists of nine tracks. There are fairly close recreations of the studio versions of "Kokomo" (with lead vocals by Love and Terry Melcher), "Disney Girls (1957)" (Johnston), and a version of "Darlin'" (lead vocals by Matt Jardine, and featuring a totally unnecessary lounge sax solo), all with a symphony orchestra providing unnecessary embellishments in the style of arrangement George Bernard Shaw memorably described as "big guitar" orchestration (and in the case of "Darlin'" totally replacing the rhythm section, removing any groove the song ever had).

Then there's a version of "God Only Knows", sung by "contemporary Christian" artist Tammy Trent, who gasps every word, and a version of "Wouldn't It Be Nice" with the melody line played on an electric guitar. In all these cases (except "Darlin'") the orchestra is essentially providing a pad behind a rock band, doing a job that could have been done as well by someone with a Casio keyboard set on "string pad" playing along with the chord sequence.

The same goes for "Just For Fun...All Surf!", a four-minute medley of various of the surf-based hits, introduced by a horrendous stack of Adrian Bakers, which has vocal harmonies (with Love, Johnston, and Baker all prominent) singing all the backing vocals, while the melodies are stated by various brass and woodwind instruments, playing over a standard rock rhythm section.

The nadir of the album is a version of "Warmth of the Sun", which while it has a nice orchestral introduction and tag (playing with the melody of the chorus line and also the middle eight of "Keep An Eye On Summer"), is performed in a totally *a capella* arrangement with multiple Adrian Bakers caterwauling their way through the song in a piercing shriek.

But the real reason for the album is apparently the two actual orchestral tracks, arranged by Bob Alcivar, who had arranged several actual good records, so presumably knew better. The "Overture" (a four-minute medley of melodic themes from eleven different songs) is just a mess – "here's a melodic theme from one song. Here's a melodic theme from a different song. You want some kind of development or connection between them? You'll have to pay extra for that..."

But the last track, the twenty-three-minute "Water Planet Suite", actually starts off kind of promisingly – the opening few minutes, with "Heroes & Villains" going into "Help Me Rhonda", have a Hollywood Western grandeur, sounding like Aaron Copland by way of Alfred Newman. Had this been sustained through the rest of the track – or better yet, the whole rest of the album – this could have been a really interesting take on the Beach Boys' music (it actually sounds very like the suite based around Brian Wilson's music that Van Dyke Parks wrote for the start of Wilson's own orchestral concerts a couple of years later, with a similar Americana feel to it). But at almost exactly the three minute mark, one can feel Alcivar giving up, and the next twenty minutes and twenty-two seconds are back to "play the record, but with strings going rum-tum and a trumpet playing the vocal line" adequacy.

The whole thing is a fascinating example of what happens when a rock musician has a desire for false legitimacy as a "serious" musician. It's clearly a labour of love – Johnston had been one of the big proponents of a plan for the Beach Boys to tour with a symphony orchestra in 1998, playing some of their more serious music, a plan which had been cancelled when Carl Wilson's illness became obviously terminal, and Johnston recorded this album to make up for that cancellation. And Johnston is clearly a very good, knowledgeable, musician.

Yet this feels like the work of someone who thinks that the only reason people think of orchestral music as superior to rock is because of the instruments used, and that if you just get a massive orchestra to play "Surf City" that somehow makes it more sophisticated than having Jan and Dean sing it.

No doubt somebody, somewhere, enjoys this album, but I can't imagine who or why. No lover of orchestral music is going to choose to listen to this instead of Messiaen, Bach, or Stravinsky, because it has none of the sophisticated development of themes and understanding of the nuances of the orchestra for which one listens to art music. But no Beach Boys fan is going to choose to listen to this over *Pet Sounds* or even the *Surfin' USA* album, because it has neither the intelligence and imagination of the former nor the energy of the latter.

A curious combination of hubris and lack of ambition.

Endless Harmony

In 1998, the Beach Boys released what was the closest they've come to a career-spanning documentary in the style of *The Beatles Anthology*. *Endless Harmony: The Beach Boys' Story* was directed by Alan Boyd, who has worked in some capacity on most Beach Boys archival releases since the mid-90s, and who had directed *Nashville Sounds*, the documentary on the making of the *Stars & Stripes* album. Combining archival footage, interviews recorded with Carl during the *Stars & Stripes* sessions, and new interviews with the other surviving 60s band members (Blondie and Ricky weren't interviewed), along with interviews with other musicians who admired the band and collaborators such as Tony Asher and Daryl Dragon, it told the band's whole story up to that point in a reasonable amount of detail.

But while the documentary was fairly good, what was more impressive was the soundtrack album, compiled by Boyd. With the exception of the title track, which had been released on *Keepin' the Summer Alive*, the album consisted entirely of unreleased recordings and alternate versions. Some, not covered in this essay, were merely things like a live recording of a surf/car medley from the sixties, or an alternate version of "Help Me Rhonda" with extra backing vocals – though even these contained much that was worthwhile (the stereo mix of "Kiss Me Baby", for example, is infinitely preferable to the mono album version, while Brian's guide vocal on "Breakaway" is heartbreaking).

But as well as these tracks (and ones like an extended mix of "Til I Die" or a great live version of "Heroes & Villains" from the early 70s) the album contained several songs which had never been released before. One of these, "All Alone", I have already dealt with in the essay on *Pacific Ocean Blue/Bambu* in the previous volume, but even ignoring that the remaining tracks include several songs as good as or better than much of the band's released material.

Soulful Old Man Sunshine (writing session excerpt)

Songwriters: Brian Wilson and Rick Henn

Lead vocals: Brian Wilson

The opening track is this forty-three second solo piano demo by Brian Wilson, covering the first two verses and chorus of the next song.

Soulful Old Man Sunshine

Songwriter: Brian Wilson and Rick Henn

Lead vocals: Carl Wilson

This 1969 track was, for many, the surprising highlight of the collection. Co-writer Rick Henn was a member of the Sunrays, the Beach Boys soundalike band that Murry Wilson, the Wilson brothers' father, put together after he was sacked as their manager. Henn also produced the backing track, while Brian Wilson produced the vocals.

Starting out with an *a capella* intro, this then turns into a strange combination of Motown-flavoured soul and Count Basie-style big band music, quite unlike anything the band did before or since (other than a couple of tracks on the unreleased *Adult/Child* album). Structurally, it's also very odd, consisting of (after the extended intro) two eight-bar verses followed by a twelve-bar chorus (in part of which all the instruments except a single harpsichord drop out), an eight-bar and a nine-bar verse followed by an eleven-bar chorus.

There's then a new sixteen-bar section ("Hey, old man shine your love on me"), rising up over a totally different, almost lift-music, instrumental track, all heavenly flutes, and then a further ten-bar section ("Suddenly the light shines through...") before going a final verse and a repetition of the eight-bar verse musical material, with wordless vocals.

The track is much better than almost anything from the *Sunflower* album, but was apparently not completed at the time. Carl Wilson's lead vocal has been said to have been compiled from multiple takes, and certainly there's an audible change of ambience at the line "soulful old man sunshine shine your light divine on me". Wilson also sings that line wrong, singing "soulful old man shunshine..." – apparently this mistake embarrassed him enough that he vetoed the track's inclusion on the *Good Vibrations* box. It's a shame, as this really is an excellent track, one which manages to be utterly unique in the band's discography while still remaining recognisably a classic Beach Boys recording.

Heroes & Villains (demo)

Songwriter: Brian Wilson and Van Dyke Parks

Lead vocals: Brian Wilson

For those who weren't most impressed by "Soulful Old Man Sunshine", the highlight of the set was this glimpse into what *Smile* would have been. Recorded on the fourth of November, 1966, this is Brian at the piano performing the first two verses of "Heroes and Villains" for DJ "Humble Harv" Miller. But then, after those verses, he goes into a song which had never been heard before – "I'm in Great Shape".

The studio backing track of that had been bootlegged, but we'd never known what the melody line was, and until this CD was released it wasn't even widely known among the fan community that a recording of Brian singing it existed.

And after that, *another* fragment – "Barnyard", another song whose studio backing track had been heard but whose vocal was previously unknown. Brian sings at the piano, coaxing Van Dyke Parks into making animal noises.

These piano-and-vocal demo fragments are not, of themselves, particularly musically interesting ("Barnyard" and "I'm in Great Shape" are two of the least interesting pieces of *Smile*), but to have them come out unannounced like this was astonishing for those who wished to better understand the puzzle that was *Smile*.

Wonderful/Don't Worry Bill

Songwriters: Brian Wilson and Van Dyke Parks/Ricky Fataar, Blondie Chaplin, Steve Fataar and Brother Fataar

Lead vocals: Carl Wilson and Blondie Chaplin

A live recording from a widely-bootlegged Carnegie Hall show from 1972, this medley doesn't really work, but is interesting nonetheless.

After an intro from Mike Love (saying *Smile* would be coming out that summer – a plan which sadly never materialised) the band perform "Wonderful" in an arrangement similar to that of the *Smile* recording, with a piano replacing the harpsichord (with what sounds like glockenspiel doubling it) and with Carl Wilson taking the lead vocal. It's an absolutely stunning performance, with some of the band's best vocals.

But then after the line "she'll sigh and thank God for won-won-wonderful", instead of ending, the band goes into a totally different song.

"Don't Worry Bill" had been a song on *The Flame*, an album released two years earlier by the band of the same name. Blondie Chaplin and Ricky Fataar had both been members of The Flame before joining the Beach Boys, and Carl Wilson produced that album, so it was natural that they would perform it live.

And it's a decent song. It's no masterpiece, but like much of *The Flame* it's a very solid blues-rock track. *The Flame* is an album that splits the sonic difference between Creedence-style swamp rock and late-period Beatles material, and this song is no exception, sounding like a funkier version of the Beatles' "I've Got a Feeling".

However, as enjoyable as it is, there's no way to make a swampy 70s funk-rock jam, ninety percent of whose lyrics are "mama won't you hold on?", fit stylistically or emotionally with a song like "Wonderful", and the transition is jarring, as is the end, when the band go back into a final, quiet, repeat of the last verse of "Wonderful".

Sail Plane Song

Songwriters: Brian Wilson and Carl Wilson

Lead vocals: Brian Wilson

An absolutely beautiful little demo recording from 1968, by the full band (Brian on piano, Carl on bass, Al guitar, Bruce on organ, and Dennis on drums) but an arrangement so sparse as to almost sound like a solo recording, with Brian providing the only vocal parts. Brian sings in a fragile falsetto about flying and how "up above the clouds there's no rain", and large parts of the track are instrumental – just the guitar, bass, piano, and organ all playing the same simple, lumbering, riff while a bass drum thumps (there are no drums at all on the vocal sections). The track ends with Brian making "nyeown" aeroplane noises over the bass riff, and the whole thing is a delightful example of the kind of beautiful eccentricity that characterises *Friends, Smiley Smile*, and the later *The Beach Boys Love You*.

Loop de Loop (Flip Flop Flyin' in an Airplane)

Songwriters: Brian Wilson, Carl Wilson and Al Jardine

Lead vocals: Al Jardine

...And then Al Jardine rather messed the song up. "Loop de Loop (Flip Flop Flyin' in an Airplane)" is a rewrite by Jardine of "Sail Plane Song", attempting to turn it into something of a musical comedy number. There are sound effects – recordings of multiple planes, sirens, tubas, what sounds like a Swanee whistle – and a fake fade out, the bass riff has now become Love singing the title line, and the whole thing sounds like an attempt to recreate the sound of Carl Stalling's cartoon music.

The 1969 recording of this had been widely bootlegged, and had rather a good reputation until this CD came out with Jardine's track paired with the original "Sail Plane Song". Hearing the two back to back, this sounds rather like someone drawing a Groucho Marx moustache, glasses, and eyebrows on Michelangelo's David.

This is also the only "new" recording on the album, in that while the instrumental track and backing vocals date from 1969, Jardine recorded new lead vocals in 1998. Fortunately, as Jardine is the only member of the band whose voice never noticeably aged, this doesn't detract from the recording.

It's a pleasant enough track, and fun enough in its own way, but "Sail Plane Song" is the way to listen to this material.

Barbara

Songwriter: Dennis Wilson

Lead vocals: Dennis Wilson

One of a very small number of songs written solo by Dennis Wilson (who more often than not worked with lyricists), this is a demo from 1971, recorded with Beach Boys touring keyboardist Daryl Dragon (later the Captain in The Captain & Tennille) and an unknown guitarist. This is very much in the mould of "Cuddle Up" – the later song is not quite a reworking of the same musical material, but clearly bears a strong resemblance to it – and according to Dragon had it been completed it would have had a similar orchestral arrangement to the later song.

But in fact, this simple recording of Dennis' song for his second wife is probably better than a completed version would have been. While Dennis' productions at this time had a tendency to go for Wagnerian grandeur, this song suits this simple recording, with Dennis playing a standard piano part while Dragon fills in what would have been the string lines on a second piano.

Quite, quite lovely, and one of the best things Dennis Wilson ever did.

Brian's Back

Songwriter: Mike Love

Lead vocals: Mike Love and Carl Wilson

A track recorded in 1978 for Mike Love's unreleased solo album *First Love,* with Carl guesting on chorus vocals, this is a nice sounding record, with some of Love's best soft vocals and a fairly restrained arrangement by producer Paul Fauerso, but the song itself, a tribute to Brian Wilson, is fairly horrible.

Different people will have different opinions about Love's sincerity in singing "they say Brian is back/I never knew that he was gone" and paying tribute to his cousin, but the combination of lyrics like "I still remember you sounding sweet and tender, singing 'Danny Boy' on grandma's lap/And those harmony highs could bring tears to my eyes, I guess I'm just a sentimental sap" with Love's patented technique of referencing every old Beach Boys song title he can ("Fun Fun Fun", "Good Vibrations", "I Get Around" and *Pet Sounds* are namechecked lyrically, while there are musical quotes from "Good Vibrations" and "You Still Believe in Me") makes one cringe.

There's also only two minutes' worth of song here, stretched out to four with a rather dull acoustic guitar solo by Jerry Donahue and multiple repetitions of the chorus (including a truck-driver's key change). By the end, this has more than outstayed its welcome. But it's far from the worst thing Love's been involved in musically, and it's pleasant enough as a background track.

Ultimate Christmas

The next in Capitol's short-lived series of Beach Boys archival releases, from the same team that brought out *Endless Harmony*, was *Ultimate Christmas*. This was essentially a rerelease of the 1964 Christmas album (dealt with in volume one of this series), with bonus tracks to almost double the album's length.

Some of those tracks came from the 1964 sessions, but most are from 1977 – during the retreat that produced the *MIU Album*, the band (primarily at that point Mike, Al, and Brian, as Dennis and Carl took little part in those proceedings) also produced an unreleased album, *Merry Christmas From the Beach Boys*. Many of the songs, in fact, used the same backing tracks as songs from *MIU*, and it seems to have been at least in part a way to get two albums out of one set of sessions.

The results remained unreleased until this CD came out in 1998 with most (though not all) of the tracks from those sessions. The results are. . . well, the best way to put it is to say they're not as bad as "half an album of outtakes from *MIU Album* with Christmas lyrics" sounds.

line-up

Brian Wilson, Carl Wilson, Dennis Wilson, Al Jardine, Mike Love

Little Saint Nick (alternate version)

Songwriters: Brian Wilson and Mike Love

Lead vocals: Mike Love and Brian Wilson

A really strange recording, this is Mike and Brian singing the lyrics to "Little Saint Nick" over the backing track of "Drive-In" from *All Summer Long*. The lyrics actually fit fairly well to the tune of "Drive-In", though the middle eight has slightly different lyrics. Towards the end Brian starts singing in a "Grinch" voice, and it generally seems to have been done as a joke, but one taken seriously enough to double-track the vocals.

This CD also contains several re-recordings of the original "Little Saint Nick" done as charity jingles in the 70s.

Child of Winter

Songwriters: Brian Wilson and Stephen Kalinich

Lead vocals: Mike Love and Brian Wilson

A Christmas single released in December 1974, this is mostly interesting for the Moog parts buried in the mix, but it's really a bit of a mess. The lyrics by Kalinich don't scan properly, the musical material is pretty dire, and for some reason there's a whole verse of "Here Comes Santa Claus (Down Santa Claus Lane)" stuck in the middle. Brian gets to do his Grinch voice again, but there's little positive to be said about this.

Santa's Got an Airplane

Songwriters: Brian Wilson, Al Jardine and Mike Love (and, uncredited, Carl Wilson)

Lead vocals: Mike Love and Al Jardine

The first of the 1977 recordings, this is actually the 1969 recording of "Loop De Loop" with new lead vocals. Now "Loop de loop flip flop Santa's got an airplane", apparently. As an attempt to recapture the magic of "Little Saint Nick" by once again singing about Santa's mode of transport, it's a failure, and the extended fade includes some playing with the stereo spectrum that's *really* annoying if you're listening with headphones.

Christmas Time Is Here Again

Songwriters: Buddy Holly, Norman Petty, and Jerry Allison, with new lyrics by Al Jardine

Lead vocals: Al Jardine

This is the *MIU Album* version of "Peggy Sue", with Jardine singing Christmas lyrics instead of the originals. Jardine's vocal is strong, but the new lyrics are easily the worst Jardine's ever written, and the result is tiring and joyless.

Winter Symphony

Songwriter: Brian Wilson

Lead vocals: Brian Wilson

This, on the other hand, is absolutely gorgeous. A recording from 1975 which was finished by Brian and Al in 1977, this is a lovely, simple, song about winter with one of the very best examples of Brian's "low and manly" vocal – Brian's the only voice on this, and while he doubles himself faintly at the octave, what's really impressive is the sensitivity with which he was singing in his roughened lower range at this point.

The song's artificially doubled in length with an extended instrumental break featuring French horn and piccolo trumpet, but even so it doesn't outstay its welcome. This isn't a song about which there's much to say – it's very simple, and much of the power is in the vocal performance. But it's a gentle, warm-spirited, little track which stands up as some of the best work from the band in the latter half of the 70s.

I Saw Santa Rockin' Round the Christmas Tree

Songwriters: Brian Wilson and Al Jardine

Lead vocals: Al, Matt and Adam Jardine

A reworking of an unreleased Brian song called "Hey There Mama", one of a large number of boogie-woogie tracks Brian wrote in the mid 70s, this features spoken verses, with Al's sons Matt and Adam talking about spying on Santa kissing their mother, and a sung chorus by Al (with backing vocals from Brian's young daughters Carnie and Wendy).

It's a forgettable trifle, probably cute if you find young children cute.

Mellekalikimaka (Kona Christmas)

Songwriters: Al Jardine and Mike Love

Lead vocals: Al Jardine and Mike Love

This is "Kona Coast" from *MIU Album*, with the addition of some sleigh bells and some tiny lyrical changes – Mike now wants to spend Christmas where he digs it the most in Hawaii, rather than going surfing where he digs it the most, and Mellekalikimaka is apparently "how they say it in the island talk-a". But it's the same track apart from some annoying sleigh bells and a mix which has had less time spent on it, so it's more apparent how off-key Brian's falsetto is.

Bells of Christmas

Songwriters: Al Jardine, Ron Altbach and Mike Love

Lead vocals: Mike Love

Another song from *MIU* with a different lyric, this is "Belles of Paris" with Christmas lyrics – "the bells of Christmas go ring-a-ling-ling, they toll for the saviour and the peace he'll bring". This is one of the more successful Christmas versions, in that it doesn't sound like another song hastily rewritten, and Love's vocal is quite pleasant. Lines like "the omnipresent spirit of the world will sing" are clunky, as is rhyming "sing" with "Nazarene" (if you can call it rhyming), but far, far worse has been done in the name of Christmas music. Very listenable.

Morning Christmas

Songwriter: Dennis Wilson

Lead vocals: Dennis Wilson

A solo track by Dennis, featuring none of the other Beach Boys, this is far and away the highlight of the 70s Christmas material. For the most part this is a simple three-chord song, built around piano arpeggios, bass harmonica, and ARP string synthesiser, with Dennis singing almost lyrics that are almost haiku-like in their simplicity ("Holy holy/Halo glowing/Candle burning/Christmas evening"). There's a chilly, wintry grandeur to the music, which combined with the lyrics' evocation of children playing manages to do a far better job of evoking the feeling of Christmas than anything else on the album. Absolutely lovely.

Hawthorne, CA

The final release in Capitol's series of late-90s/early-2000s rarities releases was this double-CD set compiled by Alan Boyd. Essentially *Endless Harmony vol. 2*, this set was another one which combined a few previously-unheard songs with instrumental and *a capella* mixes and stereo versions of previously-known tracks.

Disc one covers the early 60s, with the emphasis firmly on 1965 – there's an *a capella* version of "Kiss Me Baby", demos of "Little Deuce Coupe" and "Surfin' USA", instrumental backing tracks for "Surfin' USA" and "Good To My Baby", and alternate mixes or versions of songs like "Dance Dance Dance", "And Your Dream Comes True", "The Little Girl I Once Knew" and "Barbara Ann".

Disc two, meanwhile, covers 1967 through 1969 (along with one track from a few years later, the instrumental track to "Sail On Sailor". By far and away the better of the two discs, it contains some absolutely lovely versions of songs like "With Me Tonight", "Vegetables", "Let the Wind Blow", and "Break Away".

The need for this set to appeal both to hardcore fans and the casual buyer meant it fell somewhat between stools – there's about one CD of really interesting material here, primarily on the second disc, along with a few tracks that (to my ears anyway) have only been included in order to put some familiar song titles on the tracklist, and a few uninteresting bits of interview talk or DJ promo material.

But what is there is enough to make the set worthwhile for any Beach Boys fan.

As is normal for these rarities releases, I'm only going to discuss the truly new songs here, but the whole set is worth obtaining – though if you're like me, you'll listen to the second disc far more.

Happy Birthday Four Freshman

Songwriters: Mildred and Patty Hill

Lead vocals: Brian Wilson

The oldest track on the set dates from 1960, and is a recording Brian made of himself, using two reel-to-reel tape recorders to overdub his own voice multiple times. It's an *a capella* recording of "Happy Birthday", arranged by Brian in the style of the Four Freshmen, and it shows that even as a teenager Brian was already capable of the sophisticated harmony arrangements he'd build his career on.

Lonely Days

Songwriter: Unknown, probably Brian Wilson

Lead vocals: Carl Wilson and Bruce Johnston

A fifty-second snippet from the *Wild Honey* sessions, this is a sloppily-performed, but quite gorgeous, fragment of a ballad that fits perfectly into Brian's songwriting style around the time of *Friends* and *20/20*. Alan Boyd's liner notes credit the lead vocals to "Carl, Brian, and Al", but to my ears it breaks down as Carl on "dark and dreary, the afternoons are weary", Bruce on "crowded highway going my way", Carl again on "still I somehow get the feeling...", and Bruce and Al doubled (with Bruce more prominent) on the rest of the song – and it definitely doesn't sound like Brian's falsetto on the last "me oh my".

This is a gorgeous little fragment about feeling alone in a crowd, and deserved to be completed – and it possibly was. Just as this book went to press, Universal Music Group announced a new double-CD set focusing on the band's 1967 recordings, which includes a version of this song that's 1:45 in length. That should be very interesting...

A Time to Live in Dreams

Songwriters: Dennis Wilson and Stephen Kalinich

Lead vocals: Dennis Wilson

An absolutely lovely song by Dennis from 1968, very much in the vein of his "Be Still" from *Friends*, this is only let down by Kalinich's usual clunky lyrics. This is almost certainly an entirely solo performance by Dennis, who croaks and whispers his way through the gentle melody, accompanied mostly by simple piano chords, with only an organ and a celeste adding any additional instrumental texture. It's the celeste that makes the song, actually – the clusters of "wrong" notes on the words "wonder" and "beauty", much like the rough texture of Dennis' voice, allow the song to be more than just sentimental gushing.

The Lord's Prayer (stereo remix)

Songwriter: Albert Hay Malotte

Lead vocals: Group

The final track on the album is this *a capella* recording of "The Lord's Prayer" (as in the King James version of the Bible, with "debts" rather than "trespasses", and with the doxology included), in the style of the Four Freshmen. It was originally the B-side to "Little Saint Nick", and was included on some reissues of *The Beach Boys Christmas Album*, but not on *Ultimate Christmas*. This is a stereo remix, never before released.

The performance uses Albert Hay Malotte's melody, but the arrangement differs wildly from his setting in most other ways, and owes far more to the Four Freshmen than to choral music. Personally, I've always thought setting the prayer to music to be a bad idea – it's not written for scansion, but for clarity, and the melody has to contort itself to the syllabics – but the Beach Boys here make it sound as graceful as possible.

Live at the Roxy Theatre

While *Imagination* was not especially successful, either commercially or critically, it did mark a new point in Brian Wilson's solo career. Before 1998, Wilson had always relied on the Beach Boys to be his live "messengers" (as Dennis Wilson had famously put it) – even his first solo album had been promoted by Wilson doing odd guest spots at Beach Boys shows. Now, however, with the Beach Boys basically split, Wilson had to work on a proper solo career, and that meant live performances.

While Wilson had, of course, toured with the Beach Boys on occasion, and had even performed consistently with them from 1976 through to the early 1980s, he hadn't toured regularly since the death of his brother Dennis, and had only performed a handful of solo shows, so a band had to be formed for the *Imagination* tour. As the core of the band, four members of the Los Angeles-based powerpop band Wondermints were chosen – keyboardist Darian Sahanaja, percussionist Mike d'Amico, guitarist Nick "Nicky Wonder" Walusko, and multi-instrumentalist Probyn Gregory. To them were added several Chicago-based musicians who had worked with Joe Thomas – keyboard player Scott Bennett, vocalist Taylor Mills, Styx drummer Todd Sucherman (replaced after the initial tour by Jim Hines, who plays on this album), bass player Bob Lizik, woodwind player Paul von Mertens – along with Thomas himself on keyboards and Steve Dahl miming theremin while Gregory played. Jeffrey Foskett, who had played with the Beach Boys throughout the 1980s, also joined the band, playing guitar but also covering the falsetto vocals.

Tensions within this early line-up surfaced even before the first tour, though, as Sahanaja and Thomas clashed over the arrangements. According to Sahanaja, Thomas wanted to create new arrangements of the classic Beach Boys songs to make them more AOR – Sahanaja described Thomas' arrangement of "Caroline, No" as a "sexy, Sade kind of thing" – and Sahanaja eventually put his foot down and insisted that the arrangements stick close to Wilson's arrangements. Sahanaja became the musical director[6], Thomas left the tour after the first leg (as did Dahl and Sucherman, although Sucherman would play with Wilson on occasion again), and the band settled into what would be to the latter decades of Wilson's career as the Beach Boys and Wrecking Crew had been for the early ones.

While the band has seen occasional line-up changes, and band members sitting out occasional tours due to other commitments, it has remained remarkably stable, and Sahanaja, Walusko, Gregory, d'Amico, von Mertens, and Lizik remain members of the band, while Foskett only left in 2014 and Bennett in 2016.

And this band, along with the other musicians who occasionally substituted for or augmented them, became quite possibly the best live band in the world. Their attention to detail combined with their multi-instrumental and singing abilities meant that for the first time songs like "Let's Go Away For A While" or "Til I Die" could be performed live, in arrangements that were identical to the recordings. Sahanaja, and later von Mertens, ensured that the instrumental performances matched those in the studio, while Foskett performed a vital function in the early shows as onstage MC and also as a vocal safety net, doubling Wilson while he was still unsure about carrying a whole show by himself, and covering if he forgot a lyric.

The combination was extraordinary, and the band managed to provide enough support for Wilson that even though he suffered (and sometimes still suffers) not only from stage fright but from his well-documented mental problems, he was still able not only to perform, but to perform *well*. And *Live at the Roxy*, recorded over two nights in April 2000, shows that.

While there has been a certain amount of in-studio fixing up (some of Wilson's vocals sound a little *too* sweet, perhaps), there has been much less than one might imagine from listening to it. While the performances sound too good to be live, my own experiences of seeing this band (starting less than two years after these recordings, when they first toured the UK) say that yes, this is what they sound like. And the result is a nearly impeccable live recording.

There are faults, of course – latter-day Wilson, even at his best as he is here, is still an acquired taste vocally, and while the harmonies are superb they're a little top-heavy compared with the Beach Boys originals (the parts that Mike Love sang are often absent or very low in the mix). But as a live record of the artier side of Brian Wilson, focusing especially on the 1965-66 period of his songwriting, it couldn't be bettered.

The album was released in 2000 through the Internet only, on Wilson's own BriMel label, with subsequent reissues with bonus tracks, and is currently out of print. The tracklisting of the UK version (the most

---

[6]Von Mertens later took over this role.

comprehensive of the releases) is:

Disc one

- Little Girl Intro (the introduction to the show – an audio recording of Wilson directing the musicians in the studio session for "The Little Girl I Once Knew", which would go into the band playing the song live)

- The Little Girl I Once Knew

- This Whole World

- Don't Worry Baby

- Kiss Me Baby

- Do It Again

- California Girls

- I Get Around

- Back Home

- In My Room

- Surfer Girl

- The First Time

- This Isn't Love

- Add Some Music To Your Day

- Please Let Me Wonder

Disc two

- Band Intros

- Brian Wilson

- Til I Die

- Darlin'

- Let's Go Away For Awhile

- Pet Sounds

- God Only Knows

- Lay Down Burden

- Be My Baby

- Good Vibrations

- Caroline, No

- All Summer Long

- Love And Mercy

- Sloop John B (bonus track, only on some versions)

- Barbara Ann (bonus track, only on some versions)

- Wouldn't It Be Nice (bonus track, only on some versions)

- Help Me Rhonda (bonus track, only on some versions)

- Interview With Brian (bonus track, only on some versions)

I won't, in this piece, look at each song individually – too often I'd have nothing to say about it other than "it's like the record, but with an older Brian singing", but will instead focus on the few new or otherwise interesting tracks.

The First Time

Songwriter: Brian Wilson

This song dates back to 1983, when it was demoed as "In The Night Time". While a couple of words have been changed in the lyrics for this version, the lyrics are still utter gibberish – little more than mouth noises to give the melody some shape (examples "House of the rising sun/enough love for everyone/happy just to be", "I've heard your voice so sweet/Strangers until we meet/Til the dark side of the moon"). The arrangement is also perfunctory – for the most part just piano chords, drums, and "ooh" backing vocals, along with a sax solo from von Mertens that just restates the melody.

Despite all this, it still works surprisingly well, mostly because the melody itself is exquisite, especially the last section, when it climbs in a way that only Wilson's melodies do – seeming to strain for something outside experience.

It's not a great song – truth be told it's not even a very good song – but it's one that is nonetheless always a pleasure to hear.

This Isn't Love

Songwriters: Brian Wilson and Tony Asher

In the mid 90s, Wilson briefly teamed up again with Tony Asher, with whom he had written most of *Pet Sounds*. This track was one of the two songs to result (the other, "Everything I Need", appeared in two versions – on *The Wilsons*, featuring Brian, Carnie, and Wendy Wilson, and on Jeffrey Foskett's *Twelve and Twelve* album, featuring Foskett, Darian Sahanaja, and Brian Wilson). It was originally released on a various artists compilation of piano instrumentals, *Songs Without Words*, before being featured in a vocal version in *The Flintstones in Viva Rock Vegas*, sung by Alan Cumming. On this live version, Wilson talks excitedly about how "it's gonna be in a movie!", which is possibly the most excited anyone has ever been about that film.

The song itself is fairly decent, with Asher reprising his trick from "God Only Knows" of starting the song with a surprising negative that he turns to a positive, in this case "this isn't love, this is destiny". It does, however, show signs of having lyrics applied to a pre-existing melody, as the syllabics don't really work. Pretty, but insubstantial.

Brian Wilson

Songwriter: Stephen Page

A single verse and chorus of the then-recent hit by the Barenaked Ladies, about "lying in bed just like Brian Wilson did", which remained a regular self-deprecating joke in Wilson's set for another couple of years.

Lay Down Burden

Songwriters: Brian Wilson and Joe Thomas

The one song from *Imagination* that remained in Wilson's live set as of 2000, this is also one of the very small number of songs that he performed in a radically different arrangement. Here the song is stripped down to just piano and vocals for almost the entire song (along with some unobtrusive percussion, and a guitar part so low in the mix towards the end that I couldn't swear it's there at all), and it manages to improve the song ten thousandfold. It's still not great, but it shows the solid song that's there in a way the *Imagination* version doesn't.

Be My Baby

Songwriters: Jeff Barry, Ellie Greenwich, and Phil Spector

A surprisingly accurate rendition of Wilson's favourite ever record – the band showing they could do the wall of sound live just as well as they could do Wilson's more delicate arrangements.

Love and Mercy

Songwriter: Brian Wilson †

Another stripped-down version, again just piano and vocals, this removes the *a capella* section from the original and recasts it as a gentle, intimate, plea. This version has remained the regular closing song in Wilson's live set to this day.

Live In Las Vegas

We've already dealt with the touring Beach Boys – Mike Love, Bruce Johnston, and (for a while) David Marks – and with Brian Wilson's live performances. But what of the other surviving Beach Boy?

After Al Jardine discovered he was no longer part of the touring Beach Boys, he started two projects of his own. The first, which never came to fruition, was a folkish album with his sons Matt and Adam, to be titled *The Jardines*. Little studio work came out from Jardine for more than a decade, though – other than his overdubs on "Loop De Loop" for the *Endless Harmony* soundtrack, and a cover of the Garth Brooks song "Papa Loved Mama" for a tribute album, very little was heard from him in terms of studio work.

The other project, though, had slightly more success initially. Jardine formed, in 1998, his own band, "The Beach Boys Family and Friends". When initially announced, the band had quite an impressive lineup – along with Jardine himself and his two sons (Matt had been for many years the Beach Boys' touring falsetto vocalist) were longtime Beach Boys backing band members Billy Hinsche (himself earlier the singer on several 60s top forty hits with his earlier band Dino, Desi, and Billy), Ed Carter, Bobby Figueroa, and Richie Cannata, all of whom had lost their jobs with the Beach Boys two years earlier; Brian Wilson's daughters Carnie and Wendy (who had had several big hits themselves a few years earlier with their band Wilson Phillips); Daryl Dragon, best known as the Captain from The Captain & Tennille; and Owen Elliot (later Owen Elliot-Kruger), the daughter of Cass Elliot of the Mamas & the Papas.

After an early TV appearance on *Regis & Kathy Lee*, both Elliot and Dragon dropped out, but the band (now including guitarist Craig Copeland and keyboardist Tom Jacobs) started to play dates, gaining very favourable audience response. The plan was that they would play sets incorporating music from all eras of the band's career, not just the touring jukebox that the Beach Boys had become in later years, and in their early sets they incorporated a handful of less-performed songs.

Unfortunately for Jardine, this wasn't to last. Legal disputes with BRI, the company that owns the Beach Boys trademark (co-owned by Jardine, Love, Brian Wilson, and the estate of Carl Wilson) meant that Jardine soon had to stop using the Beach Boys name in his band name, and soon after that the Wilson sisters left the band. Jardine's band performed under various different names before settling on The Endless Summer Band, but from 1999 through 2012 they played very few gigs, and Jardine was most likely to be seen playing corporate events as part of the Surf City All-Stars (a band formed after the death of Jan Berry of Jan & Dean, consisting of Jan & Dean's former backing band plus some or all of Dean Torrence, Jardine, and David Marks).

It's shame, because on the evidence of *Live in Las Vegas* (the one record of their live performances, released as by "Al Jardine, Family & Friends") they were a very, very good band. Recorded in November 1999 and released only through Jardine's website, and now out of print, this recording consists of twenty-six live versions of Beach Boys classics, along with one studio recording of a new song by Jardine. That new song, "California Energy Blues", is a semi-humorous protest song, in torch blues form, about the rolling blackouts and electricity price hikes affecting California in the early 2000s. While it includes a spoken introduction (a fairly common feature of Jardine's folkier songs) explaining the crisis, little of the lyric will be of much interest to anyone not intimately acquainted with the vagaries of local California energy policy from 1999 to 2003. Musically, it bears a slight resemblance in feel to 50s songs like "Fever", although amusingly the backing vocal part ("I can't get enough of the megawatts") sounds almost exactly like Weird Al Yankovic's *Smile* parody "Pancreas".

While I won't discuss every individual track here, there are a few observations that are common to the whole performance. The lead vocals are split more or less evenly between the three Jardines and two Wilsons (other than "Sail On Sailor", which is sung by Figueroa and Hinsche, both of whom had taken the lead on the song during Beach Boys tours in the past), often swapping between them, and all are very competent singers, though Al and Matt Jardine are by far the best. The Wilson sisters' lead vocals have a little too much stage-school sheen about them, though fans of their early-90s pop records will no doubt find much to enjoy in their performances, but the harmonies are sublime. Al Jardine had always been the crucial element in the Beach Boys' blend, and when combined as he is here with Matt, Billy Hinsche, and Bobby Figueroa, all of whom had sung in the Beach Boys' live performances for many years, the vocal blend is the closest thing one could get to the real Beach Boys after Carl Wilson's death.

Similarly, the instrumental performances are all superb, replicating the fuller arrangements of the 1970s touring band rather than the shoddy Casio keyboard mess the live Beach Boys had deteriorated into by the 1990s. This band was in every way superior to the touring Beach Boys of the time, and while the current touring iteration of the Beach Boys has become a truly spectacular live band by the time of writing, it's a shame that more people didn't have a chance to see this band.

Full tracklisting:

- Dance, Dance, Dance

- Do You Wanna Dance

- Catch a Wave

- Hawaii

- Do It Again

- Darlin'

- Wild Honey

- Come Go with Me

- Surfer Girl

- Don't Worry, Baby

- Shut Down

- Little Deuce Coupe

- I Get Around

- In My Room

- Girl, Don't Tell Me

- Break Away

- Sail On Sailor

- God Only Knows

- Sloop John B

- Wouldn't It Be Nice

- Good Vibrations

- Heroes and Villains
- Help Me Rhonda
- Surfin' USA
- Barbara Ann
- Fun, Fun, Fun
- California Energy Blues

Pet Sounds Live In London

After the initial shock of Brian touring solo had worn off, his management needed a new hook to keep people coming to the shows, and they found one quickly – in 2000, Brian started touring full performances of the whole *Pet Sounds* album, along with the normal hits and rarities he'd been doing on previous tours.

The US dates for these shows were initially performed with a full orchestra, as well as Brian's band – the orchestra added little to the arrangements, however, and was dropped after the first tour.

And then it was announced he would be playing the UK – four shows in London, in January 2002. And this is where I can't be truly objective (even to the extent I usually am) about this album.

This album was recorded over the four shows at the Royal Festival Hall in January 2002, and I was at two of them – my first two Brian Wilson shows. And at the time, I assumed they would be my *only* two Brian Wilson shows – no-one among the fanbase expected him to continue touring for another fifteen years.

I've since seen him a further twelve times, and have a ticket to see him the month after this book comes out, and four of those shows have been *Pet Sounds* shows. All have been excellent, but none have affected my life the way those first two shows did. Seeing Brian Wilson on that stage, with a crowd who came as much to show their love for the man in what they thought would be a once-in-a-lifetime event as to see the show, performing songs like "Til I Die", "Busy Doin' Nothin'", and "Surf's Up" which I never thought I'd see played live, was a peak experience it's impossible to recapture.

And this album is the product of those shows (a DVD. was also released, a few months later, which featured footage from those shows and from a second run of shows at the same venue in June 2002), and it makes it clear that those performances really were as special as they seemed.

We have the whole *Pet Sounds* album, with some minimal audience interaction (Brian trying to see if the audience can yell louder than him, that kind of thing) performed with Brian singing every lead. On more recent *Pet Sounds* tours, as his voice has aged, he's taken to sharing the leads with others, but here, while his voice isn't what it was in 1966, he's still strong and on-key, singing as well as he has in his solo career.

The recordings are so good, in fact, that it would be easy to believe that they were touched up in the studio, but I have good quality audience recordings of the two shows I went to (the first two shows of the run), and at least some of the performances are taken absolutely unaltered from those two shows – enough of this is the Tuesday show, in particular, that I'm willing to believe that all the recordings are from one of the four shows. If I'm wrong, then the studio work is so inconspicuous that even after fifteen years I've not noticed it.

The band – on this occasion Darian Sahanaja (musical director, keyboards, and vocals), Jeffrey Foskett (MC, guitar and vocals), Nick Walusko (guitar and vocals), Probyn Gregory (guitar, keyboards, banjo, French horn, trumpet, tannerin, percussion and vocals), Scott Bennett (keyboards, guitar, percussion, and vocals), Paul von Mertens (sax, harmonica, and flute), Andy Paley (percussion and vocals), Taylor Mills (vocals), Jim Hines (drums) and Bob Lizik (bass) – perform note-perfect renditions of every song, with the only deviations from the arrangements on the record being during the instrumentals, where the band members were allowed to show off slightly – von Mertens adding some unnecessary sax solos to both, and an extended percussion duel on the title track which was more fun to watch live than to listen to on the record.

I imagine that for anyone who hasn't seen Brian perform *Pet Sounds* live, this is a little inessential – and if you *have* seen Brian perform *Pet Sounds* live, and you weren't at these particular shows, the later DVD release would probably be a better memento. But...two days after this was released, I saw Brian again, on his first proper UK tour. I got to go backstage and meet him and his band for the first time, and they all signed my copy of this CD. This is special to me.

Gettin' in Over My Head

2004 was a big year for Brian Wilson. On February 24, he performed live, for the first time, a completed version of *Smile*, the unfinished album that had hung over his head and dominated all discussions about him for nearly forty years. In September, he released a studio version of that completed *Smile* which became his most successful solo album.

The completion of *Smile*, though, overshadowed another album he released that year. *Gettin' in Over My Head* was the first studio album he had recorded in six years, and the first with his touring band.

The album was widely disliked by fans, and it's easy to see why. The performances by the backing band are exemplary, but Wilson himself sounds tired, and is frequently off-key (not helped by the decision, thankfully never made again, to have him sing nearly all the harmony parts himself). There were rumours at the time that Wilson was unhappy to be working on the album at all, and that he was largely unresponsive in the studio, and whatever the truth of those rumours, the vocals on much of the album certainly give one that impression.

But what the fans were ignoring was everything else about the record. This is understandable in many respects – most of the songs on the album dated back many years, to the Andy Paley sessions of the mid-nineties, to the unreleased *Sweet Insanity* album, or in some cases as far back as the early 1980s. Bootlegs of those versions had been available for years, often with more engaged vocals on Brian Wilson's part. So it's easy to see why this was seen as a set of inferior remakes. And it certainly didn't help that the cover, by Peter Blake, looked cheap and nasty, more like a collage made by a five-year-old than the work of one of the most acclaimed artists of the last sixty years.

In many ways the album seems to be trying to present a crafted image of a Brian Wilson album, aimed at a target market, but falling between two stools – the arrangements, for the most part, are Pet-Sounds-esque, full of vibraphone and bass harmonica, but the special guests appearing on the album are the kind of "classic rock" that simply doesn't mix well with that – Eric Clapton, Paul McCartney, Elton John.

But if you come to this not listening to it as a collection of remakes of songs you've already heard, and especially if you're not listening to it while counting the hours til *Smile* finally comes out, there's a lot to like about this album. Wilson's backing band are all superb musicians, the instrumental arrangements have a lot of interesting touches. In particular we hear for the first time something that will become very much the secret weapon of Wilson's later solo work: the string arrangements of Paul von Mertens. Von Mertens' orchestrations here are, on the handful of tracks in which he gets to demonstrate them, spectacular, with violin lines almost reminiscent of Bartók or Eastern European folk music, but also rooted in the same kind of Americana that Van Dyke Parks (who wrote new lyrics for a Wilson song here for the first time in thirty years) has mined so productively in his solo work.

And the songs themselves are, taken on their own merits, occasionally superb. The quality here is *very* variable, but even the least enthusiastic listener will admit that "Soul Searchin'", the title track, "Rainbow Eyes", and "Don't Let Her Know She's An Angel" are among the best work of Wilson has produced since the early 1970s.

So something of a curate's egg, then. But one that genuinely *is* good in parts – and one that has more good parts than not. And it's probably the most honest, unfiltered, *Brian Wilson* album of all his solo albums. It's an album that's long been overdue a reevaluation.

(All lead vocals Brian Wilson except where noted.)

How Could We Still Be Dancin'?

Songwriters: Brian Wilson and Joe Thomas

Lead vocals: Elton John and Brian Wilson

The opening track is a song (and apparently, at least in part, a backing track) left over from *Imagination*, and rather better than much of that album, though little more than disposable fluff.

The verses could, in fact, easily have been a minor hit for Elton John, who sings lead on them (and plays piano – reportedly Wilson told him to "play it like Billy Joel"). John has the unenviable task of trying to sing "how could" at the start of almost every line in a single syllable, and so at times sounds almost like Vic Reeves' "club singer" character, singing "HA! we still be...", but the verses are a lot of silly, goofy, fun, with some great honking saxophone.

Unfortunately, the bridges and intro, which feature a stack of off-key Wilsons singing far too high for his range, are almost unlistenable. Notably, when Wilson performed this song live, he took lead on the verses but gave those sections to his band to sing.

Soul Searchin'

Songwriters: Brian Wilson and Andy Paley

Lead vocals: Carl Wilson and Brian Wilson

This song – and track – dates back to the mid-90s Beach Boys sessions for an album of Wilson/Paley songs that never happened. Only this song and "You're Still A Mystery" were ever completed, and the album had been shelved.

For this album, Brian Wilson took Carl Wilson's lead vocal from a session co-produced by Don Was and synched it to an earlier backing track largely cut by Andy Paley, largely replicating a mix that had been circulating on bootlegs for several years. He replaced the other Beach Boys' backing vocals with his own (and replaced Carl Wilson's lead vocal on the middle eight) and got Paul von Mertens to add a saxophone solo over the original organ one, but otherwise it's largely identical to that bootlegged version.

(A mix of the full Beach Boys version was later released on the *Made in California* box set, and is vastly superior, in particular for Mike Love's bass vocals).

The song itself is a 60s soul ballad pastiche, largely the work of Paley, it's the kind of thing that would have made a very serviceable single for James Carr, but is elevated to greatness by Carl Wilson's vocal – the last lead he would ever record for a Beach Boys song, and one of his best.

You've Touched Me

Songwriters: Brian Wilson and Stephen Kalinich

And this song sums up everything that is frustrating about this album. It's another reworking of old musical material, this time a ballad Wilson had written in the 80s with Gary Usher, "Turning Point", turned into an uptempo, bouncy piece with some lovely bass harmonica playing and string arrangements. (The reworking is more thorough than on many of the other songs, but compare the descending chords on "I'm on top of the world/I'm just floating on clouds" to "So hard waiting for you/So hard working it through" on the earlier track) Wilson also does a far better job on the lead here than on many of the other songs.

But the lyrics...ouch. Stephen Kalinich is someone with whom I share many mutual friends, so I don't want to say anything too harsh about his lyrics, but lines like "You are a part of me/You make my spirit whole" would be banal at best, but when fitted to a melody for which their stress patterns are completely inappropriate they make the whole track sound amateur.

Gettin' in Over My Head

Songwriters: Brian Wilson and Andy Paley

This, on the other hand, is heavenly. Another song dating from the Paley sessions of the mid-90s, this recording is actually a remake co-produced by Joe Thomas around the time of the sessions for *Imagination* (though presumably sweetened somewhat in 2004, as it sounds very like the rest of this album). With a vibraphone part that hints at the similar part of "Til I Die", and a far better lead vocal than many of the rest on the album, this just *sounds* like Brian Wilson on top form (though as with many of the Paley songs it's hard to tell what's Wilson's own contribution and what's Paley imitating Wilson. My guess is that the verse melody is Wilson, the middle eight Paley – the descending "I just might not ever come back from this" is very, *very* Paley to my ears, and the chorus could be either).

A gorgeous ballad that, other than the older lead vocals, could have fit easily on *The Beach Boys Today!*, this is one of the best things Wilson's solo career has produced.

City Blues

Songwriters: Brian Wilson and Scott Bennett

And this is one of the worst. This song dates back originally to 1981, and frankly it sounds it. This is something that should have been on a soundtrack to the type of film that starred Michael J. Fox, perhaps performed by Kenny Loggins or Survivor – though in truth what this sounds most like is the musical stylings of David Hasselhoff. Eric Clapton guests on guitar but squeals all over it rather than playing anything interesting, and the whole thing is a noisy, unpleasant, mess.

The song is mainly interesting in retrospect from a purely historical perspective, as it's the first song to credit Scott Bennett as a co-writer (he added additional lyrics to finish off the song). Bennett would be a frequent collaborator with Wilson over the next decade, and we will discuss his contributions more on future albums.

Desert Drive

Songwriters: Brian Wilson and Andy Paley

Another song originally from the Paley sessions in the mid-90s, this is the only track on the album to feature vocals from Wilson's band – Paley (who was at the time of recording still playing percussion in Wilson's band), Jeffrey Foskett, Darian Sahanaja and Scott Bennett all add vocals, and the difference is immediately obvious. *This* is how the vocals on the whole album should have sounded.

The song itself is a fun bit of fluff – a car song, mostly the work of Paley, based loosely around the riff from "Salt Lake City", about taking a drive into Las Vegas, wearing "shades in case the rays get mean" and watching Wayne Newton's show.

A Friend Like You

Songwriters: Brian Wilson and Stephen Kalinich

Lead vocals: Brian Wilson and Paul McCartney

This is, while not the worst song in Brian Wilson's solo career, certainly the biggest missed opportunity. Given the opportunity to duet with Paul McCartney (who also plays guitar on the track), he has McCartney sing literally one solo line – the line "a friend like you, a friend like you". Wilson takes all the verses himself, and drowns McCartney's vocals on the other lines of the chorus in a stack of his own voice.

Which wouldn't be too bad were this in any way a good song, but it's not. The one song on the album that (as far as I'm aware) doesn't date back to much earlier, it's also the weakest song, as a song, on the album, with music that has no points of interest and lyrics that barely rise to the level of Hallmark cards.

Dreadfully, dreadfully disappointing.

Make a Wish

Songwriter: Brian Wilson

A song dating back to the *Sweet Insanity* sessions, and apparently inspired by the Make A Wish Foundation, this is a perfect example of the generic feelgood protest-generally-bad-things songs that were inexplicably popular for a few minutes in the late 80s. Apparently racial peace, equality, cures for all diseases, enough food for everyone, and love replacing hate would all be good.

Fair enough, one doesn't look to Brian Wilson to provide coherent analysis of the structural inequalities that prevent those things happening, any more than one looks to Noam Chomsky to write catchy pop songs. But frankly Chomsky could probably come up with a better melody than this one.

Rainbow Eyes

Songwriter: Brian Wilson

And now we're back to loveliness again. This song is another *Sweet Insanity* leftover, and one of the best things recorded for that album, with its gorgeous nursery-rhyme melody.

This isn't one of the better-produced tracks on the album – there's some heavy-handed drumming which feels out of place, Wilson's slurring the words, and the mix seems badly balanced – but if you can get past that, this is a wonderful, wonderful, little song, with some gorgeously bizarre chord changes under the simplistic melody.

Saturday Morning in the City

Songwriters: Brian Wilson and Andy Paley

This is, with the exception of a few small overdubs, a recording from the mid-nineties Paley sessions (and thus featuring Paley on backing vocals) of a song that had been started in the 1980s. And it's utterly wonderful, and utterly different from anything else on the album. A glorious little slice-of-life song, it sounds like something written for a Muppet or Disney film setting the scene – describing the people washing their cars (and one minor change from the Paley version that always disappoints me – in the original recording the people washing their cars are "new wavers", while in the version here they're just "young people" – I suppose Wilson must have noticed between 1996 and 2004 that the New Wave was no longer a thing), the garage sale next door, and the dog barking at the person delivering the post.

Musically, it's like all the most upbeat, cheerful parts of *Smile* without even a hint of the darker side – a cascade of different variations on the same basic ideas, with Swanee whistles, popping sound effects and car horns. Astonishingly, this is the shortest song on the album by a good half a minute, but it has more musical ideas than many other tracks on the record have in nearly twice its length. It's good-natured, fun, and quite, quite beautiful.

Fairy Tale

Songwriters: Brian Wilson and David Foster

Another song dating from the 1980s, this was originally a collaboration between Wilson and (allegedly) Eugene Landy, a fatuous song called "Save The Day" about how everyone in the 60s was wonderfully enlightened and marched for peace.

At some point David Foster (a record producer who has worked with Chicago and Celine Dion, among others) was called in to work on the music with Wilson, and recorded the song under the new title "Is There A Chance?", with new lyrics by Foster's wife Linda Thompson (the ex-wife of Caitlyn Jenner, not the singer formerly married to Richard Thompson). While none of Foster's changes remain in "Fairy Tale", he retains a credit.

The song as finally released by Wilson is...a fairy tale. The original lyrics are completely replaced by new ones about fighting a dragon and saving a princess.

An 80s-style power ballad, about fighting dragons, which quotes the Ronettes at the end, might not be your kind of thing – it certainly isn't mine – but the fact that this seems natural coming after "Saturday Morning In The City" shows what an odd, eclectic, and exciting album this actually is.

Don't Let Her Know She's an Angel

Songwriter: Brian Wilson

Another *Sweet Insanity* leftover, though I've seen stories that this was written as early as 1981. Which would mean that this song, the best single song of Brian Wilson's solo career, was ignored for two Beach Boys albums, the Usher sessions, *and* Wilson's first solo album before finally being recorded for *Sweet Insanity*. And then left for more than another decade.

In truth, none of the recordings of this song are perfect – this one has something of *Imagination*'s production values about it, but after listening to this, and to the three bootlegged versions from the *Sweet Insanity* sessions, a platonic ideal version of the song is now in my head.

Even this version, though, marred as it is by being a real recording made by human beings rather than an unachievable ideal, is quite startlingly lovely. Wilson once again returns to the regular theme of the woman who's so far above the man she's with that he can't begin to imagine why she'd be with him ("don't let her know she's an angel...I'm scared that she'll want to go free" – one of the things I prefer about some of the earlier versions is that that line is instead the less controlling "I'm scared that she'll want to leave me").

It's a touching, lovely song and one that really deserves a wider audience.

The Waltz

Songwriters: Brian Wilson and Van Dyke Parks

And the final track on the album is, as the title suggests, a waltz – and *about* waltzing, at a high school dance. The song is, yes, another *Sweet Insanity* leftover, when it was originally titled "Let's Stick Together" and featured Weird Al Yankovic on accordion. This version is in every way superior to that, with von Mertens' skittish fiddle arrangements working perfectly with Van Dyke Parks' new lyrics to conjure up a bygone age.

Oh yes. . . those lyrics. More than anything on this album, they caught flak from fans, and this song became the whipping boy for the whole album. Certainly lines like "She had a body you'd kill for/You hoped that she'd take the pill for/She up and said 'I'm a dancer/Don't tell me, you are a Cancer'" are not what Brian Wilson's fans were, in general, hoping for. But there's a sweet, witty, erudition to these lyrics that is perfectly Parks – the syllables fall in such a way that no other writer could have come up with them, and express Parks' own personality perfectly. If, as it does for some, Parks' Southern gentility and loquaciousness rubs you up the wrong way, then I can see why you'd dislike this. But for me, a fan of Parks almost as much as I am of Wilson, this is just sublime and easily one of the best things on the album.

Gettin' in Over My Head is nobody's favourite Brian Wilson record, but it's far more of an expression of Wilson as an artist than many would like to give it credit for. In his entire career, Wilson has only released four albums that consist entirely of songs he wrote or co-wrote and which he hadn't put on a previous album – *Smiley Smile, The Beach Boys Love You, Brian Wilson,* and *Gettin' in Over My Head* (2015's *No Pier Pressure* would count in the "standard" edition, but not in the expanded version which is what most people who purchased it actually have). Of those, this is definitely the worst, but it's very much of a piece with those earlier albums, and like them I think many people have found the flaws rather easier to see than the very real strengths.

Brian Wilson Presents Smile

Dealing with *Smile* has always been a problem in this series of books. To recap, for those who aren't completely familiar with the story, in 1966 and 1967 the Beach Boys recorded a series of sessions for an album largely written by Brian Wilson and Van Dyke Parks, to be titled *Smile*. That album remained unfinished, and a new album, *Smiley Smile*, came out in its place, containing some of the same songs, some of which had been re-recorded. Then over subsequent years, various *Smile* tracks came out as tracks, sometimes partially or fully re-recorded, on other albums. In 1993, the box set *Good Vibrations: Thirty Years of the Beach Boys* included about half an hour's worth of *Smile* material, sequenced into a rough album, but missed out some crucial elements.

Then, in 2003, it was announced that Brian Wilson would, with the help of his band members, be completing a suite of *Smile* material to be performed at the Royal Festival Hall in 2004. The suite premiered in February 2004, and a studio recording of the material – entirely new recordings, but keeping as close as possible to the sound of the originals – came out in September that year.

That album was followed, seven years later, by a five-CD and two-vinyl-album set, *The Smile Sessions*, containing pretty much every releasable note of sessions from the '66 and '67 recordings. Notably, much of the first disc was taken up with a reconstructed *Smile* album that followed the 2004 track sequence almost exactly.

So in a series of books where we are looking at individual songs, this poses some problems for analysis. My decision has been to treat the 2004 album as the final version, and for the *Good Vibrations* and *Smile Sessions* entries only to talk about those things which are substantially different in the versions used, or about outtakes which didn't make it to the 2004 album. In the entries for songs in this section I will, where appropriate, talk about the differences between the Beach Boys and Brian Wilson solo versions, other than the obvious difference of Wilson's voice.

But what is easiest for the purposes of this book and what the artistic truth is might be two very different things. There is still a lot of debate among Beach Boys fans as to what extent the 2004 album can be considered a "finished" *Smile* at all. Certainly, it's not the same recordings made in 1966 or 67 – it features none of the Beach Boys other than Brian Wilson, and his voice had changed substantially in the intervening decades. And the final sequence and arrangements owed a lot both to Darian Sahanaja, the keyboardist and (at the time) musical director with Wilson's band, who acted as his musical secretary for the project, and to Paul von Mertens, whose string arrangements fleshed out several tracks that had previously existed only as demos.

But on the other hand, it's a version of the album put together with the active involvement of Wilson, and of Van Dyke Parks, who was called in at an early stage when Wilson and Sahanaja couldn't decipher a vintage lyric, and who added new lyrics to many unfinished songs and transition sections. And while it's certainly not the album that *Smile* would have been had it been released in 1967 – it's unlikely that the album would have been released as three long movements, rather than as individual tracks – at its best (notably in the second movement) it works so well that one can't help but think that on some level this *must* have been how the songs were originally intended to sound.

Not everything works, but the whole is greater than the sum of its parts, and while a lot of the *Smile* music had seemed underwhelming when it came out in dribs and drabs on bootlegs over a near forty-year period, it worked incredibly well as part of a finished whole.

And the questions as to who did what on the finished version miss the point. Sahanaja and von Mertens both contributed a great deal, but this is still a Brian Wilson album. One of the problems with the cult of Brian Wilson as unique individual Romantic genius is that it misses the central reason *for* his genius, which is that he is, bar none, the greatest *collaborator* in popular music. Brian Wilson has always worked with other people – lyricists, session musicians, other lead singers... he is capable of creating very good music on his own, and has on occasion over the years, but that's not where he's at his best. He's best at shaping the talents of those around him, and using them to create better music than any of them could have created on their own.

And whatever the reason, the fact remains that the Beach Boys in 1967 weren't the right collaborators for him to finish *Smile*. The Brian Wilson Band in 2004 were.

(All songs written by Brian Wilson and Van Dyke Parks, and with lead vocals by Brian Wilson, except where noted.)

Our Prayer

Songwriter: Brian Wilson

Lead vocal: Group

The album opens with a short *a capella* introduction, a pastiche of baroque choral music that had been released in its original version on the Beach Boys' *20/20* album. The track is one of the most beautiful things that Wilson ever wrote, and is the perfect introduction to the record – a wordless *a capella* invocation, pure music, existing on its own terms rather than as a means to deliver lyrical content, but still perfectly giving the impression of a fresh start, a beginning.

Recently (as of 2016) Brian Wilson has taken to opening his live shows with this song.

Gee

Alleged songwriters: William Davis/Morris Levy

Lead vocal: Group

"Our Prayer" segues into a brief extract of "Gee". This was originally a hit for the doo-wop group The Crows. The song was apparently written by Crows member William Davis, with the help of another vocalist, Viola Watkins, but various different people (none of whom had any involvement in its writing) have been credited as writers over the years. The current credits are to Davis and Morris Levy, a convicted extortionist with close ties to the Mafia, who has many credits on songs written by black people he never met but who didn't want to be shot. "Gee" is often credited as the first rock and roll record to have any success with a white audience, and the song was particularly influential on the LA music scene, being covered by contemporaries of the Beach Boys as stylistically far apart as Jan & Dean and Frank Zappa.

The fragment used here, though, is a simple snatch of "dit dit" backing vocals, followed by the hook line "how I love my girl". Only a few seconds long, it perhaps serves as another starting point – as good a choice as any for the start of rock and roll, and certainly for rock and roll vocal groups, placed at the start of the album, after the initial invocation, it seems to serve as saying "this is where the Beach Boys came from – now look where we're going". Then the chant of "the heroes and villains" is struck up, leading to...

Heroes and Villains

The first song proper on the album is a version of the song that had first appeared as the single from *Smiley Smile*, and the first song that Brian Wilson and Van Dyke Parks wrote in collaboration with each other. I discussed this song in great detail in volume one of this series, in the *Smiley Smile* entry[7], and don't want to recapitulate that entry too much here, but what we have here is structurally very different from either the version that was originally released on *Smiley Smile* or the *Smile*-era edit that was released as a bonus track on the *Smiley Smile/Wild Honey* twofer.

The song starts the same as the single, with the "I've been in this town..." verses, and gets as far as the chorus before diverging, going into the "In the cantina..." section from the bonus track, before finally reverting to the original structure (after a "woo woo!" before "you're under arrest!"). But here, the chorus serves to introduce a motif that will recur throughout the album, a two-chord riff with similar intervals to the "Good Vibrations" chorus, but starting on a minor chord rather than a major. Where on the single this had served just as the chorus to a pop song, here it's a theme that will dominate the album.

On all the 1960s versions of the song, though, the same thing applies – while the verse instrumentation is dense and complex, inspired by Ike and Tina Turner's "Save the Last Dance for Me", the instrumentation on much of the rest of the track is minimal, often consisting of a single keyboard (either piano or harpsichord – though one of the criticisms levelled at Brian Wilson's solo version of *Smile* is that the harpsichord sounds are played on a synthesiser rather than on a real harpsichord; to my ears there's little audible difference). While parts of *Smile* are notable for their outstanding instrumental arrangements, much of what makes "Heroes and Villains" particularly special is the complexity of the vocal arrangements, with contrapuntal lines moving in and out of each other.

However, in the remade 2004 version, those lines are joined by a string arrangement by Paul von Mertens – a subtle addition, but one that thickens the sound considerably.

When the song ends, there's a short vocal fragment, reminiscent of "Our Prayer" (a fragment labelled "Bridge to Indians" on the *Smile Sessions* box set) – this vocal fragment is now used both by Brian Wilson's band and Mike Love's touring Beach Boys to end their renditions of the song. This is followed by an instrumental fade (the fragment labelled "Heroes & Villains: Fade") before...

---

[7]I've also written about the song in my book *California Dreaming: The LA Pop Music Scene and the 1960s*

Roll Plymouth Rock

"Heroes and Villains" gives way to another song built around the "Heroes and Villains" chorus riff. This track was originally released on the *Good Vibrations* box set as "Do You Like Worms?", a title which excited much speculation, though the only lyrics recorded in the 60s were the bridge lines "rock, rock, roll, Plymouth rock, roll over", and some pseudo-Hawaiian lines.

The track consists of several sections – a slow, plodding, section dominated by tympani, over which (in the 2004 version) the band chant lyrics (written by Van Dyke Parks in the 1960s – Wilson and Sahanaja's inability to decipher Parks' handwriting is what led to them calling Parks up and him assisting in completing the project) about the Sandwich islands and "waving from an ocean liner". Parks has said that the song is about "bringing this Euro-sensibility into the taming of the American continent, from Plymouth Rock to Waikiki".

After this, there's a bridge, with a solo bass accompanying the mass vocals singing "rock, rock, roll, Plymouth Rock, roll over". This stops, and we get a harpsichord performance of the "heroes and villains" chorus theme. After a couple of iterations of the theme, vocals enter again, with pseudo-"Indian"/Native American chanting, over which the lead vocal sings a variation of the chorus – "bicycle rider, just see what you've done/done to the church of the American Indian" (or, in the first chorus on the 2004 version, "ribbon of concrete" instead of "bicycle rider").

This musical material all repeats, and then there's a variation of the opening section (a tone up, and in a minor rather than a major key), with the percussion joined by a steel guitar, and the lead vocal singing cod-Hawaiian lyrics (according to Domenic Priore, these are a reference to a Hawaiian prayer), before going into a final version of the "Plymouth Rock" section and a last harpsichord instrumental version of the chorus.

Without the lead vocals, and shorn of context, this was one of the less impressive of the *Smile* fragments to surface on the *Good Vibrations* box – overlong and repetitious. In context, though, as part of a longer suite of songs, and with more variation added by the vocals, this works much better, though it's still not a highlight of the album by any means.

The "woo woo" from "Heroes and Villains" recurs and leads us into...

Barnyard

The original version of this song, as recorded in the 1960s, was just a simple two-chord instrumental, with some animal-noise vocals. However, in the 1990s a demo tape was discovered of Wilson and Parks playing "Heroes and Villains", "Barnyard", and "I'm In Great Shape". The few lines of lyric from that, a simple observation of countryside life, are used here (and in the box set version are flown in over the backing track). A charming little fragment, with not much to say about it.

The Old Master Painter

Songwriters: Haven Gillespie and Beasley Smith

An instrumental performance, on cello, of a jazz standard from 1949 (written by the same writers who wrote "That Lucky Old Sun", which in 2007 would inspire Wilson's next long-form piece. . .). Just a brief statement of a few lines of the verse melody, leading into. . .

You Are My Sunshine

Songwriter: Jimmie Davis

Another standard, this time radically reworked. Like much of *Smile,* the original is based on I-IV chords, but here the I chord becomes minor, and over a slow, mournful, string arrangement, Wilson, his voice heavily filtered (in the original recording it was Dennis, rather than Brian), sings the familiar lyrics, but in the past tense – "you *were* my sunshine", and with the last line of the verse changed to "*how could you* take my sunshine away?"

A mournful saxophone and a string glissando lead into. . .

Cabin Essence

The last song of the first movement is one that, again, I dealt with in the first book in this series. As the version here is as close as possible to the original recording, I'll reproduce some of my comments from that book below – for a longer discussion of the song, see volume one.

> The result is astonishing, one of the best things the band ever did - which is to say it is one of the best musical recordings of the twentieth century. Parks' punning, Joycean lyrics contrast an idyllic 'home on the range' in the verses with the 'iron horse', the railway that made the West possible, in the choruses, before at the end focusing on the immigrant labour that had built that railway. . .
>
> The verse, in 4/4 time, starts with just a banjo, evoking the old west,. . . an ascending scalar phrase, singing 'doing doing' over and over in imitation of the banjo. . . bass and piano come in, before everything drops out except a harmonica

and a harmonium, playing variations of the trumpet part from "Heroes and Villains", but in counter-movement to each other, for two bars.

This musical material then repeats, before entering into a two chord waltz-time chorus with an utterly different feel. Over clanking percussion, representing the spikes being driven into the ground to hold the rails together, the band chant 'who ran the iron horse?' over and over, while a wailing falsetto, fuzz bass and cellos race each other up and down ascending and descending scales, in much the same manner as in the similar-sounding *Smile* track "Mrs O'Leary's Cow", but much more frenzied, before collapsing back, exhausted, into the comfort of the verse.

After the second verse, we get another chorus, but this time with an additional element... a totally different, unconnected set of lyrics... buried in the mix...

We then enter a little, gentle, round as the band sing "Have you seen the grand coolie working on the railroad?" ...

And then over cello, banjo and harmonica, while the tinkling percussion continues ... "Over and over the crow cries uncover the cornfield". ...

Wonderful

The second movement of *Smile* is, to my mind, possibly the best piece of music ever recorded, and it starts with one of the greatest songs of all time. Another song I dealt with in volume one, I'll excerpt some of that below before talking about the differences between versions:

> Quite possibly the single most beautiful song ever written... telling the story of a young girl who goes off and loses her virginity, and her innocence more generally, at a young age...
>
> In many ways, this can be seen as a counterpart both of "Caroline, No" and of the Beatles' "She's Leaving Home", but where those songs are judgemental either of the girl or of the parents, this song seeks reconciliation and forgiveness on both sides and suggests that innocence can actually be regained with experience. It's a more mature, reflective song than the other two, great as they undoubtedly are.
>
> Not only that, it manages this while having concern for the aesthetics of the lyric in a way that neither of those other songs do. Both the other songs treat words functionally, as a

means of conveying a single piece of information. By contrast, Parks' lyrics are carefully chosen to be beautiful themselves, independent of the meaning they carry. At this point Parks was almost certainly the most artistically advanced lyricist in the music industry.

And the music matches this. A variant of the "Heroes and Villains" melody,... harmonically this is far closer to pieces like "Caroline, No" or "Don't Talk (Put Your Head On My Shoulder)" than the harmonically simplistic material elsewhere on the album, with a chord change almost every beat.

All that remains true for the *Smile* versions, but where the *Smiley Smile* re-recording was deliberately difficult, with Carl Wilson's calm, generous vocals set against Baldwin organ suddenly turning into a dissonant noise, here everything is much more obviously pretty. Brian (closely doubled by Jeffrey Foskett on the 2004 recording) sings the beautiful melody straight, backed by a harpsichord, horns, and nursery-rhyme-like contrapuntal backing vocals. The *Smile* version also has an extra verse, not in the *Smiley* version:

> All fall down, and lost in the mystery
>
> Lost it all to a non-believer
>
> And all that's left is a girl who's loved by her mother and father

While the last verse has a crucial lyrical change – instead of "never known as a non-believer", "just away from her non-believer".

Both interpretations of the song are valid, interesting, beautiful ones – and one of the few good things about the collapse of *Smile* is that it meant we have *Smiley Smile* – but the *Smile* version is both a more complete and a more readily palatable version of the song. Pure musical beauty.

The 2004 *Smile* version of this was released as a limited-edition vinyl single, backed with "Wind Chimes". In the UK that single became Wilson's highest-charting solo recording to date, reaching number 29.

Song for Children

"Wonderful" is followed by this piece, often bootlegged as "Look". Originally an instrumental piece based around the "ta na na" section of "Good Vibrations", here "Wonderful" segues directly into it, with a new vocal line ("Maybe not one. Maybe you too, wonderin'/Wonderin' who. Wonderful you, a-wonderin'"), and short fragments of lyrics connecting "Wonderful" and "Child is Father of the Man", with Jeffrey Foskett singing a couple of solo lines.

When bootlegged on its own, this was one of the less interesting pieces, sounding like just a set of cast-off ideas from "Good Vibrations" done in a toytown glockenspiel manner (it was the first instrumental track to be recorded after that song, and sounds like it), with the chorus that would later be used for "Child is Father of the Man" thrown in. However, adding the lyrics (particularly the chorus lyrics, "Child is father of the Sun" – a variant of the chorus to the next song) means it becomes a crucial element of the longer suite, and in its place it reveals wonderful riches.

The first time I heard the transition from "Wonderful" to "Song for Children" I actually cried at the sense of utter *rightness* – two pieces of music I knew well, but had never considered going together, fitting so beautifully and becoming something greater.

Child Is Father of the Man

This track had again been widely bootlegged without its verse lyrics, although it's best known for its chorus being used as the end of "Surf's Up". It's made up of three simple sections – a verse, consisting of E/F#, F#/B, and B chords, dominated by reverbed guitar and piano, with a haunting Morricone-esque harmonica melody (and, in the repetition of the verse, newly-written lyrics by Parks, again on the subject of children and belief); a two-chord chorus, A and E chords, with F# in the bass, over which the band chant "child, the child/father of the man"; and a tag section, again only two chords, D (or Dmaj7) and E, with B in the bass, playing a tick-tock melody similar to the first few bars of the verse.

Over this is one of the transitions, and since we haven't discussed those much until now, and since this song is one of the less musically interesting tracks, now is as good a time as any.

As you'll have seen from the entries above, *Smile* as finally released is divided into three movements, designed for continuous performance. In some cases, the transition between tracks is a simple segue, or sometimes even a momentary silence. But in other cases, newly-composed transitions have been created for the 2004 recording. These sections, usually only a few seconds long, perform a vital function in gluing a lot of pop songs and fragments into a cohesive whole.

These transitions are orchestrated by von Mertens, though I don't know whether it was him, Wilson, Sahanaja, or Parks who came up with them (the participants have remained silent about some of the nuts-and-bolts aspects of preparing *Smile* for public performance). They are all, however, based on melodic motifs from other songs – often combined in ways that bring similarities between apparently-disparate parts of *Smile* out. In this case, as in several others, the transition uses a melodic motif which splits the difference between the lines "canvas the town and brush the backdrop/Are you sleeping?" from "Surf's Up" and "Hanging down from my window/Those are my wind chimes" from "Wind Chimes", while also highlighting the harmonic similarity between the former line and the verse for "Child is Father of the Man".

Whether intentionally or not, a lot of *Smile* seems like variations on three or four melodic ideas. By highlighting the similarities between those variations, the transition sections in the 2004 re-recording make this seem intentional – and in the case of the second movement of *Smile* positively inspired.

Surf's Up

And the second movement ends with what may be the greatest song Brian Wilson or Van Dyke Parks have ever written, together or separately. Once again, this is a song I've discussed before (this time in volume two), and so I'll point readers to that essay for a detailed description of the song's structure.

But while the Beach Boys had released a version of the song in 1971, it was a Frankenstein combination of new lead vocals by Carl Wilson, a half-finished *Smile* backing track, Brian Wilson's piano demo, and Moog and backing vocal overdubs, supervised by Carl rather than Brian. This was the first time Brian Wilson had ever recorded a whole version of the song, other than piano-only demos, and so the best indication of what his vision of the song was.

And it's superb, even given the deterioration of his voice in the intervening decades. The first section follows the pattern of the 1971 recording pretty much exactly, including the additional "bygone, bygone" backing vocals, but on the highest notes, on the lines "canvas the town and brush the backdrop/Are you sleeping brother John?" Wilson is joined by two other voices, taking a low harmony while Jeffrey Foskett's falsetto soars overhead. Whether this was a result of necessity (Wilson no longer being able to hit those notes) or it had always been his intention to have those parts be harmonised, it's impossible now to say. What we *can* say is that it works beautifully.

The second section, meanwhile, keeps the same piano part that was used in the demo which became part of the 1971 recording, but embellishes it with more of von Mertens' sparse, Germanic-sounding string arrangements, adding to its austere beauty. And again, at the end, the track reverts to the style of the 1971 recording, including the "a children's song" lyrics apparently added by Jack Rieley, although rather than fade out the track comes to a strong close on the line "a child" – an artefact of this version of *Smile* being prepared for live performance.

In every version, "Surf's Up" is an astonishing recording, and while this version may not have the pure vocal beauty of the 1971 version (or of the 2011 edit which replaces Carl Wilson's vocal on that track with a vintage Brian Wilson vocal digitally flown in from the demo), it's all the more powerful for coming at the end of a movement in which its musical ideas have been properly set up and prefigured.

After this, the third movement of *Smile* can't help but be something of a disappointment, but it must be remembered that this is a relative assessment – after this, *any* other music would be a disappointment, and the third movement of *Smile* still has much to love when judged on its own merits.

I'm in Great Shape

The third movement starts with a transitional piece, reworking some of the "cantina" section of "Heroes and Villains", before going into a fragment that was originally intended to be part of that song (and which on *The Smile Sessions* is placed between "Roll Plymouth Rock" and "Barnyard" – the only sequencing decision on that set which is different from the 2004 recording). Taylor Mills, Jeffrey Foskett, and Wilson sing one line each of the three-line song about being "in the great shape of the agriculture", before a saxophone restates the same melody, and the track dissolves into a tape-delay explosion, segueing into. . .

I Wanna Be Around

Songwriters: Johnny Mercer and Sadie Vimmerstedt

Another standard, this one had been written by Mercer after Vimmerstedt (a grandmother from Ohio) was inspired to write the first line and send it in an envelope addressed only to "Johnny Mercer, Songwriter, New York, NY" after reading about Frank Sinatra and Ava Gardner's breakup.

That first line ("I want to be around to pick up the pieces, when someone breaks your heart in two") is the only one used here, with Mills echoing "your heart" and "in two" before the song turns into

Workshop

Songwriter: Brian Wilson

A short piano-based instrumental, over which the band "play" hammers, drills, saws, and other tools. The saws and so on sound, in fact, absolutely identical to the versions recorded in the 1960s, and may be the same recording, and thus the only part of the original *Smile* to be on the remade one (to hear the original tools in isolation without the instruments, listen to the end of "Do It Again"...), although various band members are credited as "playing" them.

Vega-Tables

Another song I've dealt with before in its *Smiley Smile* version, the *Smile* version of this song has a much more complex backing, adding piano and percussion to the bass, although the real strength of this track comes from the complex backing vocal lines, a cascade of overlapping vocal lines that make the song sound infinitely fuller than it otherwise would. It's still a trifle, but an entertaining one.

On a Holiday

Previously bootlegged as "Holidays", this is a joyful little track, all clarinet and marimba, with new lyrics by Parks, about pirates going on holiday to Hawaii (with a middle section spoke-sung by Nick Walusko), and incorporating both the "Plymouth Rock roll over" chorus and shouts of "child!", harking back to the earlier movements. After ninety seconds it comes to a hard stop and is replaced by a piano playing a short, plaintive melody (the same one Wilson had reused as the intro to "Happy Days" in 1998), over which Wilson sings "long, long ago, long ago" – a line from a nineteenth century folk song, which Wilson presumably knew in the version by Patti Page.

This in turn segues into a marimba-and-piano rendition of the "whispering winds set my wind chimes a tinkling" section of "Wind Chimes", here placed before the track proper rather than, as in the *Smiley Smile* version, as its tag.

Wind Chimes

The version of "Wind Chimes" on *Smile* is one of the few cases where the *Smile* interpretation of a song is definitively worse than the *Smiley Smile* version. While on *Smiley Smile* this is a sparse, gentle, unutterably strange song, one that it's almost impossible to imagine a human mind conceiving, here the main part of the song becomes a simple common-time melody, pleasant enough but nothing astonishing, before going into several variations of the two-chord one-step-apart changes we heard in, for example, the "over and over" part of "Cabin Essence" or the "Child is Father of the Man" chorus. It's pleasant, and interesting enough, but what was an astonishing highlight of *Smiley Smile* is one of the weaker points of *Smile* (though it says a lot about the general quality of *Smile* that the worst it gets is "pleasant, and interesting enough").

Mrs. O'Leary's Cow

Songwriter: Brian Wilson

And here we reach the most infamous track on the album – and the only recording for which Brian Wilson ever won a Grammy. There are many legends about this track, commonly known as "Fire", and more than any other track on the album this led to the myth of *Smile*. But taken for what it is, this is a remarkable piece of work.

The track starts with a Swanee whistle, after which simultaneous ascending/descending chromatic scales are played on a piano while more Swanee whistles are played and bells rung (this section, in its original recording, was released on *Good Vibrations* as "Heroes & Villains: intro").

That section sounds almost comical, but then there's a hard cut into what may be the most accurate musical depiction of a fire ever. Toms and bass drums crash, fuzz bass pounds away, cellos roar, and over the top the band sing wordlessly (the same vocal part used on "Fall Breaks and Back to Winter" from *Smiley Smile*). This is one of those occasions where words can't sum up the feeling of listening to the music, but this is a track that sounds astonishing even now, nearly fifty years after it was originally conceived.

In Blue Hawaii

After the fire, comes the water. "In Blue Hawaii" is based on the track originally released as "Love to Say DaDa" on the *Good Vibrations* box, and is made up of some of the same elements that were used in "Cool Cool Water" from *Sunflower,* but in a very different arrangement.

We start with an *a capella*, heavily reverbed, chant of "water water water", with strings entering, buried in the mix. Another two-chord one-tone-apart section, but this is more...well, fluid. Over the top, Wilson sings new lyrics by Parks, tying the fire and water sections of this "elements suite" together – "is it hot as hell in here or is it me?...I could really use a drop to drink".

We then have several more two-chord sections, in the vein of parts of "On a Holiday", "Song For Children" and "Wind Chimes", over which Wilson sings punning lyrics about Hawaii. It's another minor piece, once the introduction has ended, but one that's needed to relax us after the tension of "Mrs. O'Leary's Cow".

With the line "aloha nui means goodbye", the album proper ends – the song goes into an outro incorporating some of the motifs that have appeared throughout the album, before ending on a fragment of "Our Prayer".

Good Vibrations

Songwriters: Brian Wilson, Mike Love, and Tony Asher

And finally, we have this – not a part of any of the three suites, but the song that kickstarted *Smile*. The arrangement is pretty much identical to the original single for the most part, apart from Foskett (who doubles Wilson throughout the song) singing "and I'm pickin' up" just before the first chorus, until the "gotta keep those lovin' good" section, which is extended to include the "hum de ah" vocal part that had been recorded for the original but discarded, making the track run a good minute longer than the original.

The track also uses Tony Asher's dummy lyrics for the verses (apart from the first line, which is from Love's final lyric), though keeping Love's lyrics for the rest of the song (for which Asher never wrote a lyric).

The result is, it has to be said, somewhat disappointing – unlike the rest of *Smile*, the original "Good Vibrations" single was released at the time, in the way Wilson wanted it, and complete. While one can understand the desire – even the necessity – to include the song on the album, all it does is remind you how good the original is. Both vocally and lyrically, the original single is superior, and while this does an excellent job of recreating the original arrangement and atmosphere, it will never match up to it.

But that can't be said for the rest of the album. While parts of it (notably in the patchy third movement) don't quite live up to the thirty-seven years of hype and legend, what's amazing is that so much of it does. *Smile* – the completed, 2004, album – is a masterpiece, and that it exists at all is a testament to the talents not only of Wilson and Parks, but of Sahanaja, von Mertens, and the rest of Wilson's superb band.

What I Really Want For Christmas

Since Brian Wilson's solo recording career became an ongoing project, he has more or less alternated between albums of new material and recordings of other people's songs, done in his own style. *What I Really Want For Christmas* could just as easily have been titled *Brian Wilson Reimagines Christmas,* as for the most part the recordings are of traditional Christmas carols, reworked in the style of Wilson's 60s material.

Released in October 2005, it was the first recording he released after *Smile* was completed (apart from a single, "Walking Down The Path Of Life", released to benefit victims of Hurricane Katrina).

As his first work after *Smile*, it had a lot to live up to, and was rather disappointing to many fans as a result. Without those expectations, though, it's actually a rather lovely little album – no masterpiece, of course, but in the top tier of Christmas albums, and well worth a listen when in a festive mood. While it doesn't admit of as much analysis as the more major works, it's an album well worth listening to for anyone who has any Christmas spirit at all (which, of course, not everyone will).

(All songs trad. arr. Brian Wilson, with lead vocals by Brian Wilson and falsetto vocals by Jeffrey Foskett, except where noted.)

The Man with All the Toys

Songwriters: Brian Wilson, Mike Love

The album starts with one of two remakes of tracks from *The Beach Boys Christmas Album*. For the most part this is a note-for-note remake of the original track, apart from a drum intro and Wilson's aged voice, until 1:14, at which point an organ-and-sax instrumental break kicks in. There's then an extended version of the outro, before the song turns into a rather lovely fragment of "Joy To The World" (just the line "let every heart prepare Him

129

room", repeated to fade).

What I Really Want for Christmas

Songwriters: Brian Wilson, Bernie Taupin

The title song, and one of two new originals recorded for the album, is a collaboration with Bernie Taupin, who is best known as the lyricist for many of Elton John's biggest hits.

The song originally started out as a ballad written for Wilson's wife Melinda, entitled "Nobody Ever Did Me Like You Do", before Taupin added new lyrics. As with many of Wilson's songs for the last decade or so, it's a rather aimless, though pretty, song, with a verse consisting of a simple stop-start chordal melody on the piano, with Wilson singing Taupin's bland, generic lyrics about peace and happiness over the top, and with a rather more coherent chorus.

God Rest Ye Merry Gentlemen

The first of the traditional carols is arranged as a sort of surf gospel song, with throbbing, tremeloed, reverbed guitar and Hammond organ giving it a vaguely threatening feel even as Wilson sings about "tidings of comfort and joy". The organ gives it a feel vaguely like a 60s Atlantic soul record, even as the guitar roots it firmly in the surf genre. A decent track, although the closing saxophone solo is a little offputting.

O Holy Night

One of the more straightforward arrangements on the album, this version of the nineteenth-century carol places the melody over an instrumental bed similar to a stripped-down version of that for "Kiss Me Baby", with 12/8 arpeggios on guitar, an organ pad, and occasional snare drum hits making up most of the instrumentation, until an instrumental break in which a typically lovely and sparse string arrangement from von Mertens comes in.

We Wish You a Merry Christmas

Another straight take on a traditional carol, with the only unusual element being a huffing bass harmonica, until the 1:46 mark, when the song suddenly turns into a revved-up surf instrumental version of the song, with a guitar playing the melody, a flute countermelody, and the vocalists singing "oom bop didit" in the style of "This Whole World". The song ends with

Wilson's young children wishing the listener a merry Christmas and happy new year.

Hark the Herald Angels Sing

This version of the Charles Wesley hymn (with the traditional music by Mendelssohn) opens with a new *a capella* vocal intro, before going into a standard, rather martial, arrangement of the song. After the song proper ends, there's a strings-and-organ instrumental rendition of the theme, before a repeat of the intro, this time accompanied by the full band, and with a very nice countermelody on strings, fades the song out.

It Came Upon a Midnight Clear

Another one rearranged with a vaguely soulful feel, the combination of the 6/8 time signature, Hammond organ pad, and vaguely honky-tonk piano gives it something of the feeling of "Sail On Sailor", but the massed backing vocals, strings, jew's harp, and bass harmonica all make it a much lighter recording than that would suggest.

The First Noel

The main thing to notice with this song is the way in which the instrumental break and fade has a Leslie'd guitar doubled by tuned percussion (it sounds like a glockenspiel), creating the kind of unique texture that Brian Wilson's best arrangements have, and which you hear nowhere else. A lovely performance, and Wilson's straining for the highest notes on the last "noel", while very obvious, only makes it sound more human and comforting.

Christmasey

Songwriters: Brian Wilson, Jimmy Webb

The only songwriting collaboration between two of the greatest songwriters of all time is unfortunately not up to either man's highest standards. Musically, this is a rewrite of "Fairy Tale" from *Gettin' in Over My Head*, and while the changes have improved it substantially it still falls a little flat. Webb's lyrics, meanwhile, are more banal than his normal work, and the syllabics in the bridge sections don't work well with Wilson's less-than-perfect enunciation.

It's very pretty, and a favourite of many fans, but it won't win over anyone not already predisposed to like it.

Little Saint Nick

Songwriters: Brian Wilson, Mike Love

This is as close as possible to a straight note-for-note remake of the Beach Boys' original. Other than Wilson singing the lead instead of Love, most casual listeners would not notice that it was a new recording.

Deck the Halls

An uptempo version of the classic carol, taken far faster than the song usually is, with a new vocal intro which also doubles as a bridge to a new instrumental section, with ascending/descending scales on piano joined by bass harmonica and horn. One of the most joyous things on the album.

Auld Lang Syne

A remake of the *a capella* arrangement of the song from *The Beach Boys Christmas Album*, with an extra verse but otherwise keeping to the earlier arrangement exactly.

On Christmas Day

Songwriter: Brian Wilson

The first of three bonus tracks, this was originally released as a free download on Wilson's website. Wilson claimed at the time that he had the idea while at his children's school, meeting their teacher, and heard the song in his head.

This seems very likely, but what seems odd is that no-one bothered to tell him that what he heard in his head wasn't a new song, but an old one – the verse (which makes up the vast majority of the song) is melodically identical to "Bells of Christmas", the song Al Jardine, Mike Love, and Ron Altbach wrote for the unreleased 1977 Christmas album (and which was later rewritten with Wilson's collaboration as "Belles of Paris" for the *MIU Album*).

This rewrite is undoubtedly better – lyrically it has nothing as clunky as "The omnipresent spirit of the world will sing", and his new intro/bridge section makes more musical sense than the corresponding parts of "Bells of Christmas", but there's no question at all that this was an unconscious rewrite of the earlier song.

Joy to the World

Another bonus track, this one originally released on a 1997 various artists compilation, *Christmas Spirit*. This is possibly the most beautiful recording of Wilson's solo career. The track is co-produced (uncredited) by Joe Thomas, but has little of the downsides of his normal work. Over a very simple synthesiser background, a stack of Wilsons sing in harmony, almost *a capella*. The vocals are as good as Wilson's vocals always are when Thomas works with him (latterly Thomas has overused autotune, and his instrumental productions are abysmal, but he's one of the few people who can get the best possible vocal performance out of Wilson).

Like many of the tracks here, this does not have many hooks for analysis – it's a very simple, straightforward, performance of a beautiful hymn – but it's quite lovely.

Silent Night

And the album finishes with another track originally made available for free download from brianwilson.com – an *a capella* performance of the first verse of "Silent Night", by a multitracked stack-o'-Brians, followed by a brief spoken merry Christmas wish. Simple but effective.

Songs From Here and Back

In 2006 a rather odd, limited edition, release came out, which would (according to Mike Love's on-stage announcements around that time, anyway) be one of the band's best selling albums of the last few decades.

Songs From Here and Back is a compilation that was on sale only through Hallmark stores in the US, for a two-month period leading up to Father's Day 2006, with a discount when purchased with a sufficient number of greetings cards. It consisted of seven previously-unreleased live tracks from two different shows at the same venue (five from a 1989 show featuring Brian Wilson and Bruce Johnston, two from a 1974 show featuring Dennis Wilson and Ricky Fataar, and all featuring Mike, Carl, and Al), and one solo track each from Brian, Mike, and Al.

The live tracks are fairly clunky run-throughs of "Dance, Dance, Dance", "Wouldn't It Be Nice", "Surfer Girl", "Kokomo", "Little Deuce Coupe", "I Get Around", and "Good Vibrations", showing more than anything else just how joyless the 1980s version of the band could be — they're all perfectly competent, although Mike Kowalski's cymbal work can be a little unsteady, but they're mostly taken at too slow a pace, with any interesting arrangement ideas stripped away and replaced with cheap-sounding synths. Only Al Jardine and Jeffrey Foskett show any sign of life at all in the vocals (except on "Good Vibrations", one of the two 1974 recordings, which is a genuinely good version of the track, but not so good as to make the CD a worthwhile purchase absent anything else).

These tracks are clearly intended for much the same audience as the *NASCAR* CD — people impulse-buying a rough approximation of music they heard on the radio in their youth, who don't really care about the quality — and on those terms the CD is certainly a better purchase — but it's the three solo tracks that got Beach Boys fans interested.

The Spirit of Rock & Roll

Songwriters: Brian Wilson, Gary Usher, and Tom Kelly

Lead vocals: Brian Wilson

Of all the solo tracks, this one had the longest gestation. It was originally recorded in 1986 as a track for the Beach Boys, during Wilson's sessions with Gary Usher, and was a collaboration between Usher (who came up with the original idea), Wilson, and Tom Kelly, the co-writer of "Like a Virgin", "True Colors", and "Eternal Flame" among other songs, who Usher had brought in to the project to make Wilson's songs more commercial for the 80s. That recording was used, briefly, in a TV special the Beach Boys did to mark their twenty-fifth anniversary, but otherwise remained unreleased.

Another version – with what sounds like much the same backing track – was recorded for Wilson's unreleased solo album *Sweet Insanity* a few years later. That version – a duet with Bob Dylan, featuring Belinda Carlisle and Paula Abdul on backing vocals (no, I'm not joking) – also remains unreleased, though it's widely bootlegged.

This version is a remake, featuring members of Wilson's backing band (along with Joel Peskin on sax, who also appears on Love's track), but is very close to those versions – slightly less synth-heavy, a less oppressive drum sound and better guitar tone but otherwise almost identical (although it has a nice *a capella* tag missing from the earlier recordings). In any version it's simply not very good, being as it is a dull piece of 80s Boomer nostalgia, and it sounds like the throwaway it is.

PT Cruiser

Songwriter: Al Jardine

Lead vocals: Al Jardine with Matt Jardine

This track was the only one on the album to have been previously released, as it was released as a promotional single (along with an *a capella* version of the track) by Chrysler in 2002 to promote their then-new PT Cruiser range of convertibles.

As one might expect for what is essentially a song-length jingle, this isn't the greatest recording ever made. On the other hand, it's more fun than it needed to be. The song doesn't even pretend to be original, being made up of stitched-together bits of "Little GTO", "Hey Little Cobra" and "Shut Down", but the band (mostly the better members of the 70s and 80s Beach Boys touring band, along with Jardine's sons Matt (himself a touring Beach Boy for much of the 80s and 90s) and Adam) give it a surprising amount of life, and Jardine's vocal is strong.

Cool Head, Warm Heart

Songwriter: Mike Love

Lead vocals: Mike Love and Christian Love

And surprisingly, Mike Love's solo track is the best thing on the album.

It's relative, of course – this is by no means a great track – but it's a very, very listenable mid-tempo ballad, sung in Love's relaxed low baritone (the part of his range that has held up best, especially in the studio). This was originally recorded for a still-unreleased solo album that at various times was titled *Unleash the Love* and *Mike Love, Not War*, and Love, like Jardine, features one of his sons on the track.

Christian Love, who would later join the touring Beach Boys for several years, sounds here quite extraordinarily like Carl Wilson; Mike Love's vocals are slightly over-processed at points but are some of his best studio vocals of the last few decades, and Adrian Baker, who I've criticised with good reason before, does a good job with the vocal arrangements.

The production (by Paul Fauerso) is uninspired but not unpleasant, and the same could largely go for the song itself. It's based on a saying of Maharishi Mahesh Yogi, and like many of Love's songs about transcendental meditation it relies too much on Love's sincere belief in the song's message and not enough on actual craft.

It would have made a perfectly serviceable album track for any post-1980 Beach Boys album, and while it wouldn't have been the best song on any of those albums, it would have been closer to the best than the worst on all of them. As it is, the song remained an occasional appearance in Love's touring Beach Boys' shows for the next few years

Songs From Here and Back might be the least essential Beach Boys release of new or previously-unreleased recordings ever. It is not, however, anything like the worst. It's a perfectly listenable collection. It's just rather pointless.

That Lucky Old Sun

And this is one that I've been reluctant to write about...

That Lucky Old Sun is Brian Wilson's greatest new work since at least *The Beach Boys Love You*. It is a latter-period masterpiece that almost matches *Smile* in its ambition and scope, and is to this date the last truly great work from Wilson.

It is also, though, largely co-written with Scott Bennett, a member of Wilson's band who was, a few months ago as I write this, convicted of rape.

How one deals with that kind of situation when it comes to appreciation of art is a difficult question, and will vary from person to person and from subject to subject. Trying to get to a point where I could sort my own feelings about this out enough to write about the album delayed this whole project a good six months. I've written about that sort of thing before, but generally where both art and offence are distanced in time. In this case, given that I committed to write this book before the events in question, my options were limited. To be very clear, though, I do *not* think rape is ever excusable, and nor do I think one should separate the art and the artist in cases like this.

But on the other hand, Bennett is not the principal artist, and I want to deal fairly with the work of Wilson and his other collaborators.

The best solution I've come up with is to try, in so far as I can, to write only about the music on tracks Bennett co-wrote, on the assumption that his contribution was primarily (though not by any means solely) lyrical. I'm not at all sure that an objective assessment of his lyrics is either possible or desirable this close to his conviction, though I'm aware that a lack of that is a flaw in this essay.

So be it.

Anyway, about the album itself...

The album's gestation began with *What I Really Want For Christmas*, and with Wilson thinking about classic arrangers who'd worked on other versions of the Christmas songs on the album. He got the version of "That

Lucky Old Sun" which Gordon Jenkins had arranged for Louis Armstrong stuck in his head, bought a CD with it on, and decided to work out his own version.

Wilson had also been obsessed for years with "Proud Mary", and specifically with a version of the song recorded by Ike and Tina Turner, which he incorrectly thought Phil Spector had produced. From at least the early 90s he had been trying to record a version of the song, usually with a "rock, roll, rockin' and a rollin'" vocal part added.

That vocal part combined with the line in "That Lucky Old Sun" about "rolling round heaven all day", and those two songs between them seemed to become the two poles to which all Wilson's new songs were drawn.

Wilson was in his most productive period since the late nineties (and to date his last truly prolific period for new material) and he recorded many songs with his band members in Bennett's home studio. When the Southbank Centre in London asked him to come up with a new song cycle for the reopening of the Royal Festival Hall, where he had performed his first UK solo shows in 2002 and had premiered *Smile* in 2004, he took the best of the songs and got Van Dyke Parks to write linking narratives, which Wilson recited over music repeating themes from the songs (Darian Sahanaja came up with the music for these sections based on Wilson's musical themes, and edited many of the songs to fit the structure, while Paul von Mertens orchestrated them).

The result, when it premiered in live performance in 2007, was an absolutely glorious half hour or so of music. By careful selection and linking, Wilson and his collaborators had managed to draw together what could have been a very disparate group of songs, emphasising themes they have in common, and creating a suite that is simultaneously a set of songs about memory and nostalgia, a story of a single day that starts with sunrise and ends at midnight, and a travelogue of California. The whole is greater than the parts, and some of the parts are pretty great.

While *That Lucky Old Sun* worked best as a live performance piece, the album is still the best new work Wilson has done since 1977, and is in the handful of albums (along with *Pet Sounds, Smile, Smiley Smile,* and *Love You*) I'd point anyone to as an example of why people say he's a genius.

(All songs have lead vocals by Brian Wilson, except where noted.)

That Lucky Old Sun

Songwriters: Haven Gillespie and Beasley Smith

The album's opener is also its only cover version. "That Lucky Old Sun" was written in 1949 by Haven Gillespie and Beasley Smith, who also wrote

"The Old Master Painter", which Wilson had recorded for *Smile*. The original song is a rather heartbreaking ballad about the myriad tiny ways that work and life can grind one down, and the hope for eventual release from that condition, which has become a standard performed by (to take a few of my favourite versions) Johnny Cash, Jerry Lee Lewis and Ray Charles, among many others.

Wilson creates a new group *a capella* vocal intro before singing only the first and last verses, solo, over a backing of woodwinds, strings and piano. The effect is to evoke the dawn, with the "up in the morning" opening being reflected in many of the later songs, and to provide a gentle introduction to the album much like "Our Prayer" provided for *Smile*.

Morning Beat

Songwriters: Brian Wilson and Scott Bennett

And the opening track goes straight into a vocal chant – "Maumamayama Glory Hallelujah" – which Wilson had first mentioned as a musical idea in an interview in the early 1970s. (On a personal note, hearing the voices come in singing that line at the live premiere of this was the first moment I was sure that this piece would be something special. It was a breathtaking moment.)

This leads into a couple of verses based on a more rock and roll version of the same basic musical idea – a two-chord riff leading into a rising bridge, which is recycled from an unreleased song, "Walkin'", from the late 60s. This is one of those ideas Wilson often returns to – a very similar musical phrase is also used in his section of the song "Bells of Madness" which he recorded with his daughter Carnie in the 90s. This is all accompanied by crunchy guitars, garage-pop organ, and "rock rock rock" backing vocals, to create some of the most uplifiting uptempo music Wilson had done since *Love You*.

After three repetitions of this basic musical material (with the melody varied slightly the second time through, making it sound more like a chorus) and a repeat of the "Maumamayama glory hallelujah" vocal part, a totally different section ("hear those guitars gently strumming") comes in – very strongly reminiscent of some of the "Cherokee trail" parts of "Rio Grande", before going back into the "Walkin'" riff.

Brian Wilson has often, in recent years, talked about wanting to make a rock and roll album. This track is the best evidence in his solo career that he would be able to make such an album interesting.

Narrative: A Room With A View

Songwriters: Brian Wilson and Van Dyke Parks

And here we have the first of several narrative sections. In these, Van Dyke Parks provides rhyming couplets recited by Wilson over music (in this case a simple variant on the "Morning Beat" verse material). Parks' words are, as one would expect from him, witty, intelligent, and articulate. This one describes a dawn view in LA, the city waking up and human activity starting, as the sounds of nature, coyotes and owls, die away for the day.

Good Kind of Love

Songwriter: Brian Wilson

Lead vocals: Brian Wilson with Taylor Mills and Scott Bennett

The only solo Brian Wilson composition on the album is also one of the best. It has some of Wilson's best solo lyrics ever ("he loves her when she's sleeping/And all the dreams she's keeping/She keeps them in a jar but not too far from her heart"), and a completely unorthodox structure.

There's a typical verse ("he loves her when she's sleeping..."), which is slightly reminiscent of "Our Team", a 1970s outtake, and a standard chorus ("they have the good kind of love..."), but then the track goes into a long bridge section ("just him and her..." through "They have the good kind of love") which somehow makes perfect musical sense even though it goes all over the place. There's then a whole new section ("the sun keeps on shining/it rolls round heaven above"), an instrumental repeat of the bridge, a repeat of the last bridge line, and an ascending piano part which leads into the next song.

It's absolutely beautiful, somewhat reminiscent of the Zombies' "Friends of Mine" in the way it celebrates the love of two other people, but with a triplet swing that is quintessentially Brian Wilson.

Forever She'll Be My Surfer Girl

Songwriters: Brian Wilson and Scott Bennett

This, on the other hand, is one of the weaker songs on the album. One of an increasing number of mid-tempo ballads looking back at high points of Wilson's career that pepper his later albums, this song is supposedly about Judy Bowles, who was also supposedly the subject of the original "Surfer Girl".

But really, this is just about "remember this song I wrote when I was younger?", and has little more merit than Mike Love's similar attempts. It's only saved because of the album structure, where it links a song about love and a narrative about the beach, and where that California nostalgia is part of the aim of the album. Musically mediocre, it does its job in the context of the album, but it's not one that really stands up outside that context.

Narrative: Venice Beach

Songwriters: Brian Wilson and Van Dyke Parks

"Venice Beach is popping like live shrimp dropped on a hot wok"

Another narrative with Parks lyrics, another picture of an area in LA, this one Venice Beach, with its artists, hucksters, and homeless people all painted exquisitely in a few words.

Live Let Live

Songwriters: Brian Wilson and Van Dyke Parks

And this, the only song with Parks' lyrics, is far and away the best thing on the album. I still remember being in the audience for the first performance of this suite, and my breath being literally taken away by the opening line of this one: "I've got a notion we come from the ocean and *God almighty*".

Originally written for the film *Arctic Tale*, where it had different, inferior, lyrics (also by Parks), the song owes more than a little to "Sail On Sailor" – in particular the "live let live not die" chorus is almost identical to the earlier song's "sail on, sail on, sailor". But where that earlier song was a heavy, distraught, rock song, this is a gentle, life-affirming, waltz. The impressionistic lyrics about whales, the Pacific Ocean, the love of a benevolent God, and the smallness of humanity compared to the vastness of the world, fit perfectly with the simple but catchy melody, to create something that perfectly fits with the album's recurring themes and motifs (heartbeats, the water, rebirth, California) but transcends them. A beautiful little song.

Mexican Girl

Songwriters: Brian Wilson and Scott Bennett

Lead vocals: Brian Wilson with Scott Bennett

This, on the other hand, is generally considered the weakest song on the album by most fans. I can see the argument for it being weak – lyrics like "hey bonita muchacha/let me know that I gotcha" are not the strongest, and the song itself is fairly simple. But there's a catchiness and joy to this simple exercise in pseudo-Mexican pop that gives it a freshness that's welcome. Not everything can be a masterpiece, and this doesn't attempt to be anything more than a frivolous, light, interlude. On those terms, it works.

(Note: I've credited the lead vocals here to Wilson and Bennett, but there's no credit in the album liner notes. Someone other than Wilson clearly takes lead on the "hey bonita muchacha" section, and to my ears it sounds like Bennett – on the live DVD, and in live performances, Wilson sang lead on that section, with Foskett harmonising, but it's clearly different on the recording.)

Narrative: Cinco de Mayo

Songwriters: Brian Wilson and Van Dyke Parks

Another short narrative section, this time about Mexican-Americans in LA, but connecting up to the themes of the next song, about the cinema.

California Role/That Lucky Old Sun (reprise)

Songwriters: Brian Wilson and Scott Bennett/Haven Gillespie and Beasley Smith

Lead vocals: Brian Wilson with Scott Bennett

This was apparently originally written in the 1980s, under the title "Wondering What You're Up to Now". A ukulele-and-clarinet-driven vaudeville song reminiscent of 1920s pop (with a musical quote in the second verse from "Rhapsody in Blue"), this is another song about the California of the past, and of today. Its catchy swinginess (for the most part just shuffling between two chords) belies a rather downbeat lyric, about settling for something other than one's dreams. (Bennett sings the lead on the first two verses, with his voice distorted as if through a megaphone, *a la* Al Bowlly or Rudy Vallee).

This segues into a vocal round, almost gospel-style, based around the phrase "roll around heaven all day", with only tenuous connection to the song it's ostensibly reprising (it sounds more like parts of Wilson's own "Rio Grande").

Narrative: Between Pictures

Songwriters: Brian Wilson and Van Dyke Parks

Another short narrative section. "People fill their tanks with flights of fancy/Actors waiting tables with a method they can't share".

Oxygen to the Brain

Songwriters: Brian Wilson and Scott Bennett

Another song which hits many of the late-Brian-Wilson-lyric cliches – Brian had a bad life, but now it's good, and exercise is a good thing – but one that works very well, partly because of the contrast between the opening verse (sung almost as a nursery rhyme, "open up, open up, open your eyes/time, it's time, it's time to rise") and the upbeat chorus. This is very similar to "Happy Days" from *Imagination*, but has little of that song's discordant, jarring nature. Here the dark past is *very* firmly past, something to be looked at from a distance, not something still affecting the singer, while the upbeat chorus is immediately catchy. A lovely little minor work.

Can't Wait Too Long

Songwriter: Brian Wilson

A fragment of the 1967 song, lasting under a minute, played almost exactly as it was originally recorded. In live performance, this was one of the most moving parts of the suite, as footage of Wilson with his dead brothers was projected as the band sang "been...too...long". It's still impossible for me to hear this without thinking of that and being deeply moved. How well it works without that context, I couldn't judge.

Midnight's Another Day

Songwriters: Brian Wilson and Scott Bennett

And this one is a song that is *definitely* improved by the context. A download of the demo was made available on Wilson's website, and I thought it was a dull dirge with little to recommend it. Coming where it does in the album, though – and with slightly fuller production – this is heart-stoppingly beautiful.

Surprisingly, given that this is such a slow, emotional, ballad, it started life as an uptempo song called "Beatle Man", in which Wilson asked how Paul McCartney and Elton John were doing these days and what they were up to (sadly, if a demo of that exists, it hasn't made its way to me...).

However, Bennett felt that the suite as it stood was too lightweight – Wilson was happy, and writing happy music, and the album needed some more tonal variation. He took Wilson's song, slowed down the tempo, and added new lyrics going over the old ground of Wilson having overcome his mental trouble, as well as adding the piano intro.

As a song, there's really very little here, and it trades mostly on the emotional resonance of Wilson's past. What power it has is mostly down to von Mertens' orchestration and the sparse but effective backing vocals. But as the climax of the album, hearing Wilson singing "all these people make me feel so alone" is glorious. Context is all, here.

That Lucky Old Sun (reprise)

Songwriters: Haven Gillespie and Beasley Smith

Not really a reprise of the song, this is forty seconds of the tag to "Midnight's Another Day", with various band members singing "lucky old sun" over it, before Wilson finishes it with "he rolls around heaven all day".

Going Home

Songwriters: Brian Wilson and Scott Bennett

And the album comes to what should be its close with this great uptempo rocker, based on a similar riff to "Morning Beat", and with some glorious honking bass harmonica provided by Tommy Morgan, the Wrecking Crew harmonica player who also provides the harmonica solo.

Another variation of the "rock, rollin'" riff, this had started life as a slow cowboy song in Wilson's mid-90s sessions with Andy Paley. Little survives of that here, though, apart from the line "I'm going home" and the general melodic shape of the verse. This is much, much stronger, and probably the best uptempo track Wilson has done in the last thirty years. Fuzz bass, organ, layers of backing vocals, horns, all contribute to a great riff, which occasionally breaks off to provide a change of pace with a near-*a capella* section ("at twenty-five I turned out the lights...").

This would have been the perfect closer for the album.

Southern California

Songwriters: Brian Wilson and Scott Bennett

Unfortunately, the album actually ends with one of the dullest ballads Wilson has ever written — if he did write it at all, as several fans have suggested this is entirely the work of Bennett, who sings lead on the demo (Wilson sings lead on all the others except "California Role"), and who we know wanted there to be some more emotionally-heavy ballads on the album.

I don't think it *is* all Bennett's work — certainly the chord sequence for the verses is similar enough to "Love and Mercy", "Your Imagination", and half a dozen other Wilson songs that one can imagine this being something Wilson wrote on autopilot. And melodically, the verses are very, *very* similar to "Christmasey", which Wilson had written around the same time.

So I think this is just a case of Wilson being less than inspired and knocking out a mediocre ballad which, as the end of the album, has to bear more weight than it can.

But I want to emphasise, this is dull, but isn't *bad*. In fact, there's not a single truly bad song on the entire album. The level of inspiration varies, but even at its worst (this song and "Forever She'll Be My Surfer Girl") the album is more than listenable. And even on this song, the very end (where the band go into another "Maumamayama Glory Hallelujah") sends shivers down the spine.

And after the song ends, there's a hidden track — a few seconds of a round based on the lines "roll around heaven all day" and "work, work, workin' in the sun all day".

That Lucky Old Sun is, to date, the last truly great work Brian Wilson has put out. And it *is* a great Brian Wilson album. Yes, Bennett, Parks, Sahanaja, and von Mertens all contributed, and yes their contributions were invaluable, but Wilson has always been a great collaborator, rather than a great solo artist *per se*. I've pointed out flaws with individual songs here, but far more often than not they work as songs, and it *certainly* works as an album. And what doesn't come across in discussing individual tracks is how exuberant an album this is. This is the work of a man in his late sixties, but one who has fallen in love with making music again and is as excited by it as he was in his early twenties. It's an absolute joy to listen to.

Bonus tracks

The album had bonus tracks on iTunes ("Oh Mi Amor" and "Message Man") and on a Best Buy-exclusive CD issue ("Good Kind of Love", "I'm Into Something Good", and "Just Like Me and You").

These songs don't have songwriting credits in the album liners, and the credits here are as cited by Andrew G. Doe at `http://www.esquarterly.com/bellagio/albumarchive5.html`

Oh Mi Amor

Songwriter: Brian Wilson

Another exercise in Mexican-flavoured music, this is a rather ponderous ballad that sounds, in both production and melody, like it came from the *Imagination* sessions (it sounds like a second cousin of both "She Says That She Needs Me" and "Where Has Love Been"), though in fact it dates from 2006 and the same writing sessions that produced the album proper.

It has a slight flavour of "Besame Mucho" to it, and some nice trumpet playing, but it's overlong and outstays its welcome.

Message Man

Songwriter: Brian Wilson

While "Oh Mi Amor" has a thick, layered, production, this track sounds very like Wilson's 80s demos – other than some sweetening, there's little here other than piano chords and some rudimentary drums, and some of the lead vocals are very sloppy. It's a catchy little thing, and will appeal to those who, like myself, prefer Wilson's more idiosyncratic songs, but like "Oh Mi Amor" it goes on too long – there's about one minute's worth of musical material here, and if it had stayed at just two verses, bridge, and fade, it would be nice. But it repeats over and over, and at nearly four minutes long it needed more ideas than it has.

Good Kind of Love

Songwriter: Brian Wilson

Lead vocals: Brian Wilson with Carole King and Scott Bennett

During the demo recording process, Wilson invited Carole King, one of his idols, to record with him. This version of "Good Kind of Love" was one of the two results. The basic track is the same as the one used for the album, and the only real notable difference is that King, rather than Taylor Mills, sings the harmony line on the chorus, and the song comes to a hard end rather than segueing into the next track.

I'm Into Something Good

Songwriters: Gerry Goffin and Carole King

Lead vocals: Brian Wilson and Carole King

The other product of the sessions was this take on the 60s classic, written by King with her then-husband Gerry Goffin. This sounds precisely like one would expect a late-period Brian Wilson home recording of this song to sound – bass harmonica, saxes, a sparse production, a shuffle beat, and some minor inventive changes to the song around the edges (an *a capella* "I'm in – I'm into something" break, and a repetition and key change at the end of the second middle eight). King's vocal contribution consists of taking the odd line here and there (mostly the title line) and the first middle eight.

A nice, fun, but inessential track.

Just Like Me And You

Songwriters: Brian Wilson and Van Dyke Parks

This song is not especially interesting as a piece of music, but *is* interesting as a reflection of Brian Wilson's state of mind in 2006. Because there's a writer not credited above – Murry Wilson, Brian's father.

Wilson Sr. had been a songwriter himself, and an unsuccessful one. But Brian had always loved his music, and his favourite song by his father was one that had never even been registered with the copyright office, let alone recorded – a song called "His Little Darling and You".

That song had started "When a bee loses his queen bee, his days are numbered, it's true...". Wilson reworked his father's song, starting it instead with "when a man loses his woman, his days are numbered, it's true". As it is likely that no-one living other than Wilson has ever heard Murry Wilson's song, it's impossible to tell how much of it comes from "His Little Darling and You", but a snatch of that song that Wilson once played on a TV documentary shows the melodic similarity. In his autobiography, *I am Brian Wilson*, Wilson describes the process of incorporating his father's song as "one of the ways I was proving that I wasn't afraid of making new things that were also old things. I wasn't afraid of the past."

And that's as good a way as any of summing up the entire album.

A Postcard From California

After the demise of his Beach Boys Family & Friends project, Al Jardine went back to his position of least-visible Beach Boy. He played the occasional gig with the bulk of the Family & Friends band under various names, and guested with a band called the Surf City All-Stars (who had been Jan & Dean's backing band until the death of Jan Berry, and who then recruited Jardine's son Matt, and often featured Jardine, David Marks, and Dean Torrence as guests).

He also toured with Brian Wilson briefly in 2006, performing what were billed as Wilson's last ever public performances of *Pet Sounds* (as I write this in February 2017, Brian Wilson has extended his 2016 definitely-the-last-ever *Pet Sounds* tour into the late summer of this year...), but didn't turn up for a European tour on which he had been billed to appear, saying he had to work on his solo album.

This was greeted with a certain amount of scepticism among Beach Boys fans, as Jardine had been talking about a solo album for the best part of a decade already, but in 2010 it turned out he had been telling the truth – he finally released his first ever solo studio album.

Or at least, it's credited as a solo album. In fact, Jardine surprised everyone by putting out what was in effect a new Beach Boys album. While Jardine takes lead on every song and is sole producer, the album featured Brian Wilson on four tracks, David Marks on guitar, and one track that featured archive recordings of Carl Wilson and Bruce Johnston along with a new vocal by Mike Love. This meant the album featured more Beach Boys than some actual Beach Boys albums, and was the first sign that there was enough of a rapprochement among the Beach Boys that a reunion might happen...

The Beach Boys weren't the only guests, though. Jardine has never been comfortable in the spotlight, and is at his best as a harmony singer, so the album is full of other guests – his sons Matt and Adam, Gerry

151

Beckley and Dewey Burnell of the band America, one-time fill-in Beach Boy Glen Campbell, David Crosby, Steve Stills, Neil Young, Steve Miller, and, rather incongruously, Flea of the Red Hot Chilli Peppers (who had become friendly with Jardine after using his studio to record and rehearse – according to at least one interview with Jardine, Flea provides not only bass but trumpet) and Alec Baldwin.

The result is, astonishingly, in the top tier of Beach Boys solo records, and shows what Jardine brought to the band. A concept album of sorts, it's structured to resemble a drive through California, and showcases Jardine's concern about the environment. The album is lacking in the kind of invention that makes the band's best work so exciting – half of it is remakes of the band's old work, and the new tracks are often derivative – but it's a lovely *sounding* record.

Jardine was always an underrated singer, but as the other members' voices started to deteriorate, it's become more obvious just how great he really was – he has the strongest voice and the widest range of all of them, and he may well have always been the best singer in the band on a technical level. But there's a *pleasantness*, a comfort, in this album. It's utterly unadventurous, but it's a work that's very, very, likeable indeed.

There are several different versions of this album that have been released, all under the same title. There was a promo EP with four songs released early in 2010, then a download-only release of the full album. Soon after that came a print-on-demand CD issue. In 2012, Jardine reissued the album, adding three bonus tracks (one of which, "Waves of Love" was issued in two different mixes, one on the download and one on the CD), and then a Japanese-only version was issued with two *new* bonus tracks – a third version of "Waves of Love" and a new song, "The Eternal Ballad".

To be honest, most of the bonus tracks are pretty unnecessary, but the album as originally issued is one that most Beach Boys fans will enjoy. It's no *Pet Sounds* or *Smile*, but it doesn't pretend to be, and it's certainly better than anything released under the band's name between 1979 and its release.

(All songs have lead vocals by Al Jardine except where noted.)

A Postcard from California

Songwriter: Al Jardine

Lead vocals: Al Jardine and Glen Campbell

The opening track credits Al Jardine as the writer, but should really credit Larry Weiss, as Weiss wrote "Rhinestone Cowboy", from which the verse melody of this song is taken without any acknowledgement (the chorus melody is also *extremely* familiar, but in seven years of discussion I've not been able to figure out exactly where I know it from, and have had to conclude that it merely sounds like it should be something else).

As well as being near-identical in melody, the song's arrangement also replicates the earlier track's stop-start rhythm, and most damningly the track features Glen Campbell, who had a hit with the earlier song, on joint lead vocals.

(One could, of course, also argue that "Rhinestone Cowboy" itself is suspiciously similar to "Sloop John B"...)

The song actually seems to reference several other of Campbell's hits, being structured as a goodbye letter to a partner (like the note in "By the Time I Get to Phoenix") and having a brief Morse code beep (like the telegraph wires in "Wichita Lineman"). And the song seems to be set in the same late-60s time period as those songs – the protagonist receives a letter typed on an Underwood, and tries to call his partner but has to leave a note as she's out.

All that said, though, the track is an extremely good opener, with both singers in fine voice – Campbell's vocal is clearly showing his age, but he was still one of the finest vocalists of his generation, and turns in an exemplary performance, while Jardine still sounds exactly as he did in his early twenties. It's a derivative track, but a solid performance, and one of the most listenable things here.

California Feelin'

Songwriters: Brian Wilson and Stephen Kalinich

This track, on the other hand, is much less good. The song dates to the mid-seventies, and was attempted by the Beach Boys on several occasions then, but not released in a Beach Boys version until 2013's *Made in California* box set, although Brian Wilson had released a solo version as the one new track on a compilation of Beach Boys hits a few years earlier.

The original version's unreleased status had led to it being hugely overrated by Beach Boys fans, with people talking of it as a masterpiece, but anyone who had heard the bootlegged versions could hear that it was a half-thought-out song at best. Wilson's melody is pleasant enough, but not very well structured, and Kalinich's lyrics are, like most of his work, bathetic, trying to evoke emotion by merely using words like "loveliness and beauty".

Of the four versions of the song available legitimately (Wilson's solo, the two versions on *Made in California*, and this one), this is by far the best – Jardine's vocal is absolutely sincere, and the arrangement is stripped down to just vocal and piano, with only a harmonica solo and some faint organ right at the end. Other than the brief block harmonies, this is one of the sparsest things on the album, and its stark simplicity is a much better take on the song than the other versions' kitchen-sink excess.

The track ends, as many on the album do, with ocean sound-effects cross-fading into the next song.

Looking Down the Coast

Songwriter: Al Jardine

A song that dates back to 1978, this is almost a prog-rock epic (albeit one that comes in at less than four minutes), with different movements, very much in the same vein as the earlier *California Saga*.

Here, Jardine plays a conquistador visiting the Californian shore to enslave the "natives", while also praising the landscape and the animals of the Big Sur area — the eagles, sea otters, and gray whales.

There are two main alternating sections. The first is a verse/chorus section which repeats several times and which is the missing link between "Airplane" from *The Beach Boys Love You* and Brian Wilson's much later "Walkin' the Line" — the second half of the verse/chorus ("and through the eyes of the California condor there/hasn't got a care") is almost identical to the "If I don't get my way this time I'll die/and that's no lie" section of the latter, while also resembling "the clouds in the sky..." from the earlier song.

The second section ("this must be Monterey") is very different — where the verse/chorus is uptempo country-rock with the same "Be My Baby" stop-start rhythm as the album's title track (a motif that recurs in several places in the album) the contrasting section is much slower and built around some flamenco-style nylon-string guitar, with only an organ pad, some "ooh" backing vocals, and some cymbal crashes (emulating the sound of the sea) to support Jardine's vocal.

This is definitely Jardine's most sophisticated and interesting composition, and along with "All This Is That" is the best evidence we have that he had the potential to be a songwriter on a par with his bandmates if he'd written more.

Don't Fight the Sea

Songwriters: Al Jardine and Terry Jacks

Lead vocals: Al Jardine with Carl Wilson, Brian Wilson, Mike Love and Bruce Johnston

This song dates from 1976, and was originally released by Jacks under the title "Y'Don't Fight The Sea", and credited to him alone. Jacks had been friendly with the Beach Boys in the 70s (his hit cover version of "Seasons in the Sun" was originally intended as a Beach Boys track, and bootlegs of a Beach Boys version with Carl Wilson singing lead exist), and Jardine had made attempts to record the song during the *15 Big Ones* sessions.

This version may contain elements of that track, but the basic backing track appears to have been recorded around 1980, and then left until 1989, when Carl and Brian Wilson and Bruce Johnston added vocals to the track, which was then put aside again. For the album, Jardine and his son Matt added new vocals, and Mike Love recorded a vocal part separately (apparently recorded in his hotel room on a laptop, while on tour), creating the first new Beach Boys track of the 2000s.

Unfortunately, it's not very good – Jacks' original song was bad cod-reggae disco, and a fairly terrible song, and Jardine's version is a poor yacht-rock track with additional lyrics about a polar bear in a dream telling him to protect the environment. Carl Wilson's vocal is one of his lazier ones, while Brian Wilson's is as harsh as most of his recordings from that era. It's a curiosity more than a decent record.

The track was later released as a charity vinyl single.

Tidepool Interlude

Songwriter: Stephen Kalinich

Lead vocals: Alec Baldwin

A piano playing a simple, repetitive melody, with ocean sound effects, over which actor Alec Baldwin recites a poem by Kalinich about the Californian coast, with lines like "beautiful majesty moves through me majestically". Easily the weakest thing on the album, but it's over quickly.

Campfire Scene

Songwriter: Al Jardine

Lead vocals: Al Jardine and Neil Young

This is actually just a short extract of "California Saga: California" (the "water, water..." section) performed by Jardine and Young with banjo and harmonica accompaniment, as an intro to the next track.

California Saga: California

Songwriter: Al Jardine

Lead vocals: Al Jardine and Neil Young , with David Crosby, Stephen Stills, and Brian Wilson

A remake of the *Holland* track, with what sounds like Brian Wilson's vocal flown in from that recording, this is very similar to the original (apart from a "Tumbling Tumbleweeds" piano intro, and all instrumentation except the banjo dropping out in the second "water, water", leaving it almost *a capella*), but Crosby, Stills, Jardine, and Young make up one of the few vocal groups that could seriously compete with the Beach Boys in singing those harmonies, and the song could almost have been written for Neil Young to sing. It's quite lovely to hear the harmony parts, even if the recording's not significantly better than the original – and there's a rather melancholy touch in the last verse, where Young sings the lines about going to the Big Sur festival and seeing Country Joe in the past tense. The hippie dream is long dead...

Help Me Rhonda

Songwriters: Brian Wilson and Mike Love

Lead vocals: Al Jardine and Steve Miller

A much more pointless remake – just how many versions of this song could we possibly need? This is a duet with the Steve Miller Band (plus Flea on bass), and has a certain charm to it – they replicate the arrangement of Buster Brown's "Fannie Mae", the song which originally inspired this one, and go for a sloppy harmonica-led country-blues feel. But this was never one of the band's better big hits anyway, and this is an unnecessary version – and one which doesn't fit the narrative and themes of the rest of the album.

San Simeon

Songwriter: Al Jardine

Lead vocals: Al Jardine with Gerry Beckley and Dewey Burnell

Probably the best original on the album, this has a laid-back acoustic feel, and absolutely gorgeous harmonies featuring the two current members of the band America.

There's a little of "Don't Worry Baby" in the track, but it doesn't feel derivative in the way that some of the other songs do.

There's little substance here, and little to talk about – it's another song about the California coast and its animals (in this case "making friends with the elephant seals"), but it's a gentle, pleasant grower.

Drivin'

Songwriters: Al Jardine, Stevie Heger and Scott Slaughter

Lead vocals: Al Jardine, Brian Wilson, Gerry Beckley and Dewey Burnell

Another one featuring America, along with two of Jardine's former band-mates (Brian Wilson on vocals and David Marks on guitar), this is a pleasant enough, inoffensive car song with a slow shuffle beat. Wilson adds some of his better vocals, with a decently humorous reading of some of the later lines, when the song starts talking about how the protagonist can no longer drive because of the price of petrol (and Jardine interjects "BP you're killin' me, man" – a last-minute alteration after BP's terrible handling of the Deepwater Horizon oil spill).

Unfortunately it's let down by the last bridge, sung by America (who take all the verses), where Jardine for some reason decides just to name-drop several America song titles, crowbarring them in and making a mess of the lyric in the process.

Honkin' Down the Highway

Songwriter: Brian Wilson

Lead vocals: Al Jardine with Brian Wilson

A remake of the song from *The Beach Boys Love You* – an album which Jardine has taken to enthusing about in recent years – this is fairly similar to the original, albeit with a slightly fuller production. Jardine takes the lead, as he did on the original, and the backing is provided by a stack-o'-Brians.

The only real deviation from the original comes toward the end of the track, where a voice (distorted as if through a speaker and backed with a police siren) tells the driver to slow down ("I clocked you at a hundred and forty"). There's then a short sax solo, a repeat of the lyric from "takin' one little inch" onwards, and the track ends on a mass, choral "way with girls" – a great ending, acknowledging both the ridiculousness and the beauty of that little section of melody, always the song's highlight.

It doesn't quite beat the original, but this is always a fun song to hear, and one which unlike some of the other remakes has not been overexposed.

And I Always Will

Songwriter: Al Jardine

A song that dated back to at least 1985, when it was apparently recorded during the sessions for *The Beach Boys*, this was based on a piece by Chopin (I'm not familiar enough with Chopin's work to identify it, and Jardine himself hasn't been able to remember which piece in interviews[8]). It's a bit schlocky, the kind of thing that could have been recorded by the Carpenters, and the arrangement is a little overblown (Jardine is backed by a full orchestra here), but the vocals are strong enough that this ballad just – *just* – sits on the right side of the line separating sincerity from sentimentality, and makes a fitting conclusion to the album.

If *A Postcard From California* had been released as a Beach Boys album, it would have been their best in thirty-one years. Some of the individual tracks are weaker than others, but throughout there's a warm, organic feeling to the recording and production (quite astonishing given the patchwork way in which some of the tracks were recorded). It's not as good an album as some of Brian's solo records, but it's the only Beach Boys solo album other than *Pacific Ocean Blue* that I could see recommending to a non-fan without several caveats. It's not a great record, but it's a good, solid one, and much better than one would have expected from Jardine.

---

[8]According to reader Steven Feldman, it's Etude Opus 10 No. 3 in the key of E Major, also known as "Tristesse".

Bonus Tracks

California Dreamin'

Songwriters: John Phillips and Michelle Phillips

Lead vocals: Al Jardine, Glen Campbell and David Crosby

A very stripped-down version of The Mamas & The Papas' classic hit, which had also been recorded by the Beach Boys in the 80s. Here Jardine and Glen Campbell trade off verses as Jardine had with Carl Wilson on the Beach Boys' version, with Crosby adding backing vocals in the third verse. The instrumental backing consists only of acoustic guitar, organ, hand percussion and bongos (played by John Stamos), leaving a lot of empty space for the vocalists to shine. Of all the bonus tracks, this is the only one that truly deserved to be on the album, and it's quite lovely.

Waves of Love

Songwriters: Al Jardine and Larry Dvoskin

Lead vocals: Al Jardine and Carl Wilson

This, on the other hand, is a mess. A song Jardine had been working on for decades, it's a sloppy, unformed, rewrite of "Help Me Rhonda", with some chord changes that just don't work, and with lyrics that veer from the banal to the new age.

But the worst thing is the inclusion of the recording of Carl Wilson singing the choruses. Apparently taken from a recording of a soundcheck in 1989 when the Beach Boys ran through the song (though he sounds double-tracked), it's a sloppy run-through recording of a harmony part that's been promoted to a lead vocal section on a finished recording. Wilson, frankly, sounds drunk, though he may just have been saving his voice and energy. I can understand the wish to use every fragment of Carl Wilson vocals that exists, given that he was one of the great singers of the rock era, but he was also a perfectionist who didn't allow several perfectly releasable vocals to be released because they didn't meet his standards. I can't imagine he'd have been happy with this being released.

Even had it been Wilson's best vocal ever, though, it wouldn't have salvaged the song. It's one that's clearly important to Jardine – he's released three radically different mixes of the song on the different versions of this album, and he wanted to work on it again in 2012 during the *That's Why God Made the Radio* sessions – but it's one of the worst things he's done.

Sloop John B (A Pirate's Tale)

Trad. Arr. Al Jardine

This is a re-recording with new lyrics, originally released on a CD to accompany a children's story-book Jardine had written. The song stretches out to almost double the original length, and outstays its welcome by quite a bit, to fit in Jardine's story of piratical adventure.

The Eternal Ballad

Songwriter: Al Jardine

Jardine's first Beach Boys Family & Friends gig had been at a private event for "Supreme Master Ching Hai", a new age religious guru and owner of a vegan fast-food franchising company, who Jardine admires. This song sets a poem Ching Hai had written in her twenties to a melody reminiscent of "The Night Was So Young", but not as good.

Brian Wilson Reimagines Gershwin

After completing *That Lucky Old Sun*, Brian Wilson went into one of his periodic creative slumps, discovering that he was at least temporarily unable to write new songs. Making an album of cover versions seemed the obvious option to keep his revived recording career going, and so when Disney asked him to record an album of songs from their films, he agreed – but on one condition.

Before recording the Disney songs album, he wanted to record an album of cover versions of Gershwin songs. Wilson had been inspired by Gershwin ever since, as a tiny child, he had first heard *Rhapsody in Blue* at his grandmother's house (from what he's said over the years, it was probably the Glenn Miller version, which is a leaden, lifeless thing, but which clearly contained enough of a hint of the piece's full majesty for a small child to see its beauty). *Rhapsody in Blue* had been one of the touchstone pieces of his career, one of those pieces like "Be My Baby" that one can hear echoing throughout his work, and now Wilson wanted to record an album of songs by its composer.

The Disney company agreed, and Wilson and his band went to work. Wilson and musical director Paul von Mertens selected the songs together – mostly going for the obvious choices, and selecting among them based on what was in Wilson's vocal range. Based on their discussions, von Mertens came up with rough arrangements which he taught the band, before Wilson went into the studio and reworked the arrangements.

Based on this description of the working method, it might seem that this is more *Paul von Mertens Reimagines Gershwin* than Brian Wilson, but listening to the record itself it becomes very apparent that this isn't the case. If nothing else, it's always obvious when Wilson doesn't care about the record he's making – his vocals when he's less than totally enthused can be painfully bad.

On this album, though, Wilson hits what may be the vocal peak of

161

his solo career. He's still a somewhat eccentric vocalist even here, and it's a massively courageous decision to try to take on songs which have been famously performed by Ella Fitzgerald, Sarah Vaughan, Nina Simone, Frank Sinatra, Louis Armstrong, and the rest of the greatest interpreters of American popular song. Any performance of "Summertime" or "Love is Here to Stay" will immediately invite comparison to those recordings, and the fact that sometimes the comparison isn't a laughable one is in itself a major success. Wilson apparently worked on the vocals here harder than on anything he'd done in the studio in years, and it shows.

Not everything here works, but more does than one might imagine, and while some of the arrangements might seem a little Wilson-by-numbers, there's a freshness to many of these interpretations that's a million miles away from when Wilson's contemporaries suddenly decide in their 70s that they're going to put on a smart suit and sing the Great American Songbook backed by an orchestra playing *ersatz* Gordon Jenkins or Nelson Riddle.

Interestingly, this marks the only time Brian Wilson ever got a number one album on the *Billboard* jazz charts.

Rhapsody in Blue/Intro

Songwriter: George Gershwin

The album opens with a mostly *a capella* performance of the main musical theme from *Rhapsody in Blue*. A stack of wordless Wilsons in harmony is joined by von Mertens' clarinet, until the last few bars when a full orchestration takes over. A sweet little introduction to the album – and fragments of the piece will be heard throughout the album, as orchestral linking tracks.

The Like In I Love You

Songwriters: George Gershwin, Brian Wilson, Scott Bennett

And unfortunately the first proper song on the album is one of the worst things on it. When the album was first mooted, the Gershwin estate gave Wilson access to some compositional fragments, unreleased songs, and so on, with the offer that he could turn some into finished tracks. The first and last songs on the album are the result of that, with Wilson and Scott Bennett completing Gershwin melodies.

But in this case, the melody they were completing was actually a full song – "Will You Remember Me?", a song which Gershwin and his lyricist brother Ira (whose own talents are often unacknowledged, but whose lyrics are often as subtle as his brother's music is beautiful) had written for the

1924 musical *Lady Be Good*, but which had been dropped from the finished show.[9]

Quite why it was dropped is a mystery – "Will You Remember Me?" is not in the very first rank of the Gershwins' songs, but it has a stately, sparse, beauty to it that makes it a minor classic that deserves revival.

What Wilson and Bennett do to it though, is less revival than putting it out of its misery. A new, meandering, verse melody is attached to Gershwin's refrain (which becomes the chorus and bridge of the new song), and Ira Gershwin's simple but elegant lyrics are replaced with utter drivel like "Gliding in a starless sky/'Til we found the inner light/Now we can duplicate the universe". The whole thing is turned into something that could have been a track off *Imagination*, albeit with more organic-sounding backing, and Wilson frequently has to go out of his vocal range to hit the high notes. A poor start.

Summertime

Songwriters: George Gershwin, DuBose Heyward, Dorothy Heyward, Ira Gershwin

This is much, *much* better. Most of the first half of the album is taken up by a medley of songs from Gershwin's opera *Porgy and Bess* (a racially problematic work in the way that only well-meaning white men writing about the lives of black people can be, which nonetheless contains some of the best music Gershwin ever wrote), and this arrangement of the opera's most famous excerpt gives it a slow, leisurely, languid, blues feel which suits the song perfectly.

Von Mertens' orchestrations here are much thicker and heavier than his usual sparse work, evoking a heat haze in the Deep South, and the cello part in the extended instrumental outro may be von Mertens' finest arrangement contribution to one of Wilson's records. Jeffrey Foskett and Taylor Mills add some great high wordless vocals, and the casual vibraphone answering phrases in the early parts of the song provide a crucial hint of improvisation for what might otherwise be perhaps too rigid an interpretation of the song.

---

[9] At the time of writing, Michael Feinstein's performance of this song can be heard at https://www.youtube.com/watch?v=K8FUHNcNFIo

I Loves You, Porgy

Songwriters: George Gershwin, DuBose Heyward, Dorothy Heyward, Ira Gershwin

The second of the *Porgy and Bess* excerpts is a fairly conventional treatment of one of the opera's better-known standards. There's nothing remarkable about the arrangement, and while Wilson's vocal is competent enough it's never going to compete with Nina Simone's interpretation.

What *is* remarkable about it, though, is that Wilson sang it at all. It's indicative of his increased level of self-confidence and comfort that someone who was embarrassed of his beautiful youthful voice because he thought it made him sound effeminate would now sing a song like this – a love song to a man, asking him to protect the singer from another man and not "let him handle me with his hot hands".

In that situation many singers choose to gender-swap the lyrics or otherwise alter them, but when von Mertens discussed that possibility, or the possibility of performing the song as an instrumental, with Wilson, Wilson just said "I'm gonna sing it."

I Got Plenty o' Nuttin'

Songwriters: George Gershwin, DuBose Heyward, Dorothy Heyward, Ira Gershwin

He didn't, however, sing this – the third of the *Porgy and Bess* numbers, and one of the great highlights of the album. A lovely, jaunty, instrumental take on the song, this is reminiscent of tracks like "Barnyard" from *Smile*, as von Mertens switches between harmonica and bass harmonica to play the melody, while Probyn Gregory's banjo drives the track forward. Guaranteed to raise a grin.

It Ain't Necessarily So

Songwriters: George Gershwin, DuBose Heyward, Dorothy Heyward, Ira Gershwin

And we're back to a more conventional arrangement for the final *Porgy & Bess* number. "It Ain't Necessarily So" is one of the most slyly cynical songs the Gershwin brothers ever wrote[10]. Sung in the opera by the character Sportin' Life, the lyrics wittily present his view that many of

---

[10]All the *Porgy & Bess* songs are credited to all the collaborators on the opera, but many featured just one lyricist; Ira Gershwin wrote the lyrics for this and "I Loves You Porgy", while Du Bose Heyward wrote the words for "Summertime".

the stories in the Old Testament are less than historically accurate, but what many in the opera's original audience will not have realised is that the melody he's singing is the same as the *aliyah* (the blessing sung in a synagogue before reading from the Torah).

Wilson's reading of the song, like most, cuts out the last verse (about Methuselah) and the tag, removes the Cab Calloway style call-and-response scat sections, and has a repeat of the "to get into heaven" section, giving it a more conventional song structure. The arrangement is a relatively standard one, as well – a gospel-tinged, organ-driven take, whose only unusual features are in the middle eight (some banjo arpeggios, and "bom" backing vocals that remind me a bit of "Cherish" by the Association).

Wilson's vocal is a little too earnest for the song – its dry east coast wit is not a great fit for Wilson's open sincerity – but it's still a very competent performance.

'S Wonderful

Songwriters: George Gershwin, Ira Gershwin

Wilson's take on this song, first performed by Adele Astaire in the 1927 musical *Funny Face*, is clearly inspired by João Gilberto's 1977 bossa nova version, although Wilson sings Gershwin's melody straight rather than in Gilberto's half-spoken style. While the song isn't one of the Gershwins' best, this is a decent enough performance.

They Can't Take That Away from Me

Songwriters: George Gershwin, Ira Gershwin

One of the few real missteps on the album, this classic is redone as a shuffle, with a backing almost identical to that of "Little Saint Nick", call-and-response backing vocals, and a sax solo that wouldn't be out of place on a Dion single. The uptempo poppiness clashes badly with the song's wistfulness.

It was probably necessary for Wilson to include at least a couple of songs in something approaching his early-60s pop style, but it really doesn't work well with the Gershwins' songs, and this is the most skippable track on the album.

Love Is Here to Stay

Songwriters: George Gershwin, Ira Gershwin

The very last song George Gershwin ever wrote, its lyrics added by Ira after his brother's death, this is given one of the most straightforward arrangements on the album but is none the worse for that. For the most part it's taken very conventionally, as a small-group lounge jazz arrangement, with drums played with brushes, vibraphone, and a string section playing a pad in the background. The only unusual element is Gregory's theremin solo (actually played on a tannerin, an instrument designed to sound like a theremin but be somewhat easier to play).

It works, though. It's a touching little song, and Wilson sings it well.

I've Got a Crush on You

Songwriters: George Gershwin, Ira Gershwin

A more radical restructuring this time, as Wilson turns this standard into a doo-wop ballad, all piano triplet chords and "wop wop wop wah" backing vocals. It works surprisingly well, thanks largely to the wide-eyed sincerity of Wilson's vocal.

I Got Rhythm

Songwriters: George Gershwin, Ira Gershwin

Another rearrangement into early-60s Beach Boys style, this one works much better than "They Can't Take That Away From Me", with its clanking piano, honking sax, surf guitar, and Jeffrey Foskett's wailing falsetto giving this a real feel of 1964 (though the song it sounds most like is from much later – this is very like "Desert Drive") and the simple uptempo joy of the song means that it's a perfect candidate for this kind of treatment.

We could possibly have done without the tag, in which Foskett sings "I've got, I've got rhythm" to the tune of the old Beach Boys album track "Farmer's Daughter", but otherwise this is a nice bit of fun.

Someone to Watch Over Me

Songwriters: George Gershwin, Ira Gershwin

The penultimate song proper on the album, this is also far and away the best thing on it. The song itself is one of the Gershwins' very best, a lovely, vulnerable song. Its themes of longing and insecurity, and the childlike way in which they are expressed, are perfect matches for Wilson's own songwriting – it's the only song on here that one could imagine Wilson himself having written.

Arranged here as a simple, harpsichord-driven ballad with ideas reminiscent of both "Wonderful" and "Caroline, No", this rises head and shoulders above the rest of the album, and Wilson's touchingly sincere vocal performance is as good as anything he's managed in his solo career.

Nothing But Love

Songwriters: George Gershwin, Brian Wilson, Scott Bennett

The second of the reworked Gershwin fragments, this is based on a song from 1929, "Say My Say", which as far as I know has never been heard by the public.

It's a better song than "The Like in I Love You", though it doesn't sound very Gershwin to my ears (apart from some of the chord changes around the line "I'll tell you what's timeless/Nothing but love"). In fact, it sounds like nothing so much as some of the uptempo tracks from *That Lucky Old Sun* – it has some of the same chugging rock feel as, say, "Morning Beat".

According to von Mertens (in a 2015 interview with David Beard), the basic rhythm track was recorded before the melody and lyrics were written, and Wilson improvised a wordless melody line over the track, to which Bennett later added the lyrics.

It's not a great song, by any means, and has none of the best of either Wilson or Gershwin in it, but it's listenable enough.

Rhapsody in Blue (Reprise)

Songwriter: George Gershwin

And the album ends with another stack-o'-Brians, singing a fragment of *Rhapsody in Blue* over strings.

bonus track

Let's Call The Whole Thing Off

Songwriters: George Gershwin, Ira Gershwin

An iTunes-only bonus track, this duet between Wilson and backing vocalist Taylor Mills was left off the album proper for good reason. Neither Wilson nor Mills sound remotely interested in their performance, and none of the care which is evident on the rest of the album is here. The song itself is a classic, of course, but this performance won't ever take the place of Ella Fitzgerald and Louis Armstrong's version in anyone's heart.

Brian Wilson in the Key of Disney

The second of Brian Wilson's two-album deal with Disney Records is the one that Disney themselves were more interested in – an album of songs from Disney cartoons. Unfortunately, it seems like the album was less interesting to Wilson himself.

The making of the album was by all accounts an enjoyable experience for everyone, including Wilson, but where his vocals on the Gershwin album were as good as he's managed in his entire solo career, here a little of the sloshing and slurring returns. This is still an album where he's making a real effort as a vocalist – even the worst vocal here is better than much of the best of *Gettin' in Over My Head*, for example – but his level of engagement with the material seems to vary somewhat.

This may be because the album itself is split between two very different styles of musical material. With one exception, the songs come from either films made in Walt Disney's lifetime or from the "Disney Renaissance" of 1989-99, with nothing from the poorly-regarded twenty-year period between *The Jungle Book* and *The Little Mermaid*, or from after the mid-90s. (The one exception is "We Belong Together" from *Toy Story 3*, which was the most recent Disney/Pixar film at the time the album was recorded).

The material from 1967 and earlier is music from Wilson's childhood and early adulthood, and comes from a pre-rock-and-roll tradition which has strongly influenced Wilson in much the same way as the Gershwin material had. By contrast, the material from the 90s is largely written by near-contemporaries like Randy Newman and Elton John, whose songwriting is redolent of the 1970s sound they helped define. Wilson is a fan of both those men, but he is not the most comfortable interpreter of that idiom, and it shows.

The album works best when Wilson is singing the simple songs of his childhood, but is ultimately a minor work in Wilson's discography, and it

169

was released with almost no publicity. By the time it came out, it had already been overshadowed by two new developments – a five-CD box set of *The Smile Sessions* was to be released, and the Beach Boys were reuniting for their fiftieth anniversary, for a new album and tour...

You've Got a Friend in Me

Songwriter: Randy Newman

The album opens with one of the weaker tracks, unfortunately. Brian Wilson and Randy Newman are both great admirers of each other, and as two of the great Californian songwriters of their generation it might seem that the pairing would be a natural one.

Unfortunately, the strengths of their art are in almost total opposition to each other. Newman is, fundamentally, an ironist – someone whose entire *oeuvre* should be listened to in inverted commas, and which requires a knowing interpreter if it's to have any effect at all. Wilson, on the other hand, is almost the embodiment of sincerity. His art is all about direct, unmediated, emotional connection.

The result of Wilson singing a Newman song, then, is to remove all the nuance and character that defined it, and this isn't helped by him rearranging Newman's jovial shuffle into a chugging rock beat with a similar feel to "Morning Beat". The middle eight, in particular, is horribly affected by this – where Newman's lazy, laid-back, vocal makes the extra syllables of lines like "some other folks may be a little bit smarter than I am" seem like casual thoughts, Wilson here gabbles to try to get them into a tighter space, and the result sounds more like pressured speech than a friendly chat.

The Bare Necessities

Songwriter: Terry Gilkyson

This, on the other hand, is an absolute joy. The original song is a trifle, but a catchy one (and incidentally the first professional arranging work of Wilson's old songwriting partner Van Dyke Parks), and Wilson's take has a similar joy to it. Starting out as a marimba duet, with Probyn Gregory's banjo coming in for the first verse before the whole band join in, this has a wonderful sense of dynamics. The song wanders through different genres of Americana, from the *Smile*-esque intro and breakdown (where the marimbas are joined just by "bom bom" vocals), through almost country-flavoured early verses, all banjo and acoustic guitar, to a Dixieland rave-up at the end, with Paul von Mertens adding some lovely Sidney Bechet-esque clarinet.

Baby Mine

Songwriters: Frank Churchill, Ned Washington

Another song from an early Disney film, and another very good track. This lullaby from *Dumbo* is taken absolutely straight, and arranged in a similar fashion to some of Wilson's mid-sixties ballads (there's a clear family resemblance to "Kiss Me Baby"). I could have done without the answering saxophone phrases on the last verse, but otherwise this is a very restrained, stately arrangement of a pretty, gentle song.

Wilson's vocals here are the best on the album, and some of his best of his solo career. He's hitting notes here that he'd normally strain at, and doing it with a strong, clear voice and without losing the emotional thread of the song.

As with all the tracks on this album, what one thinks of this will depend heavily on one's opinion of the original song. But this is as nice an interpretation as one could hope for.

Kiss the Girl

Songwriters: Alan Menken, Howard Ashman

Or "sexually assault the girl"...

This song from *The Little Mermaid* was never one of Disney's finest moments. I've never seen the film and am reliably informed that in the context of the film the song isn't particularly creepy, but out of that context, the message of this song's lyric seems to be "just go up to the girl you're attracted to, who isn't talking to you, and kiss her without asking. She *might* like it."

(Again, I'm talking here about the song *as a song*, not as part of a larger narrative. This is a problem with excerpting songs from musicals, but that is what this album does, and how it asks to be read.)

It's such a shame, too bad – because the tune itself is insanely catchy, and Wilson's reinterpretation of it improves significantly (at least to my ears) on the calypso-tinged original. After an incongruous burst of soulful saxophone and Hammond, and a couple of descending scales as a guitar intro, the song becomes something halfway between Phil Spector's more Latin-flavoured early singles and Wilson's own early Beach Boys tracks, "Don't Worry Baby" guitar going up against "Spanish Harlem" castanets.

Wilson's vocal here sounds better than on any of the other late-period songs on this album, and the whole track is a lot of fun.

Speaking of the vocals, I'd *love* to be able to access the multi-tracks of both this and "Baby Mine" and see exactly what was done with Wilson's vocals. Both recordings have very strong, natural-sounding vocals, which if you listen closely seem put together from multiple takes and either artificially thickened (there's quite a bit of processing done on the lead vocals here, but done with a very light touch) or *very* closely multi-tracked.

That isn't a criticism at all in case it reads that way – it's exactly what every professional vocalist does in the studio, and it's very, very well done. But what's interesting to me is that there are a couple of tiny points – odd syllables like "the" in the "kiss the girl"s at the end of each chorus – which sound a little like Foskett singing. I don't think it *is* him, but I'm wondering if there's a tiny bit of him doubling Wilson here and there, mixed very low compared to Wilson's main vocal. Or possibly Foskett did a guide vocal (as he occasionally did with Wilson in the studio) and Wilson copied a little of his phrasing. Or possibly my ears are playing tricks on me. But I'd love to know for sure.

Whatever it is I'm hearing, though, if you can get past the lyrics there's a lot to love in this track.

Colors of the Wind

Songwriters: Alan Menken, Stephen Schwartz

And we now enter the sluggish middle of the album.

"Colors of the Wind" is a song from *Pocahontas,* and as the aphorism goes, it contains much that is good and original, but what is good is not original and what is original is not good.

Musically, it's clearly and blatantly ripped off from the Cascades' "Rhythm of the Rain" – the verse melodies of both songs are near identical for three of the four lines, and close for the fourth, and both titles have the same unusual pattern "[sensory impression] of the [meteorological phenomenon]". The middle eights are different, but otherwise the main difference between the songs is that "Colors of the Wind" is taken at a much slower pace, as befits its ponderous newage lyrics about oneness with the Earth and its animals.

As you may have guessed, I am not a fan of this song, and Wilson's arrangement unfortunately does little to improve my opinion of it – with its flute tootling evoking every romantic cliche about Native Americans, this could be a particularly dull 1990s Sting album track.

Can You Feel the Love Tonight

Songwriters: Elton John, Tim Rice

At least this, unlike the original from *The Lion King*, doesn't continue the Hollywood pseudo-ethnicity – Wilson is covering the version of the song released as a single by its composer, rather than the version used in the cartoon's narrative, and the arrangement is fairly closely modelled on that one.

The backing vocal arrangement is nice, but the song itself is simply not a very good one. In particular the syllabics on lines like "When the heart of this star-crossed voyager beats in time with yours" work against the melody in a way that makes it almost impossible to sing (Elton John got away with it by eliding a syllable, and singing "voy'ger"). Rice's meaningless lyrics and John's tuneless tune could never be salvaged.

We Belong Together

Songwriter: Randy Newman

This one might actually be an improvement on Newman's original in many ways. While the cover version of "You've Got a Friend in Me" that opened the album replaces Newman's swing with a more rigid rock beat, this one replaces Newman's rather clumping arrangement with a twist beat, making the song a lot more fun. And while Wilson doesn't sell humorous lines like "and I cheer up to where I'm less depressed" as well as Newman, and his vocal style doesn't suit the lyrical asides like "least I hope you do", his reading of the line "I just can't take it when we're apart", speak-singing it in a strained voice, is one of the funniest examples of Wilson's own deadpan humour on record, and a much better take on that line than Newman's.

It's not one of Newman's best songs, and as a result no recording of it is going to be wonderful, but it's not a bad take on the song at all.

I Just Can't Wait to Be King

Songwriters: Elton John, Tim Rice

Another cover version of a song from *The Lion King* which uses the lyrics from the Elton John solo version rather than the duet used in the cartoon. The arrangement here uses elements from both versions, combining the swamp rock feel of John's version with the pseudo-African rhythms of the Michael Jackson pastiche that is the film version, giving a Bo Diddley feel to the verses (though there's a jolting feel when one goes into the middle eight, which has a very different rhythm).

One's feelings about this will very much depend on whether one thinks Tim Rice is as clever as he evidently believes himself to be, as that will determine whether the juxtaposition of contrived punning lines like "it's easy to be royal if you're mighty leonine/It isn't just my right, even my left will be divine" with the rather less erudite "My reign will be a super awesome thing" seems clever or annoying to you.

Stay Awake

Songwriters: Richard M. Sherman, Robert B. Sherman

This is actually the second time Brian Wilson recorded a song by the Sherman brothers (the writers of much of the music for Disney's films in the 60s). The first was in 1965, when the Beach Boys had backed Annette Funicello on "The Monkey's Uncle", a song about being in love with a primate which includes lines such as "what a nutty family tree/a bride, a groom, a chimpanzee".

Thankfully, "Stay Awake", their lullaby from *Mary Poppins,* is slightly more memorable, and for better reasons. A clever little song, sung by Poppins in the film as she sends the children to sleep while pretending to urge them to stay awake, it has one of their prettiest melodies and Wilson rises to it in the same way as he did to the similar "Baby Mine", or to "Someone to Watch Over Me" on the Gershwin album. Backed mostly by harpsichord and celeste, Wilson gives a gentle vocal performance here that fits the song perfectly. It almost makes one wish for a Wilson album of lullabies.

Heigh-Ho/Whistle While You Work/Yo Ho (A Pirate's Life for Me)

Songwriters: Frank Churchill, Larry Morey, George Bruns, Xavier Atencio

This is great fun – a largely instrumental (apart from a couple of vocal choruses) medley of "Heigh Ho" and "Whistle While You Work", with a few interspersed interjections of "yo ho yo ho a pirate's life for me". There's all sorts going on here – bicycle bells, glockenspiel, what sounds like a sampled bicycle horn playing the melody, bass harmonica, ukulele, musical saw...this is exactly the kind of imaginative reinvention the album could have done with more of. Gloriously fun.

When You Wish Upon a Star

Songwriters: Leigh Harline, Ned Washington

And the closing track to the album is a song that meant a great deal to Wilson. "Surfer Girl", the song he often refers to as the first he ever wrote, was closely modelled on this song from *Pinocchio*, and Wilson takes the song reverently here. As with all the tracks on this album, your opinion of it will vary depending on your opinion of the original, but here Wilson is singing as well as he does on the entire record.

bonus tracks

Two bonus tracks were included on early copies of the album sold through Amazon, "A Dream is a Wish Your Heart Makes" only on the CD, and "Peace on Earth" only on the download version.

A Dream is a Wish Your Heart Makes

Songwriters: Mack David, Al Hoffman, Jerry Livingston

Unlike with some of the bonus tracks around this period, it's hard to see why this pleasant cover version of the ballad from *Cinderella* was left off the album proper. The arrangement is modelled after "Sail On Sailor", but the more complex melody and changes of the older song do interesting things when poured into that 12/8 soul ballad mould, and the combination sounds in retrospect very much like a trial run for the title track of the next album we'll be dealing with.

Peace on Earth

Songwriters: Peggy Lee, Sonny Burke

A simple, stripped-down, version of the Christmas song from *Lady and the Tramp*, this has something of the sparse splendour of Wilson's version of "Joy to the World". The vocal is much rawer than the rest of the vocals on the album, but the vocal arrangement is gorgeous and the simple instrumental backing (acoustic guitar, with a very faint organ pad, bass, hand percussion, and a few single reverbed electric guitar notes) is perfect for the song. Had this and "A Dream is a Wish Your Heart Makes" been included on the main body of the album, with maybe "Colors of the Wind" and "Can You Feel the Love Tonight" relegated to bonus tracks, I suspect the album would have received a rather warmer welcome at the time.

The Smile Sessions

In 2011, the Beach Boys finally released the most expansive – and most necessary – archival project they ever put out. *The Smile Sessions* was compiled by Alan Boyd and Mark Linnet, and came in two forms. There was a two-CD set aimed at people who wanted to finally hear what *Smile* was, and a much larger set. That larger set contained five CDs, two vinyl albums, two vinyl singles, and two books, and documented the sessions for the band's unreleased album in, if not utterly exhaustive detail, certainly enough to satisfy almost everyone.

The centrepiece of both versions was a reconstructed *Smile* album, mixed in mono. This followed the tracklisting of *Brian Wilson Presents Smile* almost exactly, except that it placed "I'm In Great Shape" in the middle of the first movement with the other pieces of "Heroes and Villains", rather than having it open up the third movement, and the version of "Good Vibrations" was the single version with Mike Love's lyrics (along with an extra section edited in – the "hum de ah" vocal section that had featured on several alternate mixes of the song.

Many of the songs had never had lead vocals recorded before the sessions had completed, and some remained instrumental or with backing vocals only, even in this version, but Linett managed to digitally include vocal parts from other sources to fill out many uncompleted or partially-completed tracks with contemporary or near-contemporary recordings. Other than "Cabinessence", which was just a mono mix of the version released on *20/20* with Carl's 1968 vocal on, many of these required great ingenuity in time-stretching and digitally extracting vocal parts, but Linnet managed to use Brian's piano demos of "I'm In Great Shape" and "Barnyard" to provide vocals for those songs, he took the vocal part from "Fall Breaks and Back to Winter" for "Mrs. O'Leary's Cow". A version of the water chant from a 1967 version of "Cool Cool Water" was used for "In Blue Hawaii", and the vocal round at the end of the *Smiley Smile* version of "Wind Chimes" was edited onto the transition between "Holidays" ("On A Holiday") and that song. And the "child" vocals from "Child is Father of the Man" were also used on the relevant parts of "Look (Song for Children)".

Most impressively, the vocal from Brian's 1967 piano version of "Surf's Up" was placed over the instrumental track for that song (while it still used Carl's 1971 "Bygone, bygone" backing vocals, and the group vocals on the tag from the 1971 version).

The end result was something that was as close as it's humanly possible to come to a reconstruction of *Smile* using contemporary materials only, while still following the template used in Wilson's live performances of the album.

But the box set contained numerous other wonders too. There was a 1967 solo piano version of "Surf's Up", different from the one we'd previously heard – more mournful and gentler. There were entire CDs devoted to different sections of "Heroes and Villains" and "Good Vibrations", there was a piano demo of "Vega-Tables" with very different lyrics, and there were innumerable false starts, instrumental tracks, and abandoned ideas. Short of being in the studio during the recording of *Smile*, it's impossible to get a better understanding of what Brian Wilson was doing and what his working methods were at the height of his powers.

I still, personally, prefer Brian's 2004 completed version of the album, but this is a monumental achievement that richly deserved the Grammy it won for Brian and its compilers for Best Historical Album.

As with all these archival releases, I'm only going to look here at the actual songs that hadn't been released elsewhere, but this is really a set that deserves a book of its own.

He Gives Speeches (Bonus Track)

Songwriter: Brian Wilson and Van Dyke Parks

Lead vocals: Brian Wilson

An interesting failure, it's easy to see why this wasn't included in the final album tracklisting – it's the song that would eventually become the first part of "She's Going Bald" from *Smiley Smile*, but with very different, allusive, lyrics by Parks – "He gives speeches but they put him back in bed where he wrote his satire..."

It's overlong and repetitive, and "She's Going Bald" is by far the better use of the musical material, but this is still interesting to have.

Tones/Tune X

Songwriter: Carl Wilson

Lead vocals: None

Other than a couple of generic surf instrumentals, this seems to have been Carl's earliest attempt at songwriting or production. An instrumental, mostly performed by a string section, this is very much in the style of his brother's work, and has much of the feel of "God Only Knows" to it, along with some musical motifs that sound inspired by some of the *Smile* material. The bridge is nice, as is the Hawaiian style guitar that comes in towards the end, but this seems to have been more of a sketch than anything else – an attempt to see what Carl could do in the studio – and there's not much of a song there.

I Don't Know

Songwriter: Dennis Wilson

Lead vocals: None

A piece by Dennis, which sounds *very* like Carl's *Tones/Tune X*, especially in its descending "Twinkle Twinkle Little Star" bassline, but with an Americana feel, with bass harmonica and banjo rather than Carl's strings. There's very little of interest here, except that it shows that both the younger Wilson brothers were trying to stretch their wings as producers even before Brian started to pull back from the band.

Three Blind Mice

Songwriter: Brian Wilson

Lead vocals: None

A song that doesn't really belong on this set, except that it had never had legitimate release earlier and it had appeared on numerous *Smile* bootlegs, this actually dates from October 1965, and seems to be Brian working out some ideas that he reused on "The Little Girl I Once Knew" a couple of days after this recording.

Teeter Totter Love

Songwriter: Brian Wilson

Lead vocals: Jasper Dailey

No-one seems quite sure what Brian was trying with this, except that it was presumably a joke. Recorded during the *Smile* sessions, with photographer Jasper Dailey on what can charitably be called vocals, it's a short percussion-and-Swanee-whistle driven song, with girl-group "yeah yeah" backing vocals. Dailey screech-sings the song, in the manner of Wild Man Fischer or The GTOs, and this is of no value except as a piece of outsider music.

Psychodelic Sounds: Underwater Chant

Songwriter: Brian Wilson

Lead vocals: Group

A spoken-word chanted round, a little like the Monkees' "Zilch", this has the different band members rhythmically repeating words like "underwater", "dolphin", and "swim fish fish". It's quite an effective little piece, for what it is.

That's Why God Made the Radio

February 5, 2011, marked the first time that there was any public confirmation that something interesting was happening with the Beach Boys. That was the date of "A Concert for America: A Tribute to Ronald Reagan," a benefit concert to mark what would have been the late President's centennial. The Beach Boys appeared at that show, and performed six songs. But this wasn't just the touring Beach Boys (at that time Mike Love and Bruce Johnston, along with Love's son Christian, Scott Totten, Tim Bonhomme, Randell Kirsch and John Cowsill, plus on that show John Stamos) – Al Jardine was also on stage with them, for the first time since 1998.

Jardine had not permanently rejoined the Beach Boys – he was absent from the band's shows for the rest of the year – but the appearance seemed to confirm that there had been a thawing in relations between the various Beach Boys camps, and that the rumours on fan message boards that something special might happen for the band's fiftieth anniversary (which would be in September 2011) might be true.

And as it turned out, those rumours *were* true. Quite how it happened is still the subject of some dispute, but it appears that Love and Brian Wilson had got together at some point in 2010 to discuss a possible new album. While the original discussions were about the idea of doing an album of rock and roll covers, at some point this changed into an album of new material, working with Joe Thomas.

Thomas, who had produced the band's last album in 1996, was by this point a successful producer of TV concert specials. He also had, from his sessions with Wilson in 1997 and 98, a stock of demos and half-finished recordings, some of which Wilson had intended for a possible future Beach Boys project. Wilson had already approached him about the possibility of doing something with those demos, and soon a plan of action was in place.

The surviving members of the band were going to get back together, and do a fifty-date tour in 2012 to mark their fiftieth anniversary. A new company was formed, "Fifty Big Ones", which was co-owned equally by Wilson, Love, and Thomas, and which got a license for the Beach Boys name from BRI. That company was to promote the shows, and produce TV specials including concert footage.

There was also going to be a new album, with the "produced by Brian Wilson" credit for the first time since 1977, although Thomas was to get a "recorded by" credit which amounted to him actually co-producing the album (Love got an "executive producer" credit). A record deal was made with Capitol on the basis of several Wilson/Thomas demos with vocals by Wilson and Foskett, and the album was to come out in spring 2012, to coincide with the tour.

But first, they had to prove they could get together in the recording studio and work together at all. In May 2011, Love, Wilson, Johnston, and Jardine went into Capitol's recording studio to cut a quick remake of their 1968 hit "Do It Again". Along with them in the studio was a backing band consisting of Totten and Cowsill from the touring Beach Boys, and from Brian Wilson's band Nick Walusko, Brett Simons, Probyn Gregory, Scott Bennett, Jeffrey Foskett, and Paul von Mertens, along with Gary Griffin (a keyboard player who had toured with both bands at different times).

That session went successfully enough that the band actually worked on a second track – a piano-and-wordless-vocals piece called "Think About the Days" – and the album was on.

The album, titled *That's Why God Made the Radio,* was recorded using a mixture of members of Wilson's backing band (and Cowsill on drums on some songs) and the session musicians Thomas preferred to work with. At some point David Marks was included in the reunion (reportedly at Wilson's request), and he added guitar to a handful of tracks, but otherwise the Beach Boys provided only vocals for the album.

And those vocals were, with some exceptions, dictated to them in advance. Wilson had Foskett record elaborate vocal demos, singing every part, and then had Love, Jardine, and Johnston drop in their parts, singing what Foskett had already recorded. The result is a vocal sound unlike that on previous Beach Boys albums, and sounding far more like the sound on Wilson's solo albums, with Wilson taking most lead vocals and Foskett prominent in the vocal stack.

The vocal sound is interesting in other ways, as well. A combination of the band members' ageing voices and the greater possibilities opened up by modern technology means that the vocal tracks are created very differently from the band's earlier recordings. The most notable way in which processing was used was the addition of autotune to the vocals – something which renders some tracks almost unlistenable, and made them sound dated as soon as they came out – but other, more subtle, processing is used.

In particular, the vocals are far more multitracked than in previous recordings, giving a much fuller sound. But the use of multitracking also means that occasionally the "lead vocalist" becomes a tricky question. Where earlier Beach Boys tracks had usually had each member singing a single vocal line each (even if double- or triple-tracked), here the inter-twining lines are often sung by two or more different singers, and each singer might also be singing two or three different lines.

This is far from a bad thing – there are inventive things done with the vocal arrangements here that Wilson had never done before, and in particular a trick he uses a couple of times here, of having a heavily-processed Love doubled an octave above by Foskett, is quite staggeringly effective.

Almost all the songs recorded were Wilson/Thomas co-writes. Their working methods varied from song to song, but both men have said in interviews that typically Thomas would provide basic chord structures, over which Wilson would come up with new melodies, and the two would then collaborate on the lyrics. However, this would vary enormously depending on the song, and I'll note in the entries for each song how it was written, if that's been made public.

There were reports of conflicts during the recording, too – Jardine wanted the band to work on another version of "Waves of Love", which Wilson refused to do, and Love came into conflict with Thomas and members of Wilson's management team over his desire to write new material alone with Wilson (although Love as "executive producer" had more influence than any of his bandmates, and did contribute lyrics to three Wilson/Thomas tracks, as well as writing the only non-Wilson/Thomas song on the album). More material was also recorded than could be used on the album – including a remake of Johnston's "She Believes in Love Again", originally from *The Beach Boys* – and the final song selection was apparently made by Capitol.

The result definitely has flaws – the sound of the final recording has, to many fans' ears (including mine), too much of Thomas and not enough Wilson in it. Many production elements which had appeared on *Imagination* but disappeared in Wilson's subsequent work (overuse of woodwinds, tinkling percussion, a lot of cymbal work, nylon string guitar) made a comeback here, and often not to the album's benefit. Also, the lyrics are rarely coherent at all (a common fault in all Wilson/Thomas collaborations) – the songs give the impression, usually through strong choruses, of having themes or subjects, but on closer analysis the words have mostly been chosen as mouth noises rather than having a meaning. Certain words turn up over and over – "time", "wine", "strange" – but seem to be signifiers detached from the things they signify.

But those flaws are, for the most part, minor ones. This is not a great album – it's nowhere near as good as *That Lucky Old Sun* in terms of Wilson's late-period work and production style, and it sags in the middle – but it's a good album. It's the first album with the Beach Boys' name on it to work as a coherent whole since at least 1979's *LA (Light Album)*, and it's a far better piece of work than most fans would have expected of the Beach Boys in 2012.

The reunion ended somewhat acrimoniously (as we'll discuss in later essays) and this is likely to be the last ever Beach Boys album. It's not a perfect way for the band to go out, but it's a *lot* better as a swan song than *Stars & Stripes vol 1* or *Summer in Paradise*.

line-up

Brian Wilson, Al Jardine, Mike Love, Bruce Johnston, David Marks
    All songs written by Brian Wilson and Joe Thomas except where noted

Think About the Days

Lead vocals: Group/Al Jardine

The opening song, a piano instrumental by Thomas to which Wilson added a wordless vocal part, and which opens with the group *a capella*, serves as an overture to the record. It's relatively pretty (if I'd been asked to listen to it without knowing the writer I'd have guessed it was written by Johnston on a good day), and at under ninety seconds it doesn't overstay its welcome.

But its main purpose is to show that this version of the band – vocally, Wilson, Jardine, Love, Johnston, and Foskett – could still sing. Other than a few French horn notes by Probyn Gregory at the end, the only instrument on the track is Joe Thomas' piano (Scott Bennett is credited as playing vibraphone on the track in the CD booklet, but several people involved in the album have said that the credits were wrong on some tracks, and there's no audible vibraphone).

The harmonies are gorgeous, and both Jardine (singing the "doo doo" vocals) and Johnston (singing the ultra-high falsetto) are in particularly excellent voice here.

That's Why God Made the Radio

Songwriters: Brian Wilson, Joe Thomas, Larry Millas, Jim Peterik

Lead vocals: Brian Wilson and Jeffrey Foskett

The album's title track (and first single) dates from 1998, and had been discussed by Jim Peterik for years before as one of his great lost songs. Peterik, best known for his time in Survivor, had referred to it as a song written by himself and Larry Millas (his bandmate in one-hit-wonder band The Ides of March), but in an interview around the time of the album's release, Joe Thomas explained that the title and basic chord structure were both the work of Brian Wilson.

And that chord structure is one of the more interesting things about the song, as the opening line basically reuses tricks from both "Warmth of the Sun" and "Your Summer Dream". The song starts out as a doo-wop progression, but after the second (vi7) chord, it changes up a tone to vii7 – that change up a tone between minor sevenths is the same change (though in a different context) as the change on "all the while" in "Your Summer Dream".

The song then takes that vii7 as being the ii7 of VI, and it continues the end of the doo-wop sequence, followed by the beginning again, in the new VI key, before dropping back down and finishing the original sequence, so the sequence goes "start of doo-wop sequence in C - end of doo-wop sequence in A - beginning of doo-wop sequence in A - end of doo-wop sequence in C" (I-vi7-vii7-III7-VI-iv#7-ii7-V7).

That's the first line of the song ("tuning in the latest star/from the dashboard of my car"), and the melody sung is very similar to that of "Your Summer Dream". The whole song proceeds this way, managing to reuse old elements in interesting ways. As well as old Beach Boys songs (there's also more than a little of "Keep an Eye on Summer" in here), the chorus melody is clearly "inspired" by John Barry, specifically the themes to "Midnight Cowboy" and "You Only Live Twice".

Vocally, the song is lovely. Brian (lightly doubled at points by Foskett and Jardine) does a great job on the verses, and the chorus harmony vocals give both Jardine and Johnston a chance to shine. And instrumentally, the track manages to do a reasonably tasteful updating of a 50s doo-wop style, with a $\frac{12}{8}$ organ-led backing track which bears some relation to "Soul Searchin'", with some great honking baritone sax (although this is let down by the middle eight, where for some reason there's a turn to terrible 80s AOR guitar sounds).

Lyrically, too, this is above-par for this album, with genuinely cute lines like "it's paradise when I/Lift up my antenna".

Yet... somehow, it's slightly less than the sum of its parts. It all feels a little too clean and manufactured, like it's been created by committee with no real inspiration. It's grown on me over the years, but there's still something a little lacking here.

Isn't It Time

Songwriters: Brian Wilson, Mike Love, Joe Thomas, Larry Millas, Jim Peterik

Lead vocals: Brian Wilson, Bruce Johnston, Al Jardine, Mike Love, and Jeffrey Foskett

This, on the other hand, is utterly wonderful, and genuinely the catchiest thing the Beach Boys had released since at least *The Beach Boys Love You* if not earlier. It's a very simple song which evolved in the studio from a ukulele-and-bass jam by Millas and Peterik, and for much of the track that's the only instrumental backing, other than some handclaps, with piano being added low in the mix for the choruses and middle eight, and something that sounds like a celeste on the middle eight.

(This is one of those occasions when I really wish that the credits on this album reflected reality. I don't hear any guitar on the track, yet David Marks is credited as playing guitar on it, but I couldn't *swear* that he's not on there somewhere – there's a possibility that the guitar is doubling the left hand of the piano, very faintly. On the other hand the credits don't mention Foskett, who is all over the track vocally, or the keyboards.)

It's very reminiscent of *The Beach Boys Love You* or *Smiley Smile* in the near-emptiness of the instrumental track and the way the song is carried almost entirely by the vocals, but it's also the most up-to-date sounding thing on the album, as there was a brief fad for the ukulele in hipsterish indie bands around that time. And while the track's ridiculously simple – for the most part it's just four chords – it's insanely catchy.

Every band member gets a chance to shine – Brian sings lead on the first verse while Love sings a gloriously dumb "doo-be-doo" bass part of his own invention (Love also wrote some or all of the lyrics), Love sings the second verse, and Jardine and Johnston split the chorus between themselves. The middle eight is the only slightly weak point, as Foskett strains to hit some of the high notes and doesn't sound quite as wonderful here as on the rest of the album.

A single version of this song was released on the compilations *50 Big Ones* and *Made in California*, with some additional instrumentation, a few lyrical changes, and with Foskett replaced by Love singing the melody in a lower range on the middle eight, but while Love does a better job on that section, overall the changes made were overegging the pudding, and the joyous version on the album is better.

This is one of three songs from the album (along with the title track and "Summer's Gone") which made it into the setlist during the fiftieth anniversary tour, and it remains an occasional part of Love and Johnston's touring Beach Boys' show.

Spring Vacation

Songwriters: Brian Wilson, Mike Love, Joe Thomas

Lead vocals: Mike Love, Bruce Johnston, and Brian Wilson

And after three songs ranging from good to great, we get the first real stinker. "Spring Vacation" is another song that originally dates from the *Imagination* sessions, where it was originally titled "Lay Down Burden". After Carl Wilson's death, that title was applied to another song, and this one was left.

For these sessions, Wilson asked Love to write new lyrics, and suggested some of the chorus lines, and Love came up with. . . adequate lyrics given the brief. Those lyrics received a certain amount of criticism from fans at first, until it was revealed that some of the lines referencing old Beach Boys hits were actually suggested by Wilson, not Love.

The real problem with the track isn't the lyrics, though – lines like "summer weather/we're back together" may be predictable, but they're fine for a song about how the band are back together and still going strong. The problem is, rather, that the music is, frankly, rubbish. Thomas has described it as being a gospel-style song, but it doesn't sound anything like gospel music except for the presence of a Hammond organ. Rather, it belongs to a particular subgenre of music I can only describe as "the kind of music you get on bad 90s American family sitcoms". I can't find a better descriptor for that genre than that, but this fits into it so well that I find it almost impossible to listen to the track without imagining an "executive producer: Linwood Boomer" credit coming up towards the end.

Along with that, this is one of those tracks where the autotune-as-effect has been applied so much to Love's vocal that he barely sounds human. Utterly without merit.

The Private Life of Bill and Sue

Lead vocals: Brian Wilson and Jeffrey Foskett

This, on the other hand, is a song which almost everyone except me thinks is awful, but which I think is a highlight of the album. A pseudo-calypso song (and one of the few where the nylon string guitar Thomas likes is stylistically appropriate to the song) about reality TV, this song was one of the newer songs written for the album. Wilson brought in the verse ("the private life of Bill and Sue/Can you dig what I'm telling you?") and Thomas added the chorus ("from California to Mexico..."), which he'd written separately but which meshes perfectly with Wilson's verse.

(Perhaps a little too perfectly – the one criticism I'd make of this song is that the verse and chorus are too similar both to each other and to "Mary's Boy Child").

It's by no means a complex song, but there's a huge amount of enthusiasm in the "um baddy addy yay" backing vocals in the chorus, and in Wilson and Foskett trading off chorus lines, while in the verses Wilson seems to be very patiently explaining his view of the world, and how bizarre he thinks it is that people are interested in the lives of reality TV stars.

Of all the songs on the album, this is the one that most provides me with what I look for in Beach Boys music, and I suspect it's not a coincidence that (if the credits are to be taken as accurate – we've already established that there are errors in them, but I think the basics are right) this is one of the relatively few tracks whose instrumental parts are played largely by members of Wilson's band rather than by session musicians. Where for much of the album the rhythm track and guitar parts are played by the kind of session players who'd played on *Imagination*, here the session players are confined to the piano and one of the acoustic guitars. Otherwise the band here is Wilson's then-current band, with the addition of Cowsill on drums and Marks on guitar.

It's fun, and light, and silly, and somehow hated by the vast majority of Beach Boys fandom, many of whom consider it literally the worst track the band ever made. Their loss.

Shelter

Lead vocals: Brian Wilson, Mike Love, and Jeffrey Foskett

One of the worse sequencing decisions in putting this album together was putting this track right after the last one. Both are very similar in tempo and rhythm, and in general sonic feel. (The credits suggest they were tracked at the same session – other than Joe Thomas on harpsichord the credited musicians on this track, both those from Wilson's band and the two session players, all appear on the previous track, although it's hard to be sure because no bass player or drummer is credited at all, though both are clearly audible. It may be that Nelson Bragg, credited for "percussion", played drums here.)

It's a shame, because it dilutes the impact of this, another real highlight of the album. The verses (sung by Wilson) are clearly modelled on early Phil Spector, especially his collaborations with Leiber and Stoller, and have a very similar semi-Latin feel to tracks like "Spanish Harlem", while the choruses (sung by Foskett, with Love doubling an octave down on the latter half) have a vaguely Roy Orbison or Gene Pitney feel.

While the lyrics are, like much of the album, utter gibberish to put it charitably, they still work very well with the music as both music and lyrics have a strange tension between sounding gently comforting and anxiously longing. This tension is, of course, implied in the title – "shelter" is obviously a good thing, but you still need to shelter *from* something.

(Joe Thomas has talked about how the song was inspired by Wilson referring to his home as his shelter, and this casual word choice seems to say a lot about Wilson's attitudes.)

Everything about the arrangement here – the chanted nearly-inaudible backing vocals in the last couple of choruses, the faint harpsichord, the trumpet and French horn parts played by Gregory, the "yayyay" interjection from Jardine – is perfect at setting a mood and creating a fine piece of Spectoresque pop.

Daybreak Over the Ocean

Songwriter: Mike Love

Lead vocals: Mike Love

This track is an odd one out in many ways. This is actually a recording from Love's unreleased mid-2000s solo album (variously titled *Unleash the Love* and *Mike Love Not War*), produced by Paul Fauerso, onto which the other Beach Boys have overdubbed a few extra backing vocals (the "bring back/wontcha bring back" sections). Most of the backing vocals, however, are actually supplied by Adrian Baker and Love's son Christian (he's the one singing "bring my baby" in a voice very like Carl Wilson).

The song itself dates back to the late 70s, and was originally recorded for another unreleased Love solo album, *First Love*. It's a nice enough song – a rewrite of "My Bonnie" – but the production here, with its digital percussion and synth layers, is not very pleasant. And while Love's vocal is decent enough, there's a truck-driver's key change up a semitone for the instrumental break, and on the chorus after that it sounds like a pitch-shifted copy of one of the other choruses has been used rather than him sing it in another key.

Not the worst thing on the album, but forgettable.

Beaches in Mind

Songwriters: Brian Wilson, Mike Love, Joe Thomas

Lead vocals: Mike Love

An exception to the general rule we've seen so far that songs with more Brian Wilson band members tend to be better, this is truly dire, and essentially "Spring Vacation part 2". This time the genre is that particular kind of lightweight AOR that was used to soundtrack 80s films with Michael J Fox in (I'm sorry for the imprecision in these descriptions – I can easily detail precisely which microgenre like freakbeat or psychobilly something falls into when it's in an area of my musical knowledge, but when it comes to stuff that was popular on US radio in the 80s and 90s, I'd only have a 50/50 chance at guessing whether something was by Huey Lewis or Foreigner).

"We'll find a place in the sun/where everyone can have fun", apparently. This would have fit perfectly on *Summer in Paradise*, and wouldn't have been the best thing on it.

Strange World

Lead vocals: Brian Wilson

The last four tracks on the album were conceived as part of a longer suite, though how completed that suite actually was is questionable – in some interviews, Joe Thomas talks about it as a complete work that just needed releasing, while in others both he and Wilson talk about it as a concept with nothing completed save what's on the album.

This first part is a rather bombastic track halfway between Phil Spector and Jim Steinman in feel, but aside from the excellent string arrangement by Paul von Mertens there's not much actually to it – it's harmonically simplistic and lyrically banal. It works largely because it's one of the best-*sounding* things on the album, but on repeated listens it palls rather quickly.

According to some sources, there was meant to be another song between this and the next track, which was cut.

From There to Back Again

Lead vocals: Al Jardine, Brian Wilson, and Mike Love

Easily the most complex song structure on the album, the second part of the suite is also one of the most musically interesting things here, and other than one fault it would be one of the best tracks on the album.

Unfortunately, that fault is a major one. Al Jardine gives a *stunning* vocal performance here, but it's processed to the point that at times he barely sounds human. Anyone who's seen Jardine performing live in recent years knows that the processing here is not to fix a flaw in his singing – he sounds like a man half his age, and I don't think it would be an exaggeration to say that he is currently the best living vocalist of his generation – so it must be a deliberate stylistic choice, but it's one that renders the track almost unlistenable to my ears.

Which is a shame, because almost everything else about the song is *exactly* my kind of thing. It gives up almost entirely on conventional song structure, and feels almost like a through-composed single piece. The only part of this "suite" that dates from 2012, this is far more sophisticated than the rest of it (fitting a pattern that, with the exception of "Beaches in Mind", the 2012 songs are much better than those started in the 1990s). Musically, it has a lot in common with songwriters like Burt Bacharach, Paul Williams, or Jimmy Webb, especially with the songs Williams wrote in the early 1970s.

There are, roughly, three different sections of the song. The first, with Jardine singing lead, is characterised by piano chords, flute, and reverbed guitar (similar to that on, say, the track "Pet Sounds"). There's very little repetition here but it *sort of* functions as a set of verses since the harmonic material (lots of Imaj9, IVmaj7 and ii9 chords) remains similar throughout – for a lot of it, it's the kind of interesting pattern you can get when you keep playing the same chord and just lifting up or putting down one finger.

This ends at around 1:46, when Brian's voice comes in with "if you just call..." (followed by the other Beach Boys singing "just fall...")

We then have an instrumental break based on the same harmonic material (with "aah" vocals) before another section, starting with Jardine and Wilson singing together ("through our compromise, paradise"), but Wilson soon takes over the lead on this section. This short section is backed mostly by another von Mertens string arrangement, and deviates a fair bit harmonically from the first section. This is in a minor key, and much more gloomy in feel.

Finally we get to the final section of the track, which is closer to the first section harmonically and instrumentally, but is much more upbeat, with Love singing wordless "ba ba ba" vocals and Jardine whistling.

Were it not for the processing on Jardine's voice, this would be a masterpiece. For those who can cope with that major flaw, it still is.

Pacific Coast Highway

Lead vocals: Brian Wilson

A very pretty fragment, dating from the late 90s, "Pacific Coast Highway" segues straight out of "From There to Back Again", and is so closely related to it that it's hard to think of it as a separate song, rather than a link between it and the final track. Starting with a block of "ooh" harmonies, we go into a short fragment of a song – about a minute of actual song in between forty seconds of "ooh" at the start and strings fading at the end – where Wilson sings "my life/I'm better off alone".

Summer's Gone

Songwriters: Brian Wilson, Jon Bon Jovi, Joe Thomas

Lead vocals: Brian Wilson

And the final track – the final track on any Beach Boys album – is another one that divides people. Specifically, everyone else loves it and I think it's a dirge. The end of the "suite", this was written in the 1990s and always intended as the last song on the Beach Boys' last album (although apparently Wilson later decided that maybe this wouldn't be the last album, before the band split up again).

A collaboration with Jon Bon Jovi, this thankfully has few of the New Jersey rocker's fingerprints on it. Unfortunately, it also doesn't have a chorus or a middle eight. The same thirty seconds or so of melody repeats over and over for the whole four minutes and forty-one seconds of the track, and while the first time it sounds quite pretty, if a bit plodding, by the end of the track it's become mind-numbingly tedious.

Melodically, it has a slight resemblance to parts of "Superstar" by Leon Russell, but slowed down and turned almost into a lullaby, while the production is clearly attempting to do something similar to "Caroline, No" as a weighty album closer.

The instrumental arrangement is interesting and the vocals are nice but fundamentally this is a fragment – a quarter of a song – stretched out to ten times its natural length.

Mike Love has taken a lot of criticism for a joke during the playback of this in the studio, when in front of a journalist he mimed blowing his own head off after the song (though few of those critics remember that immediately afterward he said "It's brilliant, beautiful"). But frankly, that's my reaction too. To an extent, the weight of the song as the last track on the last album has made it immune to criticism, and the fact that one line ("I'm thinking maybe I'll just stay") is inspired by Wilson's last conversation with his brother Carl gives the song a bit of borrowed emotional weight.

But fundamentally, and trying my best to like the song, it's simply not very interesting. It's a poor ending to what is a far better album than we could have expected.

bonus track

Do It Again (2012 version)

Songwriters: Brian Wilson and Mike Love

Lead vocals: Mike Love and Brian Wilson with Jeffrey Foskett

The first track recorded for the reunion, this sneaked out on a "ZinePak" – a magazine about the band with a free CD and postcards, distributed through WalMart – as the one new track on what was otherwise a standard greatest hits CD, before appearing as a bonus track on the Japanese version of the album.

The song (which later became the opening song every night during the reunion tour) was chosen because it was one that everyone involved knew, and no major changes were made to the arrangement. Love's voice is a little huskier, Brian Wilson sang the middle eight, and Foskett sang the falsetto Brian had originally sung, but other than that (and the fact that it comes to a hard close rather than fading) a casual listener would probably not notice the difference from the original, especially since the introduction is sampled from the 1968 recording.

Live: The 50th Anniversary Tour

To promote *That's Why God Made the Radio*, the Beach Boys set out on their first – and so far only – tour as a full band since Carl Wilson died. The band's line-up was the same as for that album – Mike, Brian, Al, Bruce, and David – and the backing band was mostly members of Wilson's band with a couple of important members from Love's touring Beach Boys.

The band featured Darian Sahanaja (keyboards, vocals, percussion), Probyn Gregory (guitar, French horn, tannerin, trumpet, vocals), Scott Bennett (keyboards, vocals, percussion), Jeffrey Foskett (guitar, mandolin, vocals), Paul von Mertens (flute, sax, harmonica), and Nelson Bragg (percussion) from Wilson's band. Wilson's normal drummer, Mike d'Amico of the Wondermints, played bass, and Wilson's normal guitarist, Nick Walusko appeared on the first few tour dates but had to quit the tour for health reasons. From Love's band came Scott Totten (guitar, vocals) and John Cowsill (drums, vocals).

This lineup of the band was, quite simply, the best live lineup the Beach Boys have ever had. Totten and von Mertens, acting as joint musical directors, managed to integrate both bands perfectly, and the resulting band could perform complex, delicate, material like "The Little Girl I Once Knew", "Heroes and Villains" and "God Only Knows" with the accuracy that Brian's band have always brought to those songs, while also managing to capture the garage-rock feel of the early surfing hits in the way Mike's band were, by that time, capable of.

I have talked many times in this series of essays about how wonderful Wilson's band are, but I must say a few words here about Totten and Cowsill. While the touring Beach Boys were woefully bad in the late 90s and early 2000s, a series of personnel changes had by this time left them with an almost entirely different lineup, and they were now also exceptional. While Love tours with a smaller band, Totten (his musical director and lead guitarist) is dedicated to reproducing the arrangements Brian created for the records as accurately as possible given that lineup (even down to singing "break up" while Bruce sings "broke up" on "Sloop John B", because Al sang the wrong word on the record and the more dedicated fans will expect the mistake to be replicated).

And John Cowsill is, hands down, the best live drummer I've ever seen, and perfect for this material. He has the power and energy of Dennis Wilson's playing, but also has the precision of a Hal Blaine or Earl Palmer.

So incorporating those two members into Wilson's band produced what really was the perfect Beach Boys touring band – and they were doing what was possibly the perfect set as well. The setlists were in Love's control, though Wilson and Jardine both suggested songs, and the shows were largely structured the same way as his longer theatre shows – forty to sixty songs, depending on the venue, starting with a medley of surfing hits, then a few mid-sixties album tracks like "Kiss Me Baby" or "Wendy", leading into "Don't Worry Baby" and a car medley ending in "I Get Around" before the intermission. After the intermission would come a run of more obscure fan-favourites like "All This Is That", leading into the singles from *Pet Sounds*, and then to "Good Vibrations" and a run of the big hits like "Barbara Ann" and "Fun Fun Fun". Carl and Dennis Wilson were represented via video footage of them singing "God Only Knows" and "Forever" while the band performed a live backing.

It's a structure that allows the show to expand to fit the space available, and to incorporate all sorts of fan-pleasing obscurities, while still having a definite, almost narrative, structure, and letting the audience leave feeling like the entire show has been one long three-hour run of hits from beginning to end. And it's a structure that worked astonishingly well for these shows.

That structure is more-or-less replicated on *Live: The 50th Anniversary Tour*, with a few minor changes – mostly cutting out songs where the lead vocal wasn't performed by one of the original Beach Boys (except "Why Do Fools Fall In Love?", a duet with Foskett and Totten singing a unison lead) – on the tour, Foskett had regularly sung lead on "Don't Worry Baby", Totten on "Ballad of Ole Betsy", and Darian Sahanaja on "Darlin'", among others.

So in theory, given that this was quite possibly the best tour the band ever performed, this should be the best Beach Boys live album?

Sadly not.

The bulk of the recordings are taken from very early shows on the tour, which had a massive flaw – on those early shows, before fan complaints made the tour management see sense, live autotune was applied to band members' vocals. This was presumably intended as a safety net – Brian can be a little pitchy live, and this was by far the longest tour he'd done in thirty years – but the result made them (especially Brian, but also very noticeably Mike on some of the early tracks on CD one) sound like robots.

Quite why these recordings were used when there exist soundboard recordings of shows without the autotune applied, I don't know, but that appalling lapse of taste wasn't even the worst thing about this album. That would be the mixing.

This was a *great* sounding band – I attended three shows and have audience recordings of half a dozen more, so I know that the sound this band made was an astonishing, thick, dense wall of music. Here half the instruments playing aren't even audible. In particular, Nelson Bragg's percussion is mixed almost completely out – and that in turn makes John Cowsill's drumming, which was intended to work with Bragg's playing, sound flat and lifeless.

And while no-one expects a live album to be completely free of over-dubs (though really, with seventy-five shows recorded, there's no reason for overdubbing), one does generally expect that previously-released studio tracks not just be dumped onto the album with some audience noise, yet the versions of "Do It Again", "That's Why God Made the Radio" and "Isn't It Time" on here are essentially just that, while the first half of "Heroes and Villains" is Brian's 2004 studio version from *Smile* with a handful of additional backing vocals.

This is all topped with crowd noise which swells and dies down more or less randomly, with little connection to anything a real audience would ever do. And just to add insult to injury, the credits in the CD liner don't credit several band members with all the instruments they played, and miss out Nick Walusko (who played on at least some of these dates) altogether.

A shorter, twenty-one-song, DVD of a single live performance was also released, and while that has some post-production sweetening, it's nothing like as bad as this CD.

If you want a (legitimate) record of the 2012 tour, that's the one to go for. This, honestly, is not even worth listening to at all.

line-up

Brian Wilson, Al Jardine, Mike Love, Bruce Johnston, David Marks

Full tracklisting.

All lead vocals by their original vocalists, with Jeffrey Foskett on falsetto, except where noted.

Disc 1

- "Do It Again"
- "Little Honda"
- "Catch a Wave"
- "Hawaii"
- "Don't Back Down"
- "Surfin' Safari"
- "Surfer Girl"
- "The Little Girl I Once Knew" (lead vocals Brian Wilson)
- "Wendy" (lead vocals Bruce Johnston)
- "Getcha Back" (lead vocals David Marks)
- "Then I Kissed Her"
- "Marcella" (lead vocals Brian Wilson)
- "Isn't It Time"
- "Why Do Fools Fall in Love" (lead vocals Scott Totten and Jeffrey Foskett)
- "When I Grow Up (To Be a Man)"
- "Disney Girls"
- "Be True to Your School"
- "Little Deuce Coupe"
- "409"
- "Shut Down"
- "I Get Around"

Disc 2

- "Pet Sounds" (lead guitar David Marks)
- "Add Some Music to Your Day" (lead vocals group)
- "Heroes and Villains"

- "Sail On, Sailor" (lead vocals Brian Wilson)

- "California Saga: California"

- "In My Room"

- "All This Is That" (lead vocals Mike Love and Al Jardine, with Brian Wilson and Darian Sahanaja doubled on the bridge, and Jeffrey Foskett on the "jai guru dev" tag)

- "That's Why God Made the Radio"

- "Forever"

- "God Only Knows"

- "Sloop John B"

- "Wouldn't It Be Nice" (lead vocals Al Jardine and Mike Love)

- "Good Vibrations" (lead vocals Brian Wilson doubled by Jeffrey Foskett)

- "California Girls"

- "Help Me Rhonda"

- "Rock and Roll Music"

- "Surfin' U.S.A."

- "Kokomo" (lead vocals Mike Love, Jeffrey Foskett, and Bruce Johnston)

- "Barbara Ann" (lead vocals Jeffrey Foskett)

- "Fun, Fun, Fun"

Made in California

The final part of the fiftieth anniversary celebrations came in 2013, with this six-CD career-spanning box set. Essentially a replacement for the earlier *Good Vibrations* set, this tells a very different story to that collection. Where *Good Vibrations* was essentially about Brian Wilson, with the other Beach Boys as bit players, this presents a more rounded version of the band as a whole. There is far more representation of Dennis Wilson here, especially, but there's also a lot more of Al Jardine and Carl Wilson – this is a set which is telling the story of a band, not an individual.

Once again Boyd and Linett, who put this set together, did Beach Boys fans proud. Of the 174 tracks on the box, a full sixty had never been released, and while I'm only dealing here with songs that have not otherwise been dealt with in this series of books, in a very real sense almost everything on this box was new. Mark Linett had remixed most of the 60s material into stereo for a series of reissues in 2012, and those versions, rather than the mono versions, were used here, along with several new-to-this-set mixes. There were live versions of songs one wouldn't normally expect, with unusual lineups of the band – a 1972 version of "Wild Honey" with Blondie on lead vocals, a version of "Help Me Rhonda" from the same period with Dennis Wilson singing, a 1995 "Sail On Sailor" with Carl on lead, a live "Vegetables" from 1993. There were live versions of "All I Want To Do", "Only With You", "Summer In Paradise" (the only acknowledgement that album received on this package), "Little Bird" and "Friends". There were instrumental mixes, single versions that had never appeared on CD before, and there were experiments like a new mix of "Sail Plane Song" that featured additional reverb and psychedelic phasing.

It's unfortunate that the box doesn't feature a couple of the tracks that are only on *Good Vibrations*, meaning that hardcore fans need both, because this really does a wonderful job of replacing it, and is probably the definitive collection of the Beach Boys' music (although curiously it doesn't include "Then I Kissed Her", the only omission a casual fan might notice).

But if you only own one Beach Boys set, this has to be the one.

Back Home

Songwriters: Brian Wilson and Bob Norberg

Lead vocals: Brian Wilson (1963 version), Al Jardine (1970 version)

Two different versions of this song, which of course was finally released on *15 Big Ones,* are included on this set, but both are so different from the 1976 version, and from each other, that they might as well be considered different songs.

The 1963 version is the closer of the two to the 1976 version. The verses are the same, and performed in a similar style, though obviously in Brian's much sweeter 1963 voice, but there's no "back home...I'll spend my summer..." chorus. Rather there's a middle eight which is missing from all the other versions. It's a pleasant enough track that would have made decent album filler, with some good honking baritone sax work.

The 1970 version, by contrast, is very much an Al Jardine song, in the vein of "California Saga", with banjo and harmonica, and while he's not credited it's clear that he rewrote the song substantially – the vocal melody is almost totally different from the other versions, and it shares no lyrics with either of them other than the title phrase. The "back home...I'll spend my summer..." chorus makes its first appearance here, but as a backing vocal part on the tag.

Both versions are fun, and worth having, but no version of this song is astonishingly wonderful.

Meant For You

Songwriters: Brian Wilson and Mike Love

Lead vocals: Mike Love and Brian Wilson

At first this alternate version of this song sounds identical to the opener of *Friends,* but then the song goes off in a strange direction. The "doo doo" ending is extended enormously, and Brian sings over the top "have you ever seen a pony run alongside of his mother/and have you ever seen a puppy dog laying his head on his brother?", before the "these feelings in my heart I know are meant for you" ending is repeated.

It manages to maintain the gentle air of the song for twice as long as the originally released version, but it's easy to see how this was edited to the more concise version we know.

Fallin' In Love (2009 Stereo Mix)

Songwriter: Dennis Wilson

Lead vocals: Dennis Wilson

Originally released as "Lady", this was (in its original mix, which didn't have the string intro this version does) the B-side of a single released under the name "Dennis Wilson and Rumbo" (Rumbo apparently being Daryl Dragon), although apparently at least some of the other Beach Boys are on this track, and it was considered for release on the album that eventually became *Sunflower*.

An attempt at writing in the style of Tim Hardin, who was a big influence on Dennis' earlier writing, this is frankly much better than a lot of Dennis' more well-respected material. The lyrics about the object of the song being "my lady" are a little dated now, but this has a gorgeous melody, interesting percussion (a very mechanical drum sound, which sounds like an early drum machine and points the way to the sound he'd use on "Steamboat" a few years later, as well as the drum sound on "Til I Die"), and it's a truly great record.

Sound of Free (Mono Single Version)

Songwriters: Dennis Wilson and Mike Love

Lead vocals: Dennis Wilson

The A-side of the Rumbo single, this is *definitely* a Beach Boys performance – Carl Wilson's vocal can be heard prominently in the mix.

Of the two tracks from the single, this is the less successful – Love's lyrics are a vague mush of mysticism, and it doesn't have the catchiness of its B-side – but it's still an interesting track. The verses and choruses are in the same style as much of Dennis' *Sunflower*-era work, while the middle eight ("the mountain so high...") sounds like it's from a completely different track, and shows the style he would later develop for *Pacific Ocean Blue*.

(Wouldn't It Be Nice To) Live Again

Songwriters: Dennis Wilson and Stan Shapiro

Lead vocals: Dennis Wilson

Before its release, this was the most anticipated track on *Made in California* – a song recorded by Dennis during the *Surf's Up* sessions, but (along with his "Fourth of July") left off that album after a dispute with Carl over sequencing.

In the forty years since, and particularly after it had been played, once, to attendees at a Beach Boys fan convention, the track (which had never been bootlegged) achieved an almost-legendary status among Beach Boys fandom, which it could never possibly live up to.

In truth, it is a powerful track (though clearly an unfinished one – the guitar solo in particular is clearly a placeholder), a stark ballad about despair and the hope to feel something after loss. It's not in the very top tier of Wilson's compositions, but it deserved a release, and it is at least as good as much of the *Surf's Up* album.

It's a Beautiful Day (Single Edit) (2012 Mix)

Songwriters: Al Jardine and Mike Love

Lead vocals: Carl Wilson, Al Jardine, and Mike Love

A non-album single from 1979, this was originally recorded for the satirical film *Americathon*, a rather strange film written by members of the Firesign Theatre, and starring Harvey Korman, Meatloaf, Elvis Costello, and George Carlin.

The song plays over the film's opening credits, which show a future America which has run out of oil and in which there are traffic jams from the number of bicycles (hence the lines about "the freeway is jammed now the car's disappeared from the scene", which otherwise make little sense).

The song itself is quite catchy, a rewrite of Love and Jardine's earlier "Skatetown USA" (another song written for a film, though that track remains unreleased), although it's the first of Love's several rather creepy references to "afternoon delights" in his late-period lyrics.

Goin' to the Beach

Songwriter: Mike Love

Lead vocals: Mike Love

An outtake from *Keepin' the Summer Alive*, this isn't anything special, but is still a better song and track than half of that album. A simple, chugging, shuffle with rudimentary lyrics about going to the beach, surfing, listening to the radio, and hanging out with one's girl, this is catchy enough and might even have been a minor hit had it been released at the time.

The track had actually been left unfinished until 2013, when Scott Totten overdubbed the lead guitar part and a final mix was made, but this is still mostly a vintage recording (though the digital reverb applied to Love's voice in the mix is definitely not a vintage sound). The song became a regular part of Love's setlist for several years after this release, and always went down very well live. Fun enough, but inessential.

Why Don't They Let Us Fall in Love?

Songwriters: Jeff Barry, Ellie Greenwich, and Phil Spector

Lead vocals: Mike Love and Brian Wilson

A cover version of a 1964 Ronnie Spector single, this was recorded in 1980 during some Brian-and-Mike sessions which also produced the version of "Be My Baby" on *Looking Back With Love*. This is, quite simply, a mess, with the worst aspects of the cover versions on both *15 Big Ones* and *Keepin' the Summer Alive*, and without any of the joy of either. A slow, plodding, song that was almost uniquely unsuited to the combination of Love's 1980 off-key nasality and Wilson's 1980 hoarse bellowing, literally the best thing about this is the count-in, when Brian says "wait" and has to count in again.

After that, well... Love's bass vocal is enjoyably goofy, but the arrangement is just rudimentary piano and organ chords and a beat-box, the vocals are astonishingly poor, and this almost makes the listener want to cry at the thought of these people, who had been involved in so much greatness, sunk so low.

Da Doo Ron Ron

Songwriters: Jeff Barry, Ellie Greenwich, and Phil Spector

Lead vocals: Carl Wilson

Another Spector cover, this time of the Crystals' hit, this 1979 recording is not much more inventive than "Why Don't They Let Us Fall In Love?", but at least Carl Wilson turns in a spirited lead vocal and the track has some energy. Pointless, and nothing like up to the standard of the original, but not actually unlistenable.

California Dreamin'

Songwriters: John Phillips and Michelle Phillips

Lead vocals: Carl Wilson and Al Jardine

A re-recording of the Mamas & Papas hit, produced by Terry Melcher, this 1986 non-album single made the lower reaches of the US chart. It features Roger McGuinn of the Byrds on twelve-string guitar (though it's such a rudimentary part it could have been anyone at all), and largely follows the template of the original – the major differences are that there are no backing vocals on the opening verse (instead there are storm sound effects), there's a horrible 80s sax all over the last half of the track, and the first verse is just repeated at the end rather than having the lyrical variation "if I didn't tell her I could leave today".

It's a fairly pointless cover, but Jardine's vocals are strong (he takes the first and last verse, with Carl Wilson on the second), and it remains in the band's setlist to this day.

An earlier version of the song, recorded in 1981 and released on a Terry Melcher-produced cassette-only compilation, *Rock and Roll City* (which also featured Dean Torrence and the Rip Chords) was used as the basis for this recording. That version had Love singing lead on the first verse.

You're Still a Mystery

Songwriters: Brian Wilson and Andy Paley

Lead vocals: Brian Wilson, Matt Jardine, Carl Wilson and Mike Love

This is one of two songs from the mid-90s sessions with Andy Paley and Don Was to see completion, both of which were released on this box set (the other, "Soul Searchin'", was discussed under *Gettin' in Over My Head*), this is possibly the best Beach Boys recording since 1977.

Over a gorgeous retro-60s track, with reverbed guitar reminiscent of a Jack Nitzsche instrumental, Brian sings simple – even simplistic – verses, before a chorus comes in with layers of chanted vocals which people have been trying to unpick since the first bootlegs of this material appeared in the late 90s. Matt Jardine sings lead on the chorus, doubled by Carl, and Love gets a single solo line ("I wish you'd help me find the key") in his bass range, but really the star of this recording is the vocal arrangement itself, which is the most inventive use of the band's vocals since the 60s.

This is not a particularly clever or complex track, or one susceptible to much in the way of analysis, but it's a wonderful piece of pop music that (other than the obvious ageing of the band members' vocals) would have fit perfectly on *Today!*

For some reason, Brian re-recorded his lead vocals (apparently with Joe Thomas) in 1999, and that re-recorded lead is what's used on this set rather than the 1995 recording fans were familiar with. I prefer the earlier vocal take myself, but this is a great track in whatever version you hear.

Runaway (Chicago 1965, with Concert Promo Intro - Mono)

Songwriters: Del Shannon and Max Crook

Lead vocals: Al Jardine

The "concert promo intro" here is an *a capella* recording of a section of the old barbershop song "Down by the Old Mill Stream", recorded to be used as a commercial for the band's live shows.

The rest of this track is a live recording from 1965 (from the shows later released on the *Live in Chicago 1965* download set). It was recorded after Brian had quit performing live, but a couple of weeks before Bruce joined the band. However, Brian is here on bass, rather than Glen Campbell, returning for one of his very rare late-60s performances with the group as a live album was to be recorded.

"Runaway" had been a massive hit for Del Shannon a few years earlier, but the main hook for the song was the otherworldly keyboard part, played on keyboardist Max Crook's own invention the Musitron. Without that, the Beach Boys' live version can only be a pale imitation, though Al gives a great lead vocal.

The Letter (Hawaii Rehearsal 1967)

Songwriter: Wayne Carson Thompson

Lead vocals: Brian Wilson and Mike Love

In 1967, the band (minus Bruce, but with Brian) flew to Hawaii to record a live album, *Lei'd in Hawaii*. For those shows, Brian transported his Baldwin organ, and the band performed new arrangements of many of their hits, reworked in the style of *Smiley Smile*. Unfortunately, the band were underrehearsed, and they went back into the studio, with Bruce, to record a "live in the studio" version of the album, which would have audience noise overdubbed on it. The album was scrapped, and replaced in the release schedule with *Wild Honey*.

Several tracks from the shows, the rehearsals, and the studio recordings have been released over the years, and as this book went to press it was announced that the full "live" album would be released on the new rarities collection *1967: Sunshine Tomorrow*.

This track, a cover of the Box Tops' contemporary hit, lacks much of the passion that made Alex Chilton's lead vocal so appealing, and is primarily interesting for pointing the way to the stripped-down, stoned, R&B sound of *Wild Honey*.

Guess I'm Dumb (Instrumental Track w/Background Vocals)

Songwriters: Brian Wilson and Russ Titelman

"Guess I'm Dumb" was one of Brian's greatest achievements of the sixties – a glorious single, equal parts Roy Orbison and Burt Bacharach, that he produced for the then-unknown singer Glen Campbell. It prefigures *Pet Sounds*, and is actually better than much of it.

However, it's not a Beach Boys track – but both Brian and Carl played on it, and sang backing vocals along with The Honeys (the vocal group that contained Brian's wife and his sister-in-law), and so it's included on this set without Campbell's lead vocal.

Without that, it's interesting but inessential – but anyone who loves this music should seek out any compilation containing the single version.

Sherry She Needs Me (1965 Track w/1976 Vocal)

Songwriters: Brian Wilson and Russ Titelman

Lead vocals: Brian Wilson

This is the 1965 backing track for the song that eventually became "She Says That She Needs Me" on Brian's *Imagination* album. At the time, it was called "Sandy She Needs Me", but the only vocal that seems to exist for that recording is the ending, with Love singing "Sandy baby it's time we said goodbye", with the band joining in to sing a rather lovely vocal tag.

In 1976, Brian recorded a lead vocal over the earlier backing track in his "low and manly" voice, and it's heartbreakingly effective (although when he goes into falsetto for the choruses we see both how hard it was for him to stay on key in that range by 1976 and how much the song owes to "Sherry" by the Four Seasons). But for this mix, the 1965 vocal tag is included, and hearing Brian's 1976 voice singing gruff "woah oh"'s while his youthful falsetto soars from 1965 is even more moving. A glorious track.

Mona Kana (Instrumental Track)

Songwriter: Dennis Wilson

An instrumental, recorded by Dennis in 1968, and for which Stephen Kalinich apparently wrote lyrics which were never recorded. This is *very* obviously indebted to Brian's *Smile*-era work, as well as to earlier Brian instrumentals like "Three Blind Mice" and "Trombone Dixie", but it's a very good imitation of that style, showing that Dennis could easily have emulated his brother, rather than finding his own style.

Where Is She?

Songwriter: Brian Wilson

Lead vocals: Brian Wilson

A solo Brian performance (or close to it – there's a guitar on there, which is not an instrument Brian usually played), very much in the stripped-down style of "Sail Plane Song", this is an absolutely beautiful little song, and possibly the best unreleased track on the box set.

A simple nursery-rhyme-style waltz, with a slight melodic resemblance to "She's Leaving Home", this is clearly a demo – the instrumentation is almost nonexistent – and it's stitched together from multiple performances. It opens with a simple piano statement of the song, and then goes into a full song performance with organ, clip-clop percussion, very rudimentary drumming, guitar, and what sounds like Moog bass with Brian multitracking himself, sketching in harmonies and countermelodies. Then there's a tag, repeating the first few lines, which sounds like it's edited in from the first verse to create a full performance.

Brian's right at the top of his range here, and his falsetto's noticeably thinner than it had been a couple of years earlier, but that just adds to the track's sparse beauty. This is a gorgeous, lonely, song which would have been a highlight of *Sunflower* had it been finished, but which actually works better in this form.

I Believe in Miracles

A twenty-one second *a capella* vocal snippet, recorded during the *Smiley Smile* sessions, but very much in the style of *Smile*. This had previously been bootlegged as part of an alternate edit of "Can't Wait Too Long", but bears relatively little resemblance to it, being closer to parts of "Vegetables" or "Child is Father of the Man".

Why (Instrumental Track)

Songwriter: Brian Wilson

A backing track recorded during the *MIU Album* sessions in 1977, this is a $\frac{12}{8}$ piano-led ballad with some of the same feel as "That's Why God Made the Radio". Not an especially interesting track, but musically better than much of what ended up on *MIU*.

Barnyard Blues

Songwriter: Dennis Wilson

Lead vocals: Dennis Wilson

A fun little track started by Dennis in 1971 and completed in 1974, this is clearly inspired by some of Brian's *Smile* music (as well as Dennis' own "I Don't Know" from the *Smile* era, which shares a very similar progression), but takes elements such as barnyard noises, bass harmonica and a "Wonderful"-esque keyboard part in a different direction, resulting in an almost swamp-rock style track which resembles Little Feat or The Band. This track clearly shows the connection between Dennis' mature, *Pacific Ocean Blue*, style and his earlier emulation of his brother, but it's a relatively minor piece.

You've Lost That Lovin' Feelin'

Songwriters: Phil Spector, Barry Mann, Cynthia Weil

Lead vocals: Brian Wilson

A rather astonishing version of the Righteous Brothers' classic, this is reportedly an entirely solo Brian performance. Recorded just before the start of the *Love You* sessions, it has Brian singing both Bill Medley and Bobby Hatfield's parts, and he sings Medley's part in the "low and manly" voice he used during that time period, but Hatfield's higher part is sung in a high tenor quite unlike anything else he did at that point – in fact he sounds spookily like his brother Carl here.

It's a rudimentary production – it sounds like Brian on tack piano, Moog, ARP string synthesiser, jew's harp, drums, and percussion – and in one of the rare instances where I can find fault with this set, the mix is very light and reverb-heavy. Bootlegged versions, with a much drier mix with more emphasis on the Moog bass, exist and sound much better than the released mix. But no matter what version you listen to it's a powerful recording, just because of Brian's wonderful vocals.

My Love Lives On

Songwriters: Dennis Wilson and Stephen Kalinich

Lead vocals: Dennis Wilson

A 1974 piano demo of a lovely, gentle Dennis song. For once Kalinich's lyrics work perfectly, and this is one of the best examples of Dennis' quiet ballads. While the song meanders a little towards the end, the opening verse is as good as anything he ever composed. Possibly the single best of the many Dennis tracks on this set.

The Big Beat 1963

In 2013, European copyright law changed. Up to that point, sound recordings had been under copyright for fifty years, after which they became public domain. Under pressure from the music industry, and not coincidentally in time for the fiftieth anniversary of the Beatles' first album, that was changed so that in Europe sound recordings are in copyright for seventy-five years – but *only* if the recordings have been released to the public within the first fifty calendar years. Thus any recordings from 1963 which remained unreleased as of December 31 2013 became public domain, but any which had been released by that date would remain in copyright – and so on for every subsequent year.

And so began the Beach Boys copyright extension series. Every year from 2013 onwards there has been at least one digital-only release of a previously-unreleased set of recordings from fifty years earlier, and often a physical CD release as well.

The first of these digital releases, *The Big Beat 1963*, isn't strictly-speaking a Beach Boys release. It's a collection of twenty-two previously unreleased tracks, a mixture of Beach Boys tracks, Brian Wilson demos, Brian Wilson productions for other artists, and five tracks by the Honeys with which no Beach Boys had any involvement but which were included because there was no more sensible home for them.

As the rest of this series is devoted entirely to the Beach Boys, and as the focus of this set is so clearly on Brian, I've decided to include this set as well for completeness' sake.

The sound quality on the set is... mixed. Many tracks come from acetate sources with a lot of surface noise, and it shows. But this is still a marvellous set, and well worth a listen for any fan of the Beach Boys' early material.

The Big Beat

Artist: Bob & Sheri

Songwriter: Brian Wilson

"Bob & Sheri" were Bob Norberg, Brian's roommate and occasional song-writing partner, and his then-girlfriend Cheryl Pomeroy. Here, with Brian on backing vocals, they sing in unison on an early version of "Do You Remember?"

Lyrically this has many of the same themes as the later version, with references to Chuck Berry, Buddy Holly, Hank Ballard and others, but the lyric is gibberish in many parts, with lyrics about Eisenhower in the shower, Uncle Remus and Aunt Jemima. The track clearly had potential, but the Beach Boys version is far superior.

First Rock and Roll Dance (Instrumental)

Artist: Brian Wilson

Songwriter: Brian Wilson

A nondescript surf-rock instrumental, with some King Curtis-esque sax by Steve Douglas and a similar start-stop rhythm to "Surfin' USA".

Gonna Hustle You (Demo)

Artist: Brian Wilson

Songwriters: Brian Wilson and Bob Norberg

A demo of a song written for Jan & Dean, which would later become a hit rewritten as "The New Girl in School" because "gonna hustle you" was seen as being too sexually aggressive. It's one of the catchiest of Brian's songs for Jan & Dean, and pretty much the whole arrangement is in place here, "doo ron day ron day" backing vocals and all. The major difference is that this lacks the *a capella* bass vocal hook added by Jan Berry.

Ride Away

Artist: Bob & Sheri

Songwriters: Brian Wilson and Bob Norberg

A call-and-response duet, in a Phil Spector girl-group style (with what sound like backing vocals from the Honeys), this was later rewritten as

"Surfer's Holiday", with Roger Christian and Gary Usher, for the film *Muscle Beach Party*. Fun enough but, as with many of Brian's productions outside the Beach Boys at this time, ultimately inessential.

Funny Boy

Artist: The Honeys

Songwriter: Brian Wilson

The Honeys were a girl group consisting of Brian's future wife Marilyn Rovell, her sister Diane, and their cousin Ginger Blake. This song, sung by Blake (easily the best vocalist of the three, but rather underutilised on the Honeys' records), was intended for a Honeys album that remained unreleased. It has a strong, gritty, lead vocal, but isn't much of a song.

Marie

Artist: Bob Norberg & Brian Wilson, with The Honeys

Songwriter: Brian Wilson

Brian takes lead here on a song clearly inspired by Dion tracks like "The Wanderer" and "Runaround Sue". With a similar feeling to "Car Crazy Cutie"/"Pamela Jean", this is derivative, and a rather sloppy performance, but a solid attempt at a style that Brian didn't try very often. Norberg provides bass vocals.

Mother May I

Artist: The Beach Boys

Songwriter: Brian Wilson

This is credited as a Beach Boys song, but according to *Becoming the Beach Boys* by James B. Murphy it's actually Brian plus session musicians, and recorded while the rest of the band were on tour. Based on the children's game, its verses alternate between Brian's normal falsetto voice and a screechy Grinch voice (similar to the Pied Piper from "Mount Vernon and Fairway"). A joke track that wasn't very funny.

I Do (Demo)

Artist: The Beach Boys

Songwriter: Brian Wilson and Roger Christian

A demo of the song that was later released as a bonus track on the *Surfer Girl/Shut Down vol. 2* twofer CD. This is the same basic arrangement, but without the driving guitar part, and slightly slower.

Bobby Left Me (Backing track)

Artist: Brian Wilson

Songwriter: Brian Wilson

An instrumental track, recorded during the same sessions as "Little Saint Nick", which has been variously stated as being intended for Sharon Marie (a girlfriend of Mike Love's for whom Brian produced several unsuccessful recordings around this time) or the Honeys.

A sax-driven track with prominent castanets, it shows the clear influence of Phil Spector.

If It Can't Be You (a.k.a. I'll Never Love Again)

Artist: Gary Usher

Songwriter: Brian Wilson

A piano-vocal demo (with a little hand percussion) which had previously been bootlegged with Larry Denton credited as vocalist, this is a standard doo-wop sounding ballad. Like many of these tracks it's a genre exercise, and a perfectly competent one, but not exceptional.

You Brought It All on Yourself

Artist: The Honeys

Songwriter: Brian Wilson

Another song in a Dion-esque style, this one features a unison vocal by all three of the Honeys for much of the track, which helps disguise the musical influences somewhat (Marilyn takes the solo lead vocal parts). At 0:55 there's a brief snatch of vocal melody which Brian later reused for both "Be True To Your School" and "Some of Your Love", while there's a truly odd key change right in the middle of the last line of the song.

The Honeys later re-recorded this for their 1980 album *Ecstasy*.

Make the Night a Little Longer

Artist: The Honeys

Songwriters: Gerry Goffin and Carole King

The first track on the set to have no Brian Wilson involvement, this is a Nik Venet production of a Goffin/King song originally recorded by the Cookies (a girl group most well known for their hit "Chains"). With a strong vocal from Ginger and a string sound reminiscent of the Drifters' records around this time, this could have been a hit had it been released.

Rabbit's Foot (Unfinished track with backing vocals)

Artist: The Honeys

Songwriter: Brian Wilson

This is a backing track that was intended as a Honeys track, but which Brian later reused as the backing track for "Our Car Club". This has no lead vocal, and has the Honeys singing "we'll keep a rabbit's foot" where the finished version has "we'll start a car club", but is otherwise identical to the released version.

Summer Moon

Artist: Vicki Kocher and Bob Norberg

Songwriter: Brian Wilson

A remake of "The Surfer Moon", with what sounds like the same backing track (though it's a scratchy acetate so hard to be certain), with Norberg and Vicki Kocher singing unison vocals. There are some slight lyrical changes, but there's not much better about this than the original.

Side Two (Instrumental)

Artist: The Beach Boys

Songwriter: Brian Wilson

A shuffle-flavoured instrumental, which to my ears sounds like another attempt at making a Dion-style recording, but which Peter Reum suggests may be an early attempt at "Little Deuce Coupe" (the chord changes aren't the same, but the track sounds similar enough that it's plausible).

Ballad of Ole Betsy (Demo)

Artist: The Beach Boys

Songwriter: Brian Wilson and Roger Christian

An instrumental take of the song, with strummed guitars, bass, and a rudimentary drum part (just a snare drum whacked once every bar). There's nothing unfamiliar here, but hearing this close to "I'll Never Love Again" shows the resemblance between the two tracks, which might otherwise go unnoticed.

Thank Him (Demo)

Artist: Brian Wilson

Songwriter: Brian Wilson

A fascinating little track, with Brian singing two-part Everly Brothers-style harmonies over a simple strummed electric guitar. Another song in the mould of "If It Can't Be You", "The Surfer Moon", "Ballad of Ole Betsy", "Surfer Girl" and the rest of Brian's doo-wop ballads from this period, this is most notable for the lyrics. They can be read as a female singer singing thanks for her boyfriend but to my ears the "Him" of the song sounds like a reference to God rather than a human man, and if that's the intention, this is the first of Brian's attempts at dealing with spirituality in his songs.

Once You've Got Him

Artist: The Honeys

Songwriters: Ginger Blake and Diane Rovell

One of several demos the Honeys recorded of songs they wrote themselves, intended for other artists, this is a fun little pop song in the bouncy style which Davy Jones of the Monkees would later make his own. This was actually intended for Hayley Mills, and the Honeys here sing in their approximation of a British accent (Mills is British) – mostly pronouncing hard ts and lengthening the vowels. This is just piano (played by Blake), vocals, and rudimentary drums (probably a single snare, played with brushes).

For Always and Forever (Demo)

Artist: The Honeys

Songwriters: Ginger Blake and Diane Rovell

Another demo, with the Honeys singing over piano, brushed snare, and Hammond organ. This was intended for the Paris Sisters, and the song bears a strong resemblance to their hit "I Love How You Love Me", though it also has more than a little of Johnny Ace's "Pledging My Love" to it.

Little Dirt Bike (Demo)

Artist: The Honeys

Songwriters: Ginger Blake and Diane Rovell

Another piano/drums/vocals demo, this is The Honeys' attempt at writing a song in the style of the Beach Boys' car songs. It stands up perfectly well as a song against tracks like "Little Honda" or "Shut Down", to which it bears a strong resemblance.

Darling I'm Not Stepping Out On You (Demo)

Artist: The Honeys

Songwriters: Ginger Blake and Diane Rovell

What these demos show is that Blake and Rovell could easily have had a decent career as songwriters – the fourth of this set of demos, it's the fourth competent song and the fourth genre. This is a honky-tonk country song, with Jerry Cole on guitar, and could easily have fit onto an early Jerry Lee Lewis or Carl Perkins album. The last line of the middle eight is clunky – "for us to be in love he could not bear" is a bad line, forced for the rhyme scheme – but the rest of it is a perfectly passable country exercise.

When I Think About You (Demo)

Artist: The Honeys

Songwriters: Ginger Blake and Diane Rovell

And the final song is another Honeys demo. This one's in the same style as "Darling I'm Not Stepping Out On You", and is decent enough but less memorable.

Live In Sacramento 1964

The first of 2014's copyright extension releases was a digital-only (initially iTunes-only) release of two concerts recorded in Sacramento in August 1964. These two shows, plus a 2013 show recorded at the same location, were the basis of the *Beach Boys Concert* album (which also contained a certain amount of studio tweaking), so it's not surprising that the shows sound much like that album.

There are recording flaws on both shows – notably on "Little Honda", the opening song from both shows, the recording doesn't appear to have been set up to record the vocal mics properly, and there are balance problems throughout, as one would expect for recordings made on primitive remote equipment and in a live situation. At times the screams of the audience overwhelm the performances altogether.

And yet. . . this is a genuinely exciting recording, of a band that could perform with a real garage-rock energy. The harmonies are solid throughout, Dennis pummels the drums, Brian is a better live bass player than one would expect, and Carl plays some ridiculously good surf guitar.

This is what rock and roll sounded like back when it was still a vital musical genre. There are missed drum beats, and flat notes, but for a band playing to a wall of screams, without the benefit of monitors, this is remarkably good.

There's little to say about it that wasn't already said in the entry on *Beach Boys Concert* in volume one, but this is a much better collection than that one, flaws and all.

Both shows have the same songs, performed in a slightly different order. Those songs are:

- **Little Honda**

- **Papa-Oom-Mow-Mow**

- **The Little Old Lady from Pasadena**

- **Hushabye**

- Hawaii
- Let's Go Trippin'
- The Wanderer
- Surfer Girl
- Monster Mash
- Be True to Your School
- Graduation Day
- Surfin' USA
- Don't Back Down
- Don't Worry Baby
- Wendy
- I Get Around
- Fun, Fun, Fun

The set also includes studio rehearsals of "Little Honda" and "Papa Oom-Mow-Mow".

Keep An Eye On Summer

The second 2014 copyright extension release was *Keep An Eye On Summer*, a collection of outtakes, vocal-only mixes, stereo mixes (including a couple that had previously been released) and BBC live recordings, covering the sessions for *Shut Down vol. 2*, *All Summer Long*, and *The Beach Boys' Christmas Album* and the first sessions for *The Beach Boys Today!*.

Much of this has, of course, been bootlegged — but here Alan Boyd and Mark Linett, the archivist and engineer responsible for the project, have culled the session tapes to what is listenable. While the bootlegs have things like "All Summer Long (takes 20-42)" or "Girls On The Beach (vocal overdub takes 1b-8b)", here there's just enough studio chat to get a flavour for what it was like in the studio, and only the musically interesting stuff has been kept. And some of it had never been bootlegged before, notably the *Shut Down vol. 2* material and the BBC recordings, the tapes for which were lost for many years.

The result contains some genuinely sublime moments. The *a capella* (more or less — the instrumental track is mixed down to *near*-inaudibility) mix of "She Knows Me Too Well" is spellbindingly beautiful, and the *a capella* "In The Parking Lot" is revelatory — this was never a favourite of mine before, but the harmonies in the massed vocal sections jump out in this new mix.

There's also stuff that's of more academic interest. We'd known for a while that the Beach Boys played on more of their tracks than they're usually credited for, but I didn't realise until this album that "Denny's Drums" was actually played by Dennis Wilson — like almost everyone, I'd assumed that Hal Blaine had played that track. The early take of the track here actually also has some minimal guitar.

And "Pom Pom Play Girl", another song I've never had much time for, seems in its remix to reveal that either Mike Love is a far better vocal impersonator than I'd credit him for or Jan Berry of Jan & Dean is doubling him, uncredited (the sessionography seems to indicate the former).

The few songs that have not been dealt with in some form before are:

Endless Sleep

Lead vocal: Larry Denton

Songwriter: Jody Reynolds

An outside production by Brian (the only one on this set, which is otherwise entirely Beach Boys material), this is a cover of an early teen-tragedy rockabilly song. Jody Reynolds' original is a pastiche of early Elvis. This version is taken at a faster pace, and with a more gravelly vocal. The song's not one of the greats, and Denton's not the world's best singer, so it's easy to see why this wasn't released.

Untitled Jam/Let's Live Before We Die (instrumental)

Songwriter: Brian Wilson

The "Untitled Jam" here seems to be a brief snatch of an attempt to record the old song "A Tisket A Tasket" in a similar style to the piano-led instrumentals on the *Surfer Girl* album. This is followed by a completed instrumental backing track which has much the same feel as "Keep an Eye on Summer" or "Why", and a middle eight that seems to owe a bit to "Graduation Day". The chord sequence is odd, and rather more complex than was normal for Brian's songwriting at the time, and it would be interesting to hear if a melody was ever written for it.

Christmas Eve

An instrumental track whose writer is unknown, but it sounds very much like Brian's work. This is a slow ballad in an orchestral arrangement by Dick Reynolds, recorded during the sessions for *The Beach Boys' Christmas Album*, and features rather Muzak-y jazz piano over Reynolds' usual lush strings.

Jingle Bells

Songwriter: James Lord Pierpoint

Another instrumental track arranged by Reynolds and recorded for *The Beach Boys' Christmas Album*, this is also dominated by jazz piano, but is a much more uptempo, big-band swing style arrangement which owes something to Count Basie. The liner notes to *Keep an Eye on Summer* suggest that this and the previous track may have been intended as easy listening seasonal instrumental tracks for the album, but that seems unlikely – this arrangement contains no statement of the melody, and indeed is unrecognisable as being "Jingle Bells" at all, though it's just about possible to see how the song's vocal line might fit the track.

The full tracklisting of the album is:

- Fun, Fun, Fun (session excerpt, followed by backing track)

- Fun, Fun, Fun (a capella)

- Fun, Fun, Fun (stereo mix)

- Why Do Fools Fall in Love (session excerpt, followed by backing track)

- Why Do Fools Fall In Love (new stereo mix)

- Don't Worry Baby (session excerpt, followed by backing track with background vocals)

- Don't Worry Baby (stereo mix)

- In the Parkin' Lot (session excerpt, followed by a capella version)

- Warmth of the Sun (session excerpt, followed by backing track with background vocals)

- Warmth of the Sun (stereo mix)

- Pom Pom Play Girl (session excerpt, followed by backing track with background vocals)

- Pom Pom Play Girl (new stereo mix)

- Denny's Drums (session excerpt, followed by alternate version)

- Keep an Eye on Summer (backing track with background vocals)

- Endless Sleep

- I Get Around (session excerpt, followed by backing track)

- I Get Around (a capella)

- All Summer Long (session excerpt, followed by backing track)

- All Summer Long (a capella)
- All Summer Long (stereo mix)
- Hushabye (backing track with background vocals)
- Girls on the Beach (session excerpt, followed by a capella version)
- Wendy (session excerpt, followed by a capella version)
- Don't Back Down (new stereo mix)
- Little Saint Nick (session excerpt, followed by Drive-In version)
- Untitled Jam / Let's Live Before We Die
- Little Honda (session excerpt, followed by new stereo mix)
- Little Honda (single version - previously unreleased)
- She Knows Me Too Well (backing track with background vocals)
- She Knows Me Too Well (a capella)
- Don't Hurt My Little Sister (session excerpt, followed by a capella version)
- Christmas Eve (session excerpt, followed by backing track)
- Jingle Bells (previously unreleased)
- When I Grow Up (a capella)
- Fun, Fun, Fun (live in the studio)
- I Get Around (live in the studio)
- I'm So Young (session excerpt, followed by new stereo mix of the 1964 version)
- All Dressed Up For School (session excerpt, followed by new stereo mix)
- Dance Dance Dance (Nashville version, new stereo mix)
- Dance, Dance, Dance (session excerpt, followed by backing track)

- Dance, Dance, Dance (a capella)
- I Get Around (live at the BBC)
- The Little Old Lady from Pasadena (live at the BBC)
- Graduation Day (live at the BBC)
- Surfin' USA (live at the BBC)
- Johnny B. Goode (Live)

No Pier Pressure

After the end of the 2012 reunion tour, the next couple of years saw a major realignment in the various parties within the Beach Boys organisations. Immediately after the end of the tour, Mike Love and Bruce Johnston went back to their touring band (at that time Scott Totten, Christian Love, Tim Bonhomme, Randell Kirsch, and John Cowsill), while Brian Wilson returned to his own band – but in 2013, a new tour was announced. On this one, Wilson and his band were supporting Jeff Beck (and would join Beck and his band for an encore merging both bands), but it wasn't Wilson alone – Al Jardine and David Marks also joined the band. And for a few dates so did Blondie Chaplin, who had been a member of the Beach Boys in the early 1970s.

Several social media posts were also made on accounts belonging to Jardine or Wilson, aimed at Love and Johnston, saying that they were ready to tour with them at any time. Jardine was quite insulting about Love in some interviews – and then suddenly changed his tune.

In early 2014, Love was given a prestigious award, the Ella Award, and invited several of his favourite singers to perform at the ceremony. Along with Love's own band, Bill Medley of the Righteous Brothers, and Micky Dolenz of the Monkees, both Jardine and Marks appeared, as did Jeffrey Foskett.

Shortly after this, it was announced that Foskett was leaving Wilson's band after fifteen years, and would be replacing Christian Love in the touring Beach Boys. Jardine and Marks were also announced as appearing with the touring Beach Boys for a special show at Jones Beach on the fifth of July – but only Marks appeared, with Jardine (and his son Matt) performing with Brian Wilson in the UK on the same day instead. Marks has continued to guest occasionally with the touring Beach Boys, but has never again performed live with Wilson's band. Jardine has become a permanent member of Wilson's band, as has Chaplin, and neither have performed since with the touring Beach Boys.

Matt Jardine replaced Foskett in Wilson's band for a few shows, before being replaced, supposedly permanently, by Brian Eichenberger, formerly of the Four Freshmen – who only played a handful of shows before going off to replace Kirsch in the touring Beach Boys. Matt Jardine replaced him permanently, but clearly in 2014-15 there was some manoeuvring between the different bands.

During much of this time, Wilson had been recording a new album, again written with Joe Thomas and recorded the same way as *That's Why God Made the Radio*, with a mixture of session musicians and Wilson's own band. Both Foskett and Matt Jardine featured on the recordings, as did Al Jardine, Chaplin, and Marks (on guitar only in the latter case), meaning this album is arguably a Beach Boys album by any other name (albeit one without the participation of Love or Johnston).

According to interviews during the recording, as much as three CDs' worth of material was recorded in some form or another for the album, including several instrumentals featuring Beck (who was scathing about Wilson's management in interviews after the conclusion of their joint tour, and who is not featured on the final album). The final album also features several guest vocalists, mostly popular young musicians who might be thought to give the album some commercial potential. (Though it doesn't feature Frank Ocean, who was planned to feature on the album until Wilson found out "He didn't want to sing. He wanted to do rap. He surprised us. We didn't know. He wanted to talk a rap talk on the track. We didn't like it, so we cancelled it.")

Unfortunately, it's easily Wilson's worst solo album and the most *mediocre* thing ever put out by the group, together or separately. The aural equivalent of wallpaper, it passes in one ear and out the other without ever troubling the brain, except on the all-too-frequent occasions when autotune-as-effect is used. This processing is used to an even greater extent than it had been on *That's Why God Made the Radio*, and to even worse effect, rendering several tracks unlistenable.

Joe Thomas apparently had less involvement in this album than in the previous one – according to several people who claim insider knowledge, he was more or less pushed out of the organisation by the time of the final mix of the album – but the album still sounds very like his co-productions with Wilson, and very unlike any recordings Wilson has made without him.

Some of this is, of course, down to songwriting choices – Thomas co-wrote all but one of the new original tracks on the album (Brian: "Joe? He brings interesting chord patterns and lyrics, and some melodies, I wrote most of the melodies but he wrote the chord patterns and a lot of the lyrics"[11]), and we once again see his unique ability to write lyrics that are compiled entirely from cliches but which don't ever say anything at

---

[11]Source: http://goo.gl/9CHzdq (Yahoo! interview)

all – but several of his production techniques (not just the autotune, but also the use of claves, hi-hat, and oboe, to give a few examples) seem to have remained from the previous album. If this is primarily a Brian WIlson production, he's learned a lot from Thomas, and not all for the good.

But having said that, Brian Wilson's name is on the album, and he has to take the final credit or blame. Too many fans either claim Brian is incapable of doing anything and is the puppet of other musicians on one hand, or on the other think that he would be producing another *Pet Sounds* every three minutes were it not for the terrible collaborators sullying his perfect genius. Neither is the case, as far as I'm aware.

So, in this review from this point on, I'll be treating Wilson as the auteur — relating things to his other work and in the context of his career. That's not meant to take credit away from Thomas, but I only know Thomas' work with Wilson anyway, and have no idea about how this album fits into Thomas' general body of work, which includes live albums by Kenny Chesney, Bon Jovi, and Stevie Nicks, and studio work with Peter Cetera and Toby Keith. (That said, if Thomas *is* responsible for the chord changes on the album, he really needs to learn some better ones – while I try to examine the songs musically in these essays, often these songs are built on three or four chords, usually with a truck-driver's gear-shift key change towards the end. I've been unable to say much about them, because there's nothing to say.)

*No Pier Pressur*e came in three different versions — a thirteen-track standard edition, a sixteen-track "deluxe", and an eighteen-track extra-deluxe one with two bonus tracks (a 2005 recording of "Love and Mercy" and a 1975 recording of "In the Back of My Mind"). This review is based on the eighteen-track version. "Don't Worry", "Somewhere Quiet", and "I'm Feeling Sad" don't appear on the thirteen-track version.

(All songs are by Brian Wilson and Joe Thomas, and all lead vocals by Brian Wilson, unless stated otherwise.)

This Beautiful Day

This is a promising opener. A simple, repetitive, song fragment (less than ninety seconds long), it starts with forty seconds of Brian singing solo over piano chords, in about the most natural voice he'll be in all album (his voice clearly cracks on the line "hold on to this feeling"), before turning into wordless vocals, while Paul von Mertens' string arrangement restates the melody of "Summer's Gone", providing a bridge to the previous album, while a trumpet plays answering phrases, before ending on a percolating synth.

There's not much song there, but it sets up a lovely atmosphere. Most of the credit there must go to von Mertens, who has been a secret weapon on all Wilson's music for the last decade or so. He's often (rightly) criticised for his sax playing being too loungey, but his string arrangements, with their vague hints of Bartok and their unflinching spareness, have been an element that was missing from Wilson's work for the first forty years. His arrangements throughout this album are, as always, exemplary.

Lyrically, meanwhile, this sets up one of the big themes of the album — trying to hold on to something slipping away, whether that be youth, life, love, or the Beach Boys' temporary reunion.

Runaway Dancer

Songwriters: Brian Wilson, Joe Thomas, Sebu Simonian

Lead vocals: Sebu Simonian with Brian Wilson

This is the polar opposite. Featuring Sebu, a member of Capital Cities (a young persons' skiffle group of some notoriety), who also co-wrote with Wilson and Thomas, musically this poor attempt at mid-tempo disco sounds like a Scissor Sisters B-side, but with added lounge sax.

Lyrically, it sets up the *other* kind of lyric we get on this album — the string of meaningless lines that sound vaguely like the kind of thing that 80s MOR acts thought was cool ("Yeah, she's been the talk of the town/She's walking round everywhere, looking for an answer/Someone caught her fooling around/Acting like she don't care, runaway dancer"). It's almost three times as long as the previous track, and has about a third of the musical interest, just hammering on its tedious chorus incessantly.

This got a lot of criticism from Beach Boys fandom for being an "EDM" track by which they seem to mean a currently popular style with a drum machine and synthesisers, but the problems with it aren't with it being EDM (it isn't, anyway), but rather with its lyrics (drivel), chord changes (unimaginative), and arrangement. With its processed vocals, fingerclicks, and lounge sax, this sounds like something Billy Joel might have done in 1983 imagining himself to be "New Wave".

Whatever Happened

This is a return to the sound of the first track, and a massive improvement. The chorus is a little too bombastic for my liking, but this is a decent attempt at making *Pet Sounds*-esque music. It also introduces a motif we'll be seeing a lot — a plucked, reverbed, trebly bass playing a descending melody much like that at the end of the chorus of "The Night

Was So Young". But what really makes this track worthwhile is the layering of vocal harmonies. Al Jardine doubles Brian at times and counters him at others, and the massed backing vocals sound like the Beach Boys for the first time on a record since at least 1996's *Stars & Stripes* album. The track doesn't break new ground, and is consciously looking back to Brian's glory days, but within the confines of what it's trying to do it does it well.

Even here though, the lyrics make absolutely no sense, the production is too clean, and the autotune on Al Jardine's voice is painfully apparent (and completely unnecessary). It's full of close-mic'd acoustic guitar and over-prominent cymbal work, and the basic song is pretty dire. But the vocals (including some of Brian's best on the album) more or less save it. David Marks guests on guitar.

On The Island

Lead vocals: Zooey Deschanel

This features She & Him, a duo consisting of the film star Zooey Deschanel on vocals and her collaborator M. Ward on guitar, and is absolutely lovely. It's a Jobim pastiche, a very good one. Deschanel sounds wonderful, almost like Peggy Lee. Some of the lyrics seem to be very Brian in their unnecessary details — specifying that the TV they bought is a colour one, for example — and while there's nothing very clever about the music, it's catchy as hell and pretty. The only downside is that Brian's "on the island" harmony line seems to have been cut and pasted over and over, rather than sung every time, which means that on the very last repetition, where he sings "'cause on the island", there's a jarring edit after "'cause". Other than that I can't find fault with this. Of all the tracks on the album, this is the only one I find myself wanting to return to two years on.

Half Moon Bay

Featuring Mark Isham on trumpet, this is a near-instrumental, just with wordless backing vocals, very much in the exotica/Jack Nitzsche style of previous instrumentals like "Diamond Head" or "Let's Go Away For A While". It's long on mood, short on actual melody, but it does set that mood very well. It also features a variant on that descending bass motif again. It's about a minute too long for my tastes, but perfectly listenable.

Our Special Love

Lead vocals: Peter Hollens and Brian Wilson

This is, frankly, horrible. According to Joe Thomas this started as a Tommy James & The Shondells pastiche, but Wilson decided he hated the instrumental track, which was too close to James' "Crystal Blue Persuasion". Instead the track was given to YouTube star Peter Hollens to turn into an *a capella* track.

The opening and closing sections, featuring layers of Wilson, Foskett, Chaplin and the Jardines, are pleasant enough if uninspired (and once again with unpleasant autotune). But then Hollens comes in with his beatboxing and lead vocals, and it starts to sound like "Title of the Song", the parody of bad boy-band songs by *a capella* group DaVinci's Notebook, but with more beatboxing. Beatboxing, for those who don't know, is someone making stupid "tsst" noises over and over, so if you listen with headphones it's like having someone spit down your ear.

Yet again, the lyrics are meaningless mouth noises, giving the impression of making sense until you examine them on a line-by-line basis and realise they're saying literally nothing.

It's not completely beyond redemption – the first thirty seconds are pleasant enough – but it's damned close to it.

The Right Time

Lead vocals: Al Jardine

This is essentially a rewrite of the earlier Wilson/Thomas song "Lay Down Burden", with a little of "Night Time" thrown in. An underwritten verse leads to an over-repeated chorus, and there are the usual gibberish lyrics, but the track is inoffensive enough and Jardine does a great vocal, although the autotune is a bit ham-handedly applied here (most noticeably on the word "never" in the first verse).

If more attention had been paid to writing a workable verse, and the autotune had been left off, this could have been a highlight of the album. As it is, it's. . . adequate.

David Marks guests on guitar.

Guess You Had To Be There

Lead vocals: Kacey Musgraves with Brian Wilson

Songwriters: Brian Wilson, Joe Thomas, Kacey Musgraves, and Andrew Saldago

This is a bouncy country-swing-sunshine-pop song in the vein of "California Girls" or "California Saga", with some nice banjo, presumably by Probyn Gregory (the banjo isn't credited on the album).

The lyrics, apparently rewritten by Musgraves, have been said to be inspired by Wilson recollecting the 1960s, and for the first time since "On The Island" are actually coherent.

This is simple, but one of the catchier things on the record. It's let down by the *astonishingly* bad autotuning on Musgraves' vocals (she sounds like a robot singing underwater) and a bad rawk guitar solo, but if you can get past that there's something enjoyable here.

Don't Worry

This is one of the songs that only appears on the deluxe version of the album, and received a huge amount of criticism from fans, largely because of the use of synth horns.

In fact, as a genre exercise in late-70s disco rock it's much better than "Runaway Dancer". That may not be saying much, but it's still definitely true. It's outside Wilson's usual songwriting range, but not so far out as to be unlistenable – there's a little of "Darlin'" in the song's feel, and an obvious nod to "Don't Worry Baby". It's all a bit ELO, but there are worse things to be.

Somewhere Quiet

Lead vocals: Brian WIlson and Al Jardine

Songwriters: Scott Bennett and Brian Wilson

Another mid-album bonus track, this is the 1965 Beach Boys instrumental "Summer Means New Love", re-recorded and given new lyrics by Scott Bennett. The lyrics are hamstrung by having to write to a pre-existing melody not designed for vocals (thus leading to some odd scansion at points), but Al Jardine does an excellent job on the middle-eight vocal. The original melody was already slightly old-fashioned fifty years ago, but with the addition of lyrics it becomes more classic than old-fashioned. While it's patterned after 50s pop ballads, with its 6/8 time signature, you could imagine someone like Nat "King" Cole or Tony Bennett singing this, and it fitting right in with the great American songbook material.

Once again, though, the autotune on Jardine's voice, particularly on the high note on "imagine", wrecks a lot of otherwise good work, and fundamentally the song didn't really need lyrics at all.

I'm Feeling Sad

Lead vocals: Brian WIlson and Jeffrey Foskett

This is the last of the deluxe-only tracks, and is just lovely — an uptempo, bouncy, duet with Foskett, with slice-of-life lyrics that could have come off *Friends*, this is musically somewhere between Paul Williams or Burt Bacharach on one side and bands like the BMX Bandits on the other — a fragile, beautiful, piece of bouncy pop.

Harmonically it's simplistic, but it has one of the catchiest melodies on the album, spirited vocals from Wilson and Foskett, lyrics that actually make sense, and vocal processing that's not so obtrusive as to spoil it. And the contrast between the joyous music and the depressed lyrics provides something like the contrast between the sentiments in "Til I Die" and the "hey hey hey" vocals at the end of that song's verses.

Genuinely enjoyable.

Tell Me Why

Lead vocals: Brian Wilson and Al Jardine

is a return to the ersatz *Pet Sounds* of "Whatever Happened", and again features a great vocal by Jardine on the middle eight, but is a blander song than that one — it's the only song on the album that doesn't have anything in it at all memorable.

I must have played this album thirty or so times, and yet I can still never remember anything about this song when it's not actually playing.

It's not unpleasant when it's playing – Jardine really does sing the hell out of his part, even though it's far too bombastic for my tastes – but there's no substance here.

Sail Away

Songwriters: Brian Wilson, Joe Thomas, Jim Peterik, and Larry Millas

Lead vocals: Blondie Chaplin, Al Jardine, and Brian Wilson

This shares its title both with the title track of Wilson's favourite Randy Newman album, and with a song Wilson performed on Van Dyke Parks' *Orange Crate Art* album. However, this track has more in common with the similarly named track by Styx. This could be by any of those bands — Styx, Journey, Foreigner, Survivor, Toto — who only had one hit each in Britain but were apparently ubiquitous in the US thirty years ago.

This seems to be attempting to evoke past glories – reusing the flute riff from "Sloop John B", and clearly referencing "Sail On Sailor" – but musically it's dull, slodgy, yacht-rock with no redeeming features as a song (though I have to admit I'm in a minority here – most fans seem to think this the standout track of the album).

Chaplin, Jardine, and Wilson all turn in strong vocals. I just wish it was for a song worthy of those vocals.

One Kind of Love

Songwriters: Brian Wilson and Scott Bennett

The new only song on the album written without Thomas, this sounds very like the big ballads on *That Lucky Old Sun* – it's definitely got a flavour of "Midnight's Another Day" or "Southern California", although the chorus is a little more bombastic than either of those.

Like "Somewhere Quiet", this has a melody that's not very singable, and the scansion of the lyrics sometimes doesn't really work, but it's one of the stronger songs on the album, and the breakdown where multiple Brians sing in counterpoint over bass and a horn is lovely, one of the finest moments on the album.

Much of the effect comes from von Mertens' string and horn parts,, and the song is notably less effective when performed live (it's the only song from the album that survived in Wilson's setlists for even a year). The tempo change between verse and chorus makes it difficult to play accurately live, but the lack of the orchestral arrangement exposes the song's fundamental flaws in a way the record doesn't.

Saturday Night

Songwriters: Brian Wilson, Joe Thomas, and Nate Reuss

Lead vocals: Nate Reuss and Brian Wilson

This song, written by Wilson and Thomas with Nate Reuss of the annoyingly-uncapitalised band fun, who sings lead, is another song straight out of 80s US radio — this time sounding like the kind of thing Kenny Loggins or Huey Lewis would write for a teen film starring Michael J. Fox, right down to a line about "playing our music too loud". There are some good arrangement touches — the banjo part (again presumably played by Probyn) is very pleasant — but this is uninspired, dull, hackwork.

The lyrics are back to being gibberish, the music is dull... this fits, exactly, the pattern of almost every Thomas co-write here, with their simplistic chord changes and pointless key changes. Dreadful.

The Last Song

This serves much the same purpose as "Summer's Gone" did on the last album — a calculated attempt to tug at the heartstrings, with the Spector kitchen sink turned up to twelve (to mix several metaphors horribly) in an attempt to disguise the lack of song.

It works slightly better than "Summer's Gone", in that there's an actual melody and some dynamic changes (though again the dynamics on this song just consist of going loud and bombastic), but it's utterly substanceless. Wilson takes most of the lead vocal, but someone else sings the high "la la la" part – it doesn't sound like Matt Jardine or Foskett, and annoyingly there are no individual credits for tracks, so my guess is that it's one of Thom Griffin or Jimmy Riley, the two session singers who are credited with additional backing vocals on the album.

In The Back of My Mind

Songwriters: Brian Wilson and Mike Love

A 1975 piano-and-vocals demo of the song which first appeared ten years earlier, on *The Beach Boys Today!*

Here Brian, in his croaky mid-seventies voice, plays through the song (including a new middle eight replacing the old one). There's more heart, musicianship, and genuine spirit in this two-and-a-half-minute busk-through of a song, with occasional off-key vocals and stumbled-over words, than in the entire rest of the album.

Love and Mercy

A recording from 2005, originally released as a medley with another song, "Walking Down The Path of Life". This is a studio recording of the arrangement Brian and his band perform live, and other than a tiny bit of double-tracking on Brian's vocal toward the end and an additional organ pad in the last verse this is exactly how the live recordings of it sound.

Overall, *No Pier Pressure* feels like the result of several different, conflicting, ambitions — to make something "adult contemporary", to make something vaguely arty that sounds a bit like *Pet Sounds*, to make something that sounds like contemporary pop radio, and to just make another Brian Wilson album of nice songs – but without the material to fulfil even one of those ambitions adequately. One could pull together an eight- to ten-track short album from this that would be much more acceptable, and could even have been good if the autotune-as-effect had not been so overused, but given that the bonus tracks are among the best things on the album, it's unlikely that whoever made the final sequencing decisions would have made the right choices when putting one together.

As it is, it's an album that receives a vigorous defence from some quarters, but always couched in terms of "supporting Brian". On its musical merits, it's not even interestingly bad.

Brian Wilson and Friends

To promote *No Pier Pressure,* Brian appeared in a PBS TV special, a live concert recording from December 2014 featuring his normal band line-up at that point (and including, for once, both Matt Jardine and Brian Eichenberger), with Al Jardine now essentially Brian's co-frontman and Blondie Chaplin joining for several songs. They were also joined by many of the guest stars who appeared on the album, and on several songs by Billy Hinsche (who would later tour with Brian's band in 2016, substituting for Darian Sahanaja, who couldn't make that tour) and Ricky Fataar.

This was initially released as a DVD-plus-BluRay package, but later reissued as a DVD-plus-audio-CD version – the audio CD cut out the songs with guest vocals, but added live versions of "California Saga" and "California Girls".

As the CD is unobtainable except with the DVD, and contains largely the same performances, I'll primarily be discussing this as a DVD rather than as a CD – and to be honest, it works better as a visual document than as a live CD.

A live DVD from this band is always welcome, of course, but there's a credit which strikes fear into the hearts of many: "produced and directed by Joe Thomas". But that fear is, surprisingly, misplaced. While I won't say there's no autotune on here for certain, what I will say is that at no point do we get the robo-voice effect that wrecks much of *No Pier Pressure, That's Why God Made the Radio,* and *Live: The 50th Anniversary Tour.* The vocal mix is much wetter than I would prefer, and there's clearly been some touching up done in the studio, but many of the vocals are definitely as live — with missed words, swallowed syllables, sloshed sibilants and all. Errors are hidden with strategic doubling and a lot of reverb, rather than by whacking so much autotune on that everyone sounds like a robot. Fundamentally, what this DVD sounds like is what you'd get if you saw this band when Brian was on a very good night but the sound engineer was a little too reverb-happy, rather than the clinical mess one might fear.

That's only my opinion, and I don't have the world's greatest ears for studio effects. But if the *50th Anniversary Tour* CD is a ten in over-autotuning, and *No Pier Pressure* is about a six, this would be at most a two or three. Certainly there appears to have been an attempt here to use autotune transparently rather than as a deliberate effect.

The show opens with a gorgeous version of **Our Prayer**, mixed with every individual voice audible, and sounding lovely, before going straight into **Heroes & Villains** with the cantina section in place. Whoever's singing the high harmony on the "dance Margarita" section does a won-derful camp vibrato on it and the whole thing sounds great, although Brian swallows a couple of syllables. It's amazing how adding Al Jardine to the harmony stack makes the band sound like the Beach Boys.

That's even more true of **Sloop John B**, where Al and Brian duet (although this is the first of a few songs where the video cuts to a long shot of Brian in a couple of places precisely when the timbre of his vocal changes and becomes more reverby, which makes the punch-ins rather obvious). But when you hear Al and Brian together, with no other voices, on "hoist up the John B sails", for all that Brian's voice has changed dramatically in the last fifty years, it still sounds like the Beach Boys.

Dance Dance Dance has never been a favourite of mine, but it does give Eichenberger a chance to shine on the choruses, and Probyn Gregory the first of several excellent guitar solos.

Good Vibrations seems to be filmed to show the people who've made fun of Al for his guitar not being in the mix that he can play — on the DVD there are a lot of shots of his fingers as he plays the guitar motif in the verses. This sounds to me like it may have been edited from two performances — there's a sudden change in the sound halfway through the first chorus that may just be a bit of sloppy mixing, but which may have been an edit. In general this seems to be one of the least "live" tracks, unless there really were multiple Al Jardines on stage at the same time.

This Beautiful Day features trumpeter Mark Isham, but also clearly has the studio vocal take, with multi-tracked autotuned Brians, used rather than a live one (the song's really out of Brian's current vocal range, so this is unsurprising). It's a nice little song though.

Runaway Dancer sounds more or less identical to the studio version, and again seems to have had a lot of tweaking. It features Sebu on lead vocals, as the studio version does. Not a highlight.

Sebu also takes lead on **Don't Worry Baby** and does a very creditable job, although his style is a little melismatic for my personal taste. The track has also been very slightly rearranged, with a little keyboard figure I don't think suits it, but it's always a great song, and I can't help but warm to Sebu when he does Mike Love-esque driving movements on the line "she makes me want to drive".

At this point, the show becomes the early-70s Beach Boys, with Al Jardine (who had been absent from the stage for Sebu's songs) returning and introducing Blondie Chaplin, Ricky Fataar, and Billy Hinsche.

We get a very good version of **Marcella**, although Brian's still a little too polite a vocalist for this one, which might have been better sung by Chaplin, but the cascading, overlapping vocal lines from the band are fantastic. Probyn also proves here that an often-made criticism of this band is false — people sometimes say that they're a little too staid and can't do rock. Probyn's solo at the end shows that they *can* do loud rock solos (which are generally far, far easier than the other stuff they pull off), they just know when it's not appropriate.

Wild Honey features Chaplin on lead, and he forgets huge chunks of the lyric, just yelling random bits that he remembers along with non-lyrical mouth noises, while pulling eye-popping faces and looking like the even-more-raddled love-child of Keith Richards and Lou Reed. This makes it the best thing on the DVD by a long way.

Sail On Sailor also features Chaplin on vocals, this time giving a much more restrained, quite beautiful, vocal performance. And with Brian Wilson, Al Jardine, and Billy Hinsche in the backing vocal stack, this sounds like the Beach Boys. This might be the best live version of the song I've heard.

Even Chaplin and Jardine can't save the overblown yacht-rock that is **Sail Away**, though. It sounds just like it does on the record, and that's a bad thing.

Mark Isham then returns (and the other guests leave) for **Half Moon Bay**, which allows the band to demonstrate their ability to play delicate, expressive music beautifully. Something like this, which is all about the empty spaces, is much more difficult to get right than a stompy rock track like "Marcella", but the band pull it off perfectly.

An instrumental take on **Don't Talk (Put Your Head On My Shoulder)** follows, with Isham playing the vocal melody on the trumpet. This sounds utterly lovely — "Don't Talk" may be Brian's very best melody as pure melody — but the song does rather miss something without its lyrics.

Nate Reuss comes on for **Saturday Night**, which sounds just like it does on the record (forgettable), before bringing Blondie and Ricky back on for a version of **Hold On Dear Brother**, their song from the *Carl & The Passions (So Tough)* album, which shows that Reuss can *really* sing — his performance is quite astonishing, as is Probyn Gregory's. Probyn manages to reproduce Red Rhodes' slide guitar solo from the record on a normal guitar, and the whole song is a lovely addition to the set, and must have been jaw-dropping live.

Reuss also sings lead on **Darlin'**, where he's merely competent rather than astonishing. Following this, the DVD cuts away to two studio tracks with She & Him. **On The Island** is the track from the album but with a different lead vocal take and with some but not all of the backing vocal parts stripped out, and works very well, but **God Only Knows** is a bit of a disaster — Deschanel sings it very nicely, and while Ward's guitar is the only accompaniment it works well, but then a truly horrible clodhopping one-man-band style drum part comes in and it wrecks it.

The DVD then returns to the live show for **The Right Time**. This works slightly better as a live track than on the record, with the harmonies sounding lovely and Al Jardine sounding even better in his seventies than he did in his twenties, and the band sounding more organic than the sterile studio version.

Wouldn't It Be Nice follows, with Al again on lead. He's either double-tracked or being partially doubled by Matt Jardine (who sounds very similar to his dad) here, but sounds astonishing (Brian is *definitely* double-tracked on the middle eight). How Al Jardine can still sound so good at his age, I can't imagine. And obviously the song itself is a masterpiece.

We then get a run-through of a few of the hits — Al singing lead again on **Help Me Rhonda** (performed in the studio arrangement, rather than the old touring band arrangement). Bob Lizik's bass playing is particularly good here; very loose and springy-sounding, just right for this song.

All Summer Long follows, with Brian back on lead, and the show proper ends with an all-hands performance of **Fun Fun Fun**, with Brian sounding a little tired and missing a couple of words, but getting by on the energy of the track (and Al doubling him on the last couple of verses to keep him going). The studio version of Guess You Had To Be There plays over the credits, with an interview with Kacey Musgraves, and there are two bonus tracks (**Pacific Coast Highway** and **Summer's Gone**) that really should have been included in the main feature.

Overall, this isn't the best possible representation of this band — it's a little too clean, a little too sterile, to get across just how good they really are — but it's a lot better than we had any right to expect, both in choice of songs and in how (comparatively) little it's been messed with in the studio. If you go and see this band live, you'll see something very close to this.

The CD tracklist is:

- **Our Prayer**

- Heroes and Villains
- Sloop John B
- Dance, Dance, Dance
- Good Vibrations
- This Beautiful Day
- Marcella
- Wild Honey
- Sail On Sailor
- Sail Away
- Half Moon Bay
- Don't Talk
- The Right Time
- Wouldn't It Be Nice
- Help Me Rhonda
- Fun, Fun, Fun
- California Girls
- California Saga
- All Summer Long

Beach Boys' Party! Uncovered and Unplugged

2015 brought two copyright-extension releases, and one of them was, for the first time, an actual CD release. This double-CD release contained a new version of the *Beach Boys Party!* album, without the party overdubs that were added to the original version, along with a CD and a half of session recordings.

There is not actually much of interest on here – the remixed, *sans* overdubs, album itself is interesting to listen to once or twice, but while the odd track is improved by being able to hear it without the background noise, more often the sparse sterility is unforgiving to the general sloppy air of many of the performances.

The session recordings, on the other hand, are more interesting, especially for the way that Carl as much as Brian is running things – while Brian was in charge in the studio, Carl was clearly the musical director on stage and the band are taking direction from him a lot of the time.

On the whole though this set is the least interesting of the various copyright-extension sets, and the one most people will return to least often.

However, it does contain performances of a number of songs which don't appear elsewhere (as well as more takes on songs that do, and run-throughs of songs like "California Girls")...

(I Can't Get No) Satisfaction

Songwriters: Mick Jagger and Keith Richards

Lead vocals: Group

Two versions of the Rolling Stones' then-recent hit are included, one of them with some perfunctory blues harmonica (presumably by Billy Hinsche). Both songs have unison lead vocals by (at least) Brian, Carl, and Al, with Carl and Al both showing the bluesier sides to their vocals that would show up a couple of years later on the *Wild Honey* album.

Blowin' in the Wind

Songwriter: Bob Dylan

Lead vocals: Al Jardine

Opening with some rather lovely twelve-string guitar chords playing an unrelated song, this is a very nice version of the Dylan classic, with Carl and Al both playing simple interlocking folk-style finger-picked parts while Al sings the song entirely straight. It's utterly unlike the bulk of the Beach Boys' music, but shows that Al could have had the folk music career he seemed, early on, to want.

She Belongs To Me/The Artist (Laugh At Me)

Songwriters: Bob Dylan/Sonny Bono

Lead vocals: Mike Love

A few bars of the Dylan song break down very quickly, and instead the band launch into a parody of Sonny Bono's hit "Laugh at Me", with comedy lyrics ("Why do you/smell like a city zoo?/Maybe it's because you just don't bathe") that had clearly been worked out before, as various band members join in on some of the lyrics.

Hang on Sloopy/Twist and Shout/You've Lost That Lovin' Feelin'

Songwriters: Wes Farrell and Bert Berns/Bert Berns/Phil Spector, Barry Mann, Cynthia Weil

Lead vocals: Group

Forty seconds of messing round, singing the listed songs over the three-chord pattern they all share.

Riot in Cell Block #9

Songwriters: Jerry Leiber and Mike Stoller

Lead vocals: Mike Love

Two run-throughs of the Leiber/Stoller classic comedy blues, a big hit for the Robins in 1954. The first take is sloppy and not particularly good, but the second version has some really rather good lead vocals from Mike, and it's clearly a song he loved (he would of course later remake it as "Student Demonstration Time" a few years later).

The Diary

Songwriters: Neil Sedaka and Howard Greenfield

Lead vocals: Bruce Johnston

A few seconds of messing about, with Bruce sing Neil Sedaka's 1958 hit. Unfortunately, this ends with him singing "when it's late at night/make sure that she's white", which is a joke one would have expected to be cut for this release...

Ticket To Ride

Songwriters: John Lennon and Paul McCartney

Lead vocals: Group

A couple of sloppy run-throughs of the Beatles' hit, mostly without lyrics, and interesting mostly for the way the guitar riff resembles that of "Sloop John B" at times.

One Kiss Led to Another

Songwriters: Jerry Leiber and Mike Stoller

Lead vocals: Mike Love

Another storytelling Leiber/Stoller R&B song (this time written for the Coasters, a group formed by members of the Robins), and again Mike sounds hugely comfortable with this material. It's not a performance of the complete song – they give up after a couple of verses – but it's a fun take on a fun song while it lasts.

Heart and Soul/Long Tall Sally/The Boy From New York City

Songwriters: Hoagy Carmichael and Frank Loesser/Robert "Bumps" Blackwell, Enotris Johnson, and Richard Penniman/George Davis and John T. Taylor

Fragments, none more than a few seconds and none of them proper attempts at performance.

Smokey Joe's Cafe

Songwriters: Jerry Leiber and Mike Stoller

Lead vocals: Mike Love

Another Robins song, another excellent performance by Love, although again sadly the performance stutters to a stop halfway through.

Live in Chicago 1965

The second copyright-extension release from 2015, and the last album we will be dealing with in this book, was a digital-only release of two shows (plus rehearsal run-throughs of four songs) recorded at the Arie Crown Theater, Chicago, on March 26 and 27, 1965. While Brian had already left the touring group at this point, it was so recently that Bruce Johnston had not yet replaced Glen Campbell in the band, and as they were recording these shows for a live album Brian rejoined, replacing Glen.

Thus this is the last recording by the original line-up of the Beach Boys, without Bruce, while they were still a regular touring unit playing a normal show (the only later recordings of just the original five members playing live were the 1967 Hawaii shows, where Brian replaced Bruce and radically rearranged the material in the style of *Smiley Smile*).

As this was recorded only a few months after the Sacramento shows, it's perhaps not surprising that the performances are very similar in quality. These are rough recordings, with Brian forgetting the lyrics to "Don't Worry Baby" and Dennis' vocal mic not working on "Do You Wanna Dance" for the first show.

But much of what was said in the essay for *Live in Sacramento* applies here too, and with an added poignancy. This is the very last moment in which the Beach Boys were the same band both on and off stage – the last time when they were a band of five people, rather than a five-man (or more) touring band and a studio-bound producer/songwriter/vocalist. You get to hear Brian sing "Please Let Me Wonder" and "Don't Worry Baby" live in his young, undamaged, voice, and that's worth the purchase price in itself.

This is a 1960s live recording, with all that that entails, but it's worth it as a historical document of the ending of something very special, and the beginning of something else.

The two shows were largely identical in song selections (though not in order), with show two having two more songs. The songs performed were:

- **Do You Wanna Dance**

- Hawaii
- Please Let Me Wonder
- Surfer Girl
- Runaway
- Louie Louie
- Fun Fun Fun
- 409 (second show only)
- Shut Down
- Monster Mash
- Surfin' U.S.A.
- Little Honda
- Wendy
- In My Room (second show only)
- Don't Worry Baby
- I Get Around
- Johnny B. Goode
- Papa-Oom-Mow-Mow

Non-Album Tracks

Over the years, the Beach Boys have recorded and released a handful of tracks that were only available as singles, on various-artist compilations, or as tracks on otherwise-uninteresting greatest hits collections. Most of those tracks are not very good, but for completeness' sake I'll cover them here. The list below is of any track released as by the Beach Boys or a single band member credited solo, where that song has not been covered in any of this book series, so it doesn't cover, for example, Mike Love's duets with Dean Torrence, but does cover his solo recordings.

(You'll Never Be) Alone on Christmas Day

Songwriters: Mike Love and Ron Altbach

Lead vocals: Mike Love

This song was originally written and recorded for the unreleased 1977 Christmas album, but for some reason it was not included on *Ultimate Christmas*, which is a shame as while it's no masterpiece it's better than much of what *was* included on that album.

However, in 2015 the band Phoenix recorded a version of the song for the Netflix Christmas special *A Very Murray Christmas*, featuring Bill Murray, and Love decided, having been reminded of the song, to record his own new solo version and release it as a digital single.

It's a very nice arrangement – a very competent Spector pastiche by producer Michael Lloyd – and Jeffrey Foskett adds some very nice falsetto, but the track is hamstrung by having so much autotune applied to Love's lead vocals that it makes *No Pier Pressure* sound warm and human in comparison. Love's lead vocal (which sounds like a good performance otherwise) is completely wrecked by this production choice, rendering the track unlistenable.

Back in the USSR

Songwriters: John Lennon and Paul McCartney

Lead vocals: Mike Love and Jeffrey Foskett

A live recording from July 4, 1985, featuring Ringo Starr (the only Beatle not to appear on the Beatles' studio version) on drums, this is a song which Mike Love often claims in interviews to have helped Paul McCartney write. The band stick closely to the Beatles' arrangement, and Love and Foskett sing a unison lead, with Bruce taking the falsetto. This was released on *Fourth of July: A Rockin' Celebration of America,* a various-artists collection, to benefit Love's own Love Foundation charity. That collection also featured Love's solo "Happy Birthday America" (see below), and live performances by the Beach Boys with special guests – "Come Go With Me" with the Oak Ridge Boys, "Surfer Girl" with Julio Iglesias, and "Barbara Ann" with Jimmy Page.

Barbie

Songwriter: Bruce Morgan

Lead vocal: Brian Wilson

This track was actually performed by "Kenny and the Cadets", a studio-only group consisting of Brian, Carl, Al, the Wilsons' mother Audree, and Val Poliuto, formerly of doo-wop group The Jaguars. This group recorded for two songs for Hite and Dorinda Morgan, the owners of Candix Records, which were released as an unsuccessful single but have later been released under the Beach Boys' name on various compilations of their pre-Capitol recordings (most recently *Becoming the Beach Boys: The Complete Hite and Dorinda Morgan Sessions*, which is the best source for those tracks).

"Barbie" itself is a rather poor love ballad, written by Dorinda Morgan but credited to her son Bruce, and inspired by the doll, which was made in Hawthorne, the Beach Boys' home town. Brian takes a decent falsetto lead, but it's not the band's greatest work.

Barbie (Living Doll)

Songwriter: Brian Wilson †

Lead vocal: Brian Wilson

And some thirty-five years later, Brian was once again singing about Barbie. This time it was for a recording (credited to the Beach Boys, but only audibly featuring Brian) to be included on a flexi-disc with the then-new California Dream Barbie.

The track has the synth-heavy, abrasive, sound of much of Brian's mid-eighties work with Gary Usher, and is a fun enough but ultimately disposable track whose main point of musical interest is a key change up a major third for the middle eight. Brian also recorded this song with different, better lyrics under the title "Christine", but that recording is still not legitimately available.

Beach Boys Stomp

Songwriter: Carl Wilson

An utterly generic surf instrumental, also known by the title "Karate" because the band shout that out during the song, recorded during the Morgan sessions.

Believe in Yourself

Songwriter: Brian Wilson

Lead vocal: Brian Wilson

A Brian solo track, very much in the style of some of his mid-eighties work, recorded around the time of the *Gettin' in Over My Head* sessions and used in an episode of the cartoon series *Duck Dodgers in the 24$\frac{1}{2}$th Century*, in which Brian guests to teach Daffy Duck to believe in himself while surfing.

The song is catchy enough, but stretches about ninety seconds of musical material to three minutes, while the lyrics are the standard "have faith in yourself and you will be OK" you'd expect for a song written for a kids' cartoon. The vocal is better than much of his work on *Gettin' in Over My Head*, there's a nice honking baritone sax and a wall-of-Brians on backing vocals, and the result, while not a masterpiece by any means, is perfectly serviceable in the context of the cartoon it was used in. It's since been released on a various-artists CD that came free with an issue of Beach Boys fanzine *Endless Summer Quarterly*.

California Sun

Songwriter: Henry Glover

Lead vocals: Brian Wilson

A remake of the Rivieras' hit, this is pretty much a note-for-note cover of their arrangement, apart from a new middle section (presumably Brian's work) – "sunshine, sunshine, California sun". This was recorded for the soundtrack of the film *Curious George 2*, and while it's an energetic enough performance it doesn't really add anything to the original.

Chasin' the Sky

Songwriter: Randy Bishop

Lead vocals: Carl Wilson

The Beach Boys' first recording after Dennis' death was for this 1984 track, recorded for the soundtrack of *Up The Creek*, an undistinguished *Animal House* rip-off. It sounds exactly like you'd expect a song from a 1980s teen comedy to sound, right down to the bad synths, rawk guitar, and rhyming "crazy" with "lady".

Country Feelin's

Songwriter: Brian Wilson*

Lead vocals: Brian Wilson

A Brian solo track from the *Sweet Insanity* period, released on the Disney charity album *For Our Children*, this features cartoon voice actor Jim Cummings providing animal noises in a similar fashion to "Barnyard". It's not a particularly spectacular track, but is fun enough and doesn't outstay its welcome.

Crocodile Rock

Songwriters: Elton John and Bernie Taupin

Lead vocals: Al Jardine and Carl Wilson

Recorded for the 1991 tribute album *Two Rooms: Celebrating the Songs of Elton John and Bernie Taupin*, this is almost exactly what you'd think an early-nineties Beach Boys take on this song would sound like. A karaoke-style backing track, with "crocodile, rock a while, crocodile rock" backing vocals, is redeemed by an incredibly strong, powerful vocal from Al, who sounds like singing this song is the most important thing in the world to him. Carl phones in his performance on the last verse but is still Carl Wilson, so the whole thing is listenable overall even if not exactly a highlight of the band's career.

Daddy's Little Girl

Songwriter: Brian Wilson*

Lead vocals: Brian Wilson

Recorded for the film *She's Out of Control* (a film starring Tony Danza, and Micky Dolenz's daughter Ami, which Roger Ebert gave zero stars), this is loosely rewritten from the *Smile* track "Look/Song For Children", but instead of musical subtlety has synths, the most out-of-tune falsetto that Brian ever committed to vinyl, and lyrics about how "daddy's little girl is all grown up" and "she's a fox and a real cutie" (this is, to be fair, the subject of the film, which is entirely about a man's disgust with his own daughter's sexual attractiveness). A track that makes one cringe in multiple different ways.

East Meets West

Songwriters Bob Crewe and Bob Gaudio

Lead vocals: Mike, Carl, Al, Brian, and Frankie Valli

A collaboration with Frankie Valli and the Four Seasons, this track has possibly the most accidentally unfortunate lyric on a Beach Boys record ever – the Beach Boys' vocal contributions, including Brian singing over and over on the tag "two different drummers playing side by side/You know the best of them will survive", were recorded literally days before Dennis Wilson's death.

Somehow the single saw release, with that line intact, anyway. It sank without a trace, though, as it's simply not very good: lyrics contrasting "nights in Hollywood" with "lights on Broadway", and the kind of cheap, tacky production we find on so many of these eighties and early-nineties oddities.

Goodnight Irene

Songwriter: Huddie Ledbetter

Lead vocals: Brian Wilson

A solo Brian version of the Leadbelly classic, recorded around the same time as his first solo album for the 1988 Woody Guthrie/Leadbelly tribute album *Folkways: A Vision Shared*.

Recorded with Andy Paley, this is sonically very close to the better parts of *Brian Wilson*, and has a nice Spectoresque quality to it, with a great sense of dynamics in the instrumental arrangement. It's a combination of song and singer which you wouldn't expect to work, especially with it being taken as a mid-tempo pop song rather than the ballad one might expect, but it really *does* work.

(Also it's nice to hear Brian singing the proper lyric, "I get you in my dreams", rather than the bowdlerised "I'll see you in my dreams").

Happy Birthday America

Songwriters: Gary Griffin and Tom Mather

Lead vocals: Mike Love

A Mike solo studio track added to the otherwise-live *Fourth of July A Rockin' Celebration of America* album, this is a piece of synth-heavy mid-eighties schlock with a particularly nasal Mike vocal. As a non-American, I'm not exactly the target audience for a song about how wonderful America is, but this is no "This Land is Your Land", and frankly it's not even up to the standard of Neil Diamond's "Coming to America", which seems to be more the kind of thing this is aiming for. I'd defy anyone not to cringe as the samples of Kennedy saying "ask not what your country", King's "I have a dream", and Neil Armstrong's "just one small step" come in towards the end.

Happy Endings

Songwriters: Bruce Johnston and Terry Melcher

Lead vocals: Little Richard, Carl Wilson, Mike Love, and Al Jardine

The combination of Little Richard with the Beach Boys could theoretically have been an interesting one but unfortunately they chose to perform what is possibly the least suited song ever for Little Richard's vocal style – a ballad very much in the style of Bruce's solo album *Going Public*, but with the electric piano sound now updated to *synth* electric piano, because this is the eighties. In fact, the middle eight at least comes from around the same time as *Going Public*, as it's lifted from a song Bruce co-wrote with Curt Boettcher around that time (a seven-minute-long electric-piano ballad tribute to the Marx Brothers titled "Brand New Old Friends").

Little Richard does his best with his sections, but the song does nothing to help him. The track was recorded for the soundtrack of *The Telephone* (a legendarily strange film, almost a completely solo performance by Whoopi Goldberg, with a script by Harry Nilsson and Terry Southern), and released unsuccessfully as a single.

Have Yourself a Merry Little Christmas

Songwriters: Hugh Martin and Ralph Blane

Lead vocals: Mike Love

This 1983 recording was for a TV movie called *Scrooge's Rock and Roll Christmas*, which featured (as "magic snow globe singers") Mike, Dean Torrence, Paul Revere and the Raiders, and The Association. A soundtrack album came out, first on Hitbound Records and later on Radio Shack's own label, to be given away as in-store premiums, under the title *Christmas Party*.

Love duets with Dean Torrence on a handful of tracks, but this is his only solo performance. It sounds better than one would expect given that it's a 1983 recording of Mike Love singing "Have Yourself a Merry Little Christmas", and is perfectly acceptable background music, although Love loses points for singing the more saccharine "hang a shining star upon the highest bough" rather than the original lyric "until then we'll have to muddle on somehow".

Hungry Heart

Songwriter: Bruce Springsteen

Lead vocals: Mike Love

Having written "Getcha Back" as an obvious homage to Springsteen's classic "Hungry Heart" (itself an equally obvious homage to the Beach Boys themselves) it made sense for Mike Love to record this solo version for a 2001 Bruce Springsteen tribute album (the imaginatively-titled *A Tribute to Bruce Springsteen: Made in the U.S.A.*).

The backing track is a fairly accurate recreation of Springsteen's original, and the vocals (by Love and various members of the then-current touring Beach Boys, plus John Stamos) are all fine, although Love's lead vocal hardly measures up to Springsteen.

Judy

Songwriter: Brian Wilson

Lead vocals: Brian Wilson

A simple twelve-bar in a style vaguely similar to Jan and Dean's early records, this is one of Brian's earliest songs, and was recorded during the Morgan sessions. Unfortunately, the performance barely even rises to demo level.

Karen

Songwriter: Jack Marshall

Lead vocals: Mike Love

A forty-second theme song for a 1964 NBC-TV sitcom, this is a standard US TV theme song of that era ("she's alarming but disarming and a really very charming modern girl"), but recorded in an upbeat surf style (with a very brief quote of Dick Dale's guitar part from "Misirlou" to open it).

Lady Liberty

Songwriters: Al Jardine and Ron Altbach

Lead vocals: Al Jardine and Carl Wilson

A partial re-recording of "Lady Lynda" from 1986, with new lyrics to celebrate the Statue of Liberty's birthday, this is badly produced enough that the original "ooh lady won't you lie lady" backing vocals leak through at some points when Al and Carl (the only Beach Boys audible singing the newly-recorded lyrics) aren't singing "ooh lady from sea lady to shining sea". This was released as the B-side to "California Dreamin'"

Lavender

Songwriter: Dorinda Morgan

Lead vocal: Group

A rather dull ballad written by Dorinda Morgan and recorded during the Morgan sessions, this mostly exists as an excuse for the band to show off their Four Freshmen style harmonies. Backed by rudimentary acoustic guitar, they do sound very good, but there's nothing special here.

Listen to Me

Songwriters: "Charles Hardin" and Norman Petty

Lead vocals: Brian Wilson

A Brian solo cover of the Buddy Holly track ("Charles Hardin" was a pseudonym for Holly, whose birth name was Charles Hardin Holley), this was recorded for *Listen to Me: Buddy Holly,* a 2011 tribute album for what would have been Holly's 75th birthday. It's a perfectly pleasant but unexceptional recording of a perfectly pleasant but unexceptional song.

The Loco-Motion

Songwriters: Gerry Goffin and Carole King

Lead vocal: Mike Love

A Mike Love solo recording, released on the Radio Shack cassette *Rock and Roll City*, which also featured the original mix of the Beach Boys' version of "California Dreamin'", Love's solo versions of "Da Doo Ron Ron", "The Letter", and "Sugar Shack", and Mike and Dean Torrence duetting on "Lightning Strikes" and "Her Boyfriend's Back". This is Mike at his most nasal singing over what sounds like a Casio keyboard. Wretched.

Love Like in Fairytales

Songwriter: Mike Love

Lead vocals: Mike Love

A song Mike originally wrote and recorded for his 1978 unreleased solo album *First Love*, this was re-recorded for his 2004 unreleased solo album *Unleash the Love*, and bootlegged under the title "Glow Crescent Glow". The 2004 version eventually saw release on a free CD with *Endless Summer Quarterly*.

It's actually rather nice. Sonically it's much like the other *Unleash the Love* songs that have seen legitimate release ("Cool Head Warm Heart", "Pisces Brothers", and "Daybreak Over the Ocean"), with a very pretty, soft, lead vocal from Love over an acoustic guitar backing. Lyrically, the references to various Greek gods get stale by the end of the song, but like many of Mike's solo ballads it's got a pretty melody that suits his voice well.

Luau

Songwriter: Bruce Morgan

Lead vocals: Brian and Group

The B-side to the original Candix version of "Surfin'", written by Hite and Dorinda Morgan's son Bruce, this is a jolly enough piece of nothing.

The Monkey's Uncle

Songwriters: Richard M. Sherman and Robert B. Sherman

Lead vocals: Annette Funicello

Written and recorded for the soundtrack of the 1965 Disney film *The Monkey's Uncle*, this features the Beach Boys backing former Mouseketeer Annette. Over a backing track that's fairly similar in feel to "Little Honda", they sing about how Annette is in love with a monkey ("I'd live in a jungle gym in order to be with him/I love the monkey's uncle and I wish I were the monkey's aunt", "What a nutty family tree – a bride, a groom, a chimpanzee").

Pisces Brothers

Songwriter: Mike Love

Lead vocals: Mike Love

Another track from *Unleash the Love*, this is a slow ballad about George Harrison, who had died not long before the *Unleash the Love* sessions, and Love's memories of their time together in Rishikesh studying with the Maharishi ("Jai Guru Dev/Little darlin' here comes the sun...Hare Krishna/We're gonna miss ya").

Some have argued that the song is a little insincere, and is Love making his connection with Harrison into something rather bigger than it was in reality, but my own view is that it's perfectly reasonable for Love to mourn someone with whom he might not have been close but who spent a very meaningful period of time with him.

The song is another of Love's soft ballads with a pretty, gentle melody rather let down by the lyrics, and Love sings it very well. The song was released as a digital single in 2014 and has since become a regular part of the touring Beach Boys' live set, where it goes down rather better for a general audience than its reputation with Beach Boys fans would suggest (I've often seen audience members in tears as Love sings in front of video footage of Harrison). It was recently (March 2017) included in the soundtrack album for *Rooted in Peace*, a documentary about transcendental meditation that features Love, along with David Lynch and Deepak Chopra.

Problem Child

Songwriter: Terry Melcher

Lead vocals: Carl Wilson, Mike Love, and Al Jardine

The title song for the 1990 children's film, this was released as a cassingle and promo CD single. The sound is that of the band's other contemporaneous recordings, and it features "nyah nyah nyah nyah nyah" childlike backing vocals and a synthesised snare drum that sounds more like an explosion than a real drum. (John Stamos mimed the drums in the video).

Unsurprisingly, it didn't chart.

Rock 'n' Roll to the Rescue

Songwriters: Mike Love and Terry Melcher

Lead vocals: Brian (with Carl and Al on middle verse)

The token new song on the 1986 hits compilation *Made in USA* (other than the single version of "California Dreamin'"), this Terry Melcher production features all the standard hallmarks of his work with the band (horrible drum sound, squealy guitars, too much reverb) along with a shouted lead vocal by Brian which is enthusiastic but not exactly tuneful. Lyrically, meanwhile, it's the standard blather about the power of rock and roll.

Rodney on the ROQ

Songwriters: Brian Wilson and Andy Paley

Lead vocals: Brian Wilson with Jeffrey Foskett

A track recorded in the early 2000s as a set of jingles for DJ Rodney Bingenheimer, this was not really intended as a full song, but as a performance which could be excerpted at various points for Bingenheimer's show. That said, it does work as a full track, and was released as such in

2003 on the soundtrack of the documentary about Bingenheimer *Mayor of Sunset Strip.*

The track is almost pastiche-Wilson, and features "Mr. Rodney Bingenheimer" being rhymed with "he shoots from the hip, he's a real good timer". As the last (so far) Wilson/Paley collaboration, it's a fun reminder of how good the music they made together was, if hardly an essential track.

Santa's Going to Kokomo

Songwriter: Mike Love

Lead vocals: Mike Love

"Arruba, Bermuda, do you wanna know/Where Santa and the missus really like to go?"

A Mike Love solo track with "cute" children's backing vocals, about Santa going to the beach and surfing on his sled once Christmas is over. It manages to be rather worse than that description makes it sound. It was released on a various artists Christmas compilation, *Juvenile Diabetes Research Foundation: More Hope For The Holidays*.

Sea Cruise

Songwriter: Huey "Piano" Smith

Lead vocals: Dennis Wilson

Recorded during the *15 Big Ones* sessions, this is a rather enjoyable cover of Huey "Piano" Smith's New Orleans classic, recorded in a similar style to the band's version of "Shortenin' Bread" with layers of keyboards, stabbing guitar, and honking sax, and with a gruff, muscular lead vocal from Dennis (the only other Beach Boy who appears to be vocally present is Brian, who sings some falsetto "ooh"s very low in the mix).

This is much better than half of the covers that made the released *15 Big Ones*, and it was eventually released on *Ten Years of Harmony* (a 1981 compilation that covered the band's work from *Sunflower* through *Keepin' the Summer Alive*, and which has never had a legitimate CD release).

Speed Turtle

Songwriters: Sandra Boynton and Michael Ford

Lead vocals: Brian Wilson

A lovely, charming pastiche of the Beach Boys' early car songs, but sung about a turtle instead of a car, this is from a 2008 children's album and songbook, *Blue Moo: 17 Jukebox Hits from Way Back Never*, for which songwriter Sandra Boynton got performers like Davy Jones of the Monkees, B.B. King, Neil Sedaka, and Gerry and the Pacemakers to record children's songs in the style of their own hits. A Brian solo track.

Stagger Lee

Songwriter: Lloyd Price

Lead vocals: Mike Love with Adrian Baker

Recorded for the various artists compilation *New Memories* (from the same label that also brought out *Christmas Party* and *Rock and Roll City*) in 1983, this is a Mike Love solo version of Lloyd Price's classic New Orleans R&B hit.

Staggerlee.com lists 428 versions of this song (and the other variants of it like "Stack O' Lee Blues" – while Price is the credited writer this is a traditional song). I haven't heard all 428, but I am fairly confident that Love's version is, if not the worst, certainly in the bottom percentile.

Sugar Shack

Songwriters: Keith McCormack, Jimmy Torres, and Fay Voss

Lead vocals: Mike Love

In theory, a version of this song by Mike Love could have been fun – the original, by Jimmy Gilmer and the Fireballs, is hardly a classic, but is very clearly a pastiche of the Leiber/Stoller songs for the Coasters Love admires so much. The original could easily be improved on by a vocal from Love with a little more swagger than Gilmer's.

Unfortunately this 1983 version from *Rock and Roll City* sees Love at his most nasal, singing over a backing track that sounds like the preset rhythm from a Casio keyboard.

Sweets For My Sweet

Songwriters: Doc Pomus and Mort Shuman

Lead vocals: Brian Wilson

A solo Brian performance of the classic Drifters/Searchers hit, recorded during the Paley sessions and released on the 1995 tribute album *Till the Night Is Gone: a Doc Pomus Tribute.* It's quite fun but it's not the best vocal Brian turned in in the mid-nineties, being more yelled than sung.

This Song Wants to Sleep With You Tonight

Songwriters: Brian Wilson and Andy Paley

Lead vocals: Brian Wilson

A gorgeous little song, originally recorded for the B-side of Brian's 1995 re-make of "Do it Again", this is utterly lovely. "This song's a little blue/'cause songs get lonely too/This song wants to sleep with you tonight". The most charming thing Brian recorded in the nineties.

This Could Be the Night

Songwriters: Harry Nilsson and Phil Spector

Lead vocals: Brian Wilson

A cover of Brian's favourite Harry Nilsson song, a track originally recorded by the Modern Folk Quartet in an attempt by Phil Spector to make a Lovin' Spoonful soundalike track. This cover version was released on *For The Love of Harry: Everybody Sings Nilsson* (a 1995 tribute album which also featured Carl Wilson singing with his group Beckley/Lamm/Wilson on their version of "Without Her").

A Brian solo track, recorded with Paley, this is a straight remake of the MFQ's original, near-identical to their version except for Brian's vocal. Brian was pleased enough with this version that he included it a few years later in the setlist for his first full solo tour.

Walking Down the Path of Life

Songwriter: Brian Wilson

Lead vocals: Brian Wilson and Taylor Mills

A 2005 solo single released to benefit victims of Hurricane Katrina, this gospel track consists of three sections, each repeated – an opening *a capella* section with the band singing "Walking down the path of life/I feel His presence day and night" as block harmonies, a Brian solo section with him singing "touch me/heal me/wash my sins away" over the piano, and a much faster call-and response gospel song (in a similar style to "He Come Down" or "That Same Song") with Taylor Mills taking the lead vocals as the rest of the band echo her.

After two minutes this segues into the version of "Love and Mercy" included as a bonus track on *No Pier Pressure*.

This is quite lovely, and one of Brian's best solo recordings.

Wanderlust

Songwriter: Paul McCartney

Lead vocals: Brian Wilson

This solo cover by Brian of the song from Paul McCartney's *Tug of War* was released in 2014 on the tribute album *The Art of McCartney*, but was probably recorded several years earlier, as Jeffrey Foskett (who left Brian's band in 2013) and Taylor Mills (who left in 2011) are audible in the vocal mix.

The original is one of McCartney's best latter-day compositions, and the arrangement here wisely sticks closely to his template, though adding some backing vocal parts which weren't on his original. The only problem is Brian's lead vocal, which is slightly mush-mouthed – he's swallowing syllables a little.

What Love Can Do

Songwriters: Brian Wilson, Burt Bacharach, and Steven Krikorian

Lead vocals: Brian Wilson

A 2009 Brian solo recording for a compilation, *New Music from an Old Friend*, which featured various musicians who had hits in the 60s and 70s performing one new song and one of their hits each. This is a collaboration with Burt Bacharach and sounds to my ears more like Bacharach's work than Wilson's, but it *also* sounds quite a bit like the songs Brian was writing around the time of *That Lucky Old Sun*.

Whoever contributed what, the result (with orchestrations by Paul von Mertens and with the woodblocks, bass harmonica, and French horn that characterised much of Brian's music around this time) is one of the best solo things Brian has ever done. His vocals (subtly doubled by Jeffrey Foskett at points, never overwhelming Wilson) are strong, the song's winding melody combines the best of both Bacharach and Wilson, and the lyrics contain a few good lines ("I know I could be wrong/although I know I'm not").

Other than a stylistically out of place guitar solo which spoils it slightly, this is as good as anything Brian has released as a solo artist.

What'd I Say

Songwriter: Ray Charles

Lead vocals: Brian Wilson

A 1964 live recording of Ray Charles' R&B classic released on an Australian-only album, *Beach Boys/Brian Wilson Rarities*, which came out in 1981 and was swiftly deleted. The recording is swamped with screams from the audience and the Beach Boys were never exactly the most soulful band ever – this is roughly as white and clean sounding as Gerry and the Pacemakers' contemporaneous version. But Mike plays some surprisingly competent sax, and they sound like they're having fun.

What Is a Young Girl Made Of?

Songwriter: Bruce Morgan

Lead vocals: Brian Wilson

The other "Kenny and the Cadets" recording, this was the B-side to "Barbie", and is similar in style to the work of Neil Sedaka or Paul Anka. Brian does his best with lyrics like "what is a young girl made of?/Mostly a young man's dreams", but there's little of interest here.

With a Little Help from My Friends

Songwriters: John Lennon and Paul McCartney

Lead vocals: Bruce Johnston

Recorded during the *Lei'd in Hawaii* sessions, this is a fairly straight cover version of the Beatles' track, done in an as-live arrangement that tries to replicate the Beatles' version, which had come out a few weeks before the session. Unfortunately the band decided to experiment with varispeeding, and so Bruce's lead vocals are slowed down and sound like he's on Valium on the finished track, which was released on the *Rarities* collection.

Just as this book went to press, a new copyright extension release, *Sunshine Tomorrow*, was released. That compilation is not covered here, but it contains both the original mix of this track and a new mix, in which Mark Linett tries, with some success, to use digital technology to match the backing track and lead vocals, recorded at different speeds, and make the lead vocal sound more natural.

Acknowledgements

This book would not have come into being without the discussions I've had for over half my life with members of the Beach Boys fan community, both online and in person. Most of my knowledge of this band comes not from books - which with a few notable exceptions are horribly inaccurate - but from these discussions. There's no way I can list all of the people who have contributed in this way, but special thanks should go to Val Johnson-Howe, Ian Alexander-Barnes, Kingsley Abbot, Margaret Dowdle-Head, Iain Harris, Andrew Doe, Tobias Bernsand, blick, topgazza, the late Bob Hanes, Van Dyke Parks, Probyn Gregory, Scott Totten, Paul Mc-Nulty, Sean Macreavy, Alex McCambley, Paul Baker, Shawn Taylor, Adam Marsland, Blake Jones, Sean Courtney, Rob McCabe, Annie Wallace, Jon Hunt, John Lane, and more generally all members of the Pet Sounds Mailing List from 1997 through to 2006 and all the regulars at Beach Boys Britain.

The book would also have been very different had I not spent many years making music myself, so I'd like to thank all members of Stealth Munchkin and The National Pep, past and present.

Three resources have been more helpful than any others in checking both the facts and my interpretations of the music. Andrew Doe's Bellagio 10452 site[12] is the definitive word as to the 'plain facts' of the band's career from 1962 through to 1999. Philip Lambert's *Inside The Music Of Brian Wilson* is the best musicological analysis of, specifically, Brian Wilson's music from 1962 through 1967 I've ever read. As you can imagine that book overlaps with this one in a number of areas, and where those overlaps exist Lambert goes into far more detail than I have space for. And finally Francis Greene's transcriptions of the chords for almost every Beach Boys song[13] have been an absolute Godsend.

Thanks should also go to all those who have encouraged me in my writing in the past, including, but not limited to, Bill Ritchie, Jennie

---

[12]http://www.esquarterly.com/bellagio/
[13]http://www.surfermoon.com/tabs.shtml#francis

Rigg, Steve Hickey, Stuart Douglas, Lawrence Burton, Simon Bucher-Jones, Philip Purser-Hallard, Al Ewing, Emily Wright, Dave Page, Eve Friday, Andrew Ducker, Andrew Rilstone, Gavin Burrows, Alex Wilcock, Richard Flowers, Wesley Osam, Iain Lee, Gavin Robinson, and my fellow bloggers at Mindless Ones. There are many more than I can possibly list here, and I have undoubtedly missed out dozens of people who deserve acknowledgement.

The book wouldn't exist at all without my backers at http://patreon.com/AndrewHickey, who have generously funded my work for the last year and continue to fund my writing.

This book was written and typeset in the Free Software text editing program LyX (http://lyx.org), so thanks go to the creators of that software, as well as to the creators of LATEX, and, ultimately, Donald Knuth, whose typesetting language TEX is the ultimate basis of all those programs. It was created on a machine running the Debian GNU/Linux distribution, so thanks to all the many thousands of people who gave their work freely to that system.

The cover design is courtesy of Mapcase Of Anaheim.

Susan Lang, Tilt Araiza, Christian Lipski, Geoff Howe and Holly Matthies have between them read through this book and its previous two volumes in draft form (not all have contributed to all volumes, but all contributed to some), and made significant corrections, not only of fact and grammar, but also of musical analysis and style.

Where this book is worthwhile and correct, the credit is due them. Where it is dull and incorrect, the blame is mine.

Song index

Index

Printed in Great Britain
by Amazon